ED'S LETTER

The Times They Are a-Changin'

SO READ ON AND TAKE CONTROL OF YOUR CAREER

T hanks for buying this book; if you're the kind of person I imagine you to be, you picked it up because you dream of playing Wembley Stadium one day. I also reckon you're smart enough to realise you won't find any guarantee of superstardom printed on the pages inside.

What I do promise you is the advice given here – from experienced, working musicians and industry professionals – will help you to avoid the potholes on music's highway and to pick out a route that best fits your style of travel. The essential talent and hard work it requires to succeed is down to you.

The old ways of the music business no longer apply. Major labels and kitchen-sink indies alike have struggled to cope with new developments in distribution, while technological advances mean professional studios and expensive producers are less relevant to the unsigned sector.

With the establishment wrong-footed, the music market is open to new faces as never before – and the best way to exploit this is to embrace the 360°, or DIY, model of artist promotion. In chapter eight, we give the first comprehensive explanation of this method and provide practical advice for recording, distributing and promoting your own music.

This guide is based on my experiences and those of my colleagues on the circuit, with contributions from old hands and big names from the business. Everything has been written with you – the musician – in mind.

We don't claim to reveal the secret to success; all we can say is talent, hard work and an understanding of the business, as outlined in this volume, can only smooth your journey up the ladder. If you have any questions or comments, visit *www. howtomakeitinmusic.com* and join the forum – we'd love to hear about your experiences.

Thanks

CONTENTS

YOUR GUIDE TO HOW TO MAKE IT IN MUSIC

1 Know your scene inside out, p12

2 Get yourself on a festival bill, p70

5 Perfecting a live recording, p118

10 Win these great prizes in our competition, p256

HOW TO
MAKE IT IN
MUSIC

EDITORIAL

Author Stuart James Smith
Copy Editor Al Spicer
Chief Sub Jo Halpin
Thanks to Rob da Bank, Jon Goody, Mark Richards, Jamie Elton, Alex Eichenberger, Tim Aldous, Dean Marsh, Patrick Bickerton, Danny Bird, Linda Duong

ART

Art Editor Mike Mansfield
Design Mat Deaves, Ian Jackson

ADVERTISING & MARKETING

Alive Advertising
Marketing Manager Tom Townsend-Smith

INTERNATIONAL LICENSING

The content in this bookazine is available for international licensing overseas.
Contact Winnie Liesenfeld. 0044 207 907 6134 winnie_liesenfeld@dennis.co.uk

MANAGEMENT

Bookazine Manager Dharmesh Mistry (0207 907 6100 dharmesh_mistry@dennis.co.uk)
Operations Director Robin Ryan
Group Advertising Director Julian Lloyd-Evans
Circulation Director Martin Belson
Finance Director Brett Reynolds
Group Finance Director Ian Leggett
Chief Executive James Tye
Chairman Felix Dennis

A DENNIS PUBULICATION

Dennis Publishing, 30 Cleveland St, London W1T 4JD. Company registered in England. All material © Dennis Publishing Limited, licensed by Felden 2008, and may not be reproduced in whole or part without the consent of the publishers.

Dennis Publishing operates an efficient commercial reprints service.
For more details please call 020 7907 6100

LIABILITY

Printed at Stones

The paper used within this bookazine is produced from sustainable fibre, manufactured by mills with a valid chain of custody.

 **recycle**
When you have finished with this magazine please recycle it.

5 RECORDING

Mixing, mastering, layered or live – who knew recording music was so complicated? And, on top of all that, you might get 'red-light fever'! But don't fret; our experts explain the studio process.

6 PUBLISHING

They may be scrawled in a pocket notebook, but your songs are copyrighted. A good publisher can exploit this and take your work from beer-mat obscurity to possible ringtone stardom! ●

7 RECORD LABELS

Reports of their demise have proved premature and signing to a major label is still the accepted route to global success. So, how to attract the attention of those elusive A&R people.

8 DIY MUSIC

If Sony aren't beating a path to your door, set up your own label to record, market and distribute your music. If it's good enough for Ned's Atomic Dustbin, it could be good enough for you, too!

9 RADIO & INTERNET

The digital revolution has created more outlets for new music than you can shake a stick at. Broadcast, podcast or webcast, just make sure you make the most of it.

10 WHAT COMES NEXT

You've read the guide from cover to cover and absorbed the pearls of wisdom. But, remember, fame costs and this is where you start paying... in sweat!

7 Find out how labels are adapting, p174

9 Get yourself on the radio the easy way, p210

8 The New Model explained in full, p192

10 Got a deal? Now the hard work really begins, p232

Reasons to be Cheerful

MUSIC IS IN FINE FETTLE, SAYS ROB DA BANK

Doom and gloom, misery, heartache, bankruptcies and redundancies. Listen to the news and you'd think the end was nigh for the music industry. But I'm having none of it – and neither should you. Hopefully, by the time you've finished reading this guide, you will feel sufficiently fired up by just how much fun and how rewarding it is to work in the music biz that you'll drop your toast, turn off daytime TV and get out there and join in!

Sure, if you work for a major record company or in a CD-pressing plant, you may be looking over your shoulder a bit more frequently, with the state of music sales in general and the decline of the CD on your mind. But delve a bit deeper into the industry, particularly in the UK, and you'll find a hive of opportunities across many fields; and all of them involve our main love – music.

We've been running an independent record label here at Sunday Best for 10 years now and, despite the prevailing industry depression, we've never been in better health, financially or sales wise. We're not driving around in Rolls Royces and burning £50 notes to light our cigars, but we're ticking over nicely. Speak to many others in the independent sector – or chat to those who aren't just in the industry for the dollar – and you'll see things could be a lot worse. Added to that, the label is being sent better music now than at any time previously.

When I get asked how I've made so many things work – two music festivals, two BBC Radio 1 shows, a record label, a publishing company and a DJ career – I put it down, firstly, to a lot of luck. The music business involves a lot of factors that could make or break whatever you want to do. Being in the right place at the right time helps, but so does turning up when you're supposed to and applying yourself 100% of the time.

Unless I'd done three years wage-free work experience at a music magazine, I wouldn't have made the contacts and won the trust of so many people in the industry. Work experience – whether you want to be a DJ, lighting technician or music publisher – is unbelievably beneficial and will help you define exactly what you want to do.

Self-promotion is also a must – have a MySpace or facebook group about what you do, no matter how boring or technical you think it might be. In today's music industry, the more visible and better networked you are, the bigger the opportunities. Good luck with all your goals!

Rob da Bank
www.sundaybest.net/www.bestival.net

INTRODUCTION

HOW YOU CAN PROFIT FROM THIS BOOK

READ THE WORDS, FOLLOW THE EXPERT ADVICE & MAKE THE MOST OF OUR EXCLUSIVE LISTINGS

This guide has been written to represent the journey many unsigned artists take during the early stages of their career. Each of the topics under discussion has been dissected by musicians and industry professionals to provide you with an overall picture of the contemporary scene, and to give you a clear explanation of today's rapidly evolving business.

Each chapter presents you with an insight into the opportunities now available to musicians, regardless of whether they are signed or unsigned. By getting a proper understanding of the New Model (see chapter eight) and applying its methods to your marketing, your music should actually get heard and, hopefully, appreciated.

Artists are less dependent on record labels these days, so it's essential they keep up to date with developments in the music industry.

Once you have got to grips with the advice provided in this guide, look to put it into practice by using the listings at the end of each chapter. We've been very selective in compiling these – it could almost be said we're offering you them on a silver platter – but, when using them, always follow the stated means of communication. This is usually by post or email, but never by phone – the numbers are only included for reference.

There are no guarantees in the music business and you'll still have to work hard – and show bags of persistence – if you intend to make a living from your art. But this guide, with its interviews with industry experts, features and listings, should pull you through some of the traps of the business and give you the know-how to become a DIY musician. Enjoy your adventure. ★

CHAPTER #1

THE STAGE IS SET

YOU'VE GOT THE BAND, YOU'VE THE SONGS – NOW TO FIND SOMEWHERE TO PLAY

Live music is thriving at present, with promoters fighting it out to line up quality acts for their increasingly popular gig nights, be it in a pub, a club or a concert venue. These nights range from solo acoustic and indie gigs to a wide range of genre-specific events – such as for rockabilly, blues and electro – at which audiences will have certain expectations of the artists who are playing. The key, therefore, is to research and approach venues and promoters who cater for the type music you play. You may find certain venues want a mixed-genre line-up – again, all it takes is a little bit of Googling and you'll find what you are looking for. ●

The social-networking site MySpace is currently the quickest and most popular means of tracking down venues or promoters and of finding out what kind of nights they run, what expectations they have of an artist and the best means of contacting them.

As you can imagine, they receive hundreds of emails from bands every week and, sometimes, getting a reply is more about timing than whether they like, or do not like, your music – so don't take it personally if you don't receive an immediate response. It's best to give promoters at least a month to reply; don't fill their inboxes with message after message because this is a surefire way of being ignored completely.

AUDIENCE LEVELS

Promoters are a strange breed of people, who have chosen to pursue a creative vocation that has the sort of stress levels more commonly associated with City traders. But there is a fine line between promoting (i.e. booking you and also advertising the gig and your band) and merely booking, with some 'promoters' frequently confusing the two.

There are only a handful of full-time

> ## Promoters pursue a creative vocation that has stress levels associated with City traders

promoters who deal exclusively with unsigned acts and most of these are simply looking to get punters though the door, often asking artists to bring up to 50 people to a gig at £8 a head. So, on top of writing, rehearsing and performing their music, artists are now expected to manage audience levels too!

But don't fret, use facebook, MySpace and other social-networking sites – as well as the more traditional 'dog and bone' – to coax family, friends and friends of friends into watching you play live. It may be tough motivating friends to keep attending your gigs week after week, but it will be worth it when you get that rousing round of applause, which will impress the promoters and increase your chances of being rebooked. ★

The State of Play

HAVE YOUR WITS AT THE READY TO STOP THAT DREAM GIG BECOMING A NIGHTMARE

G igging slots attract so much competition that you'll need to keep your wits about you at all times. For every honest, hardworking promoter you come across, expect to find an unsavoury equivalent who is simply looking for their next victim. Here are some of the most common pitfalls to watch out for:

PAY TO PLAY

Quite simply, DO NOT PAY TO PLAY. Some promoters have started demanding that artists bring, say, 50 paying guests to a gig and, if only 35 turn up, to pay for the 15 who didn't make it. If you're made this type of offer, just turn down the gig. These people don't care about your music, they're in it purely for the money.

CONTRACTS

You would be advised against signing contracts to play at venues. If it is a requirement of the venue – and you are desperate to play there – you may have to consider it. But, as with all contracts, take the time to read every detail. If you're not happy, request that the promoter makes the relevant changes. If he/she refuses, then turn down the gig.

PAYMENT

Most venues will have someone at the door whose job it is to make a note of how many people have come to see a particular artist. After about the first 15 people, the artist will usually get £2 per person; more than 25 people £3; 50 or more £4 (this may vary from

BLANKET EMAIL

THE QUICKEST AND EASIEST WAY TO GET YOURSELF AND YOUR MUSIC KNOWN TO PROMOTERS AND VENUES

Blanket emails may seem impersonal, but they are often the best way to send information about yourself to a promoter or a venue. First and foremost, they will want to know about your gigging experience and the type of music you play, so keep to the point in your email and don't be tempted to make outlandish claims that you won't be able to live up to. For example, don't promise a promoter you will bring 50 people to a gig when you know scraping together 10 will be a struggle. It is best to do a bit of research on the websites of each venue/promoter before emailing, just in case they request specific information.

Below is an example of a blanket email you could send to a venue or promoter when looking to secure a gig.

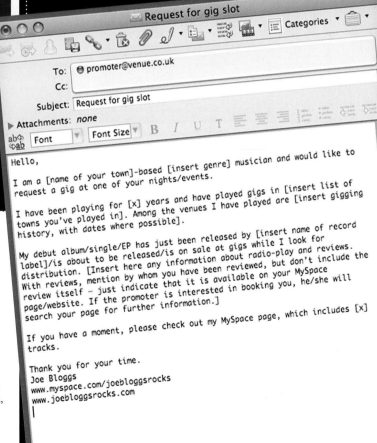

> ## Request for gig slot
>
> To: promoter@venue.co.uk
> Cc:
> Subject: Request for gig slot
> ▶ Attachments: *none*
> Font   Font Size   **B** *I* U T
>
> Hello,
>
> I am a [name of your town]-based [insert genre] musician and would like to request a gig at one of your nights/events.
>
> I have been playing for [x] years and have played gigs in [insert list of towns you've played in]. Among the venues I have played are [insert gigging history, with dates where possible].
>
> My debut album/single/EP has just been released by [insert name of record label]/is about to be released/is on sale at gigs while I look for distribution. [Insert here any information about radio-play and reviews. With reviews, mention by whom you have been reviewed, but don't include the review itself – just indicate that it is available on your MySpace page/website. If the promoter is interested in booking you, he/she will search your page for further information.]
>
> If you have a moment, please check out my MySpace page, which includes [x] tracks.
>
> Thank you for your time.
> Joe Bloggs
> www.myspace.com/joebloggsrocks
> www.joebloggsrocks.com
>
> |

venue to venue). This is by no means ideal, but, unfortunately, it's the current state of play.

Whenever possible, try to negotiate all fees beforehand. If the promoter tries to get out of paying you – even though you know you have brought in the required numbers – ask to see the door ticklist. If needs be, go around and count everyone with him, but don't let yourself be cheated out of money.

Keep focused and know what you want when talking to promoters; most are good, decent professionals who love music and want to help the live scene survive the licensing laws, noise complaints and restricted capacities that many venues now have imposed upon them. ★

Introducing...Innercity Pirate

Your Audience

THE BOOKING IS CONFIRMED: NOW TO GET A FANBASE

Securing a gig slot is only half the battle, so – if you don't want to be playing to a disinterested audience in a barely populated venue – ignite the interest of potential gig-goers early and think of ways to keep them coming back.

BEFORE THE BIG NIGHT

The best place to start is with any contacts you have on your mailing list (more about this later). As early as possible, send out a mass email with full details about the gig, including where to buy tickets, a link to Google Map and addresses of websites that offer information about the venue and other bands on the bill. Follow this up with another email the day before the gig to give people a gentle reminder.

As for friends, you can hassle them the most, but beware not to damage relationships by being too pushy. Target those mates who haven't been to see you for a while, rather than ones who have been to your past couple of gigs. Try getting your devoted fans to

form 'street teams', which go out to amass a mailing list and spread the word about your band. It's also worth sending out MySpace bulletins, creating a facebook group event and posting flyers via the comments section of MySpace. Finally, post the gig on free listings websites and include links to MySpace and to the event itself.

While you have a big role to play in creating an audience, the promoter is officially responsible and he/she should have done their share by listing the event and sending out flyers. If, after all of your efforts, you still only draft in a handful of people, try to remain positive. See the gig as having been a promotional tool.

PROMOTION AT GIGS

Playing live is the best self-promotion an unsigned artist can have, so it's important to take advantage of every gig you play.

Always have your details to hand so that, if you are approached after a gig, you can give out your MySpace/website address.

GOOD BAND-PROMO SITES

Places to post your gigs and a good resource for venues and promoters throughout the country.

WWW.
giglistings.co.uk
gigping.com
gigwise.com, *above*
gumtree.com
gigguide.co.uk
(Scotland)
nationalgigguide.com

CHEAP 'N' CHEERFUL PROMO

**IT DOESN'T HAVE TO COST THE EARTH TO RAISE YOUR
PROFILE – SOME IMAGINATION SHOULD DO THE TRICK**

Business cards or badges are effective ways of doing this – your details can be printed clearly, you can stuff a few into your pocket and you can leave them lying around a venue before you play. If they look good, people will pick them up, especially badges.

The most tried and trusted method of widening your fanbase is the mailing list; a bit of paper on a clipboard, with two columns – one for the person's name and another for their email address – and your band/artist name at the top of the page. This is the simplest and best means of building up a following around your local scene.

It might also be an idea to give away freebies: a three-track demo (make sure your details are on the artwork), stickers, t-shirts, cups, bags, bottles of champagne – if there is space to put your MySpace/website address, it's useable. Even if you grab the attention of a just handful of people, that handful could turn into 10 extra people at your next gig. ★

FACEBOOK
www.facebook.com

Create a group page, send out messages when you have a new track on your page/website and send out invitations for gigs. Along with MySpace, a quick and cheap way to spread the word.

VISTAPRINT
www.vistaprint.co.uk

Free business-card service – you only pay postage and packing – but, for a small fee, you can create cards using your own design.

MOOCARDS
www.moo.com

Create business cards and stickers using Flickr, where you upload images for 28x70mm business cards. A great twist on the traditional business card.

AWESOME BADGES
www.awesomebadges.co.uk

Cheap badges that come in a range of sizes – you only have to supply the design. They also produce posters, banners, flyers and keyrings.

BEST BADGES
www.bestbadges.co.uk

Vinyl, paper, waterproof and clear badges. You can also get t-shirts, plectrums and badges.

BAND STICKERS
www.bandstickers.co.uk

Vinyl stickers, badges and flyers. The company also makes cheap bass-drum skins.

BADGES FOR BANDS
www.badgesforbands.com

Custom t-shirts, badges, flyers and business cards.

Technically Speaking, It's Sorted

EXPECT BASIC EQUIPMENT AT MOST VENUES, BUT DON'T FORGET YOUR SPARES

Most venues have the same general set-up, so, with regular gigs, you'll get used to the equipment on offer. This will usually consist of Shure SM-58 microphones, a sound desk – 8-12 channels for small venues and 16-plus for mid-size ones – microphone stands, XLR leads and DI boxes.

Venues tend to supply only the basics and the artists fill in the gaps, while also covering breakables. Always carry a couple of spare jack-to-jack leads, some 9V batteries, guitar strings and drumsticks – basically, anything that has the potential to suddenly fall apart.

Sound engineers know their way around most kit, but the difference between a good and bad gig may be the drums being too loud or inaudible backing vocals. Getting your ideal set-up can easily be achieved with a sound check and, with practise, you should be able to work out the sound that suits you.

To keep time with each other, and to enable the singer to retain pitch control, your monitor mix should reflect everything being played. You and the sound engineer should be after a balance between every instrument, including the vocals, within the monitors and the main PA. ★

Power to the People

A BASIC KNOWLEDGE OF GIG GADGETS IS A POSITIVE BOON

N o matter what venue you play, the equipment that turns the strum of your guitar into a face-melting roar will be made up of, more or less, the same bits and pieces. The more you know about the gear and what it does, the more control you'll have over your final sound, plus, it will help you to set up quickly.

The acoustics of the room, the stage set-up and the venue's PA system will all influence how you sound – and an empty room at five in the afternoon will respond very differently to one crammed with people at 11 o'clock, so follow the advice of the sound engineer when positioning your equipment.

Here, freelance sound engineer Jamie Elton (*www.myspace.com/jamieelton*) explains the basic kit you'll find in most venues. Familiarise yourself with what it is and how it works, and watch your relationship with sound engineers blossom.

SET-UP FOR A SMALL VENUE

1 10-16 CHANNEL MIXING DESK
This is the board with loads of knobs and faders at which the sound engineer will be found, twiddling for dear life! With this, they can adjust the levels of each instrument/microphone, change the EQ to manage high, mid and low frequencies in each channel and add effects, such as delay and reverb. Generally, the smaller the venue, the smaller the desk.

2 10-16 CHANNEL MULTICORE
The box on the wall into which all of the mic leads are plugged. It sends all of the feeds to the mixing desk, which would, otherwise, have to be put next to the stage – very inconvenient.

3 FRONT OF HOUSE PA
The technical name for the sound system that directs sound to the audience. Often, this will consist of two sets of speakers, one for the higher frequencies and one for the lower frequencies (often known as bass bins).

4 MONITORS
When a band is on stage, it is useful for them to clearly hear what they are playing, so monitors are supplied to pump sound back at them. Often, a band will want a lot of vocals through the monitors because this is the hardest thing to hear on a loud stage. In a small venue, expect at least one monitor mix to be available from the mixing desk and at least one monitor speaker (often known as a wedge) to be available on stage.

5 CABLES AND MICS

Expect to find enough cables and mics plus stands to cater for the average band (three vocals, two guitars, drums, bass guitar and keyboard).

6 DI BOXES

What they do: Direct Injection boxes connect standard jack (guitar) leads to XLR leads. They can be used to split the signal of an instrument/audio feed.

When you need them: DI Boxes are commonly used for keyboards and acoustic guitars. These instruments are generally put straight into the PA, but usually only have jack outputs, so a DI Box is used. The jack lead from the instrument is plugged into the box and an XLR lead is taken from the box into the PA. If you use backing tracks from a laptop/mini-disc player, you would also use a DI Box to take the feed into the PA. DI Boxes can be used to split a signal, which means you can plug in one instrument and take two separate audio feeds. This is often done so one feed can go to the front-of-house PA and the other to a monitor or amp on stage.

Useful info: Some venues have no DI Boxes, while others seem to have hundreds of the things lying about. For a small venue, two would be a fair bet, but if your band requires a lot of keyboards and backing tracks, always take your own (one per mono channel of your instrument/backing tracks) just to be on the safe side.

Recommended purchase: Samson S Direct – usually less than £30

7 MICROPHONES

Microphones pick up the sound from musicians and their instruments. Because of the variety of instruments in even the most standard band set-up, there are different microphones; two of the most common are:

7a VOCAL MICS

What they do: To ensure the singer's voice is as loud as the rest of the band, a vocal mic is essential. In fact, in some very small venues, vocals may be the only thing put through the PA.

When you need them: Vocal mics can also be used for brass and wind instruments, guitar amps, drums and percussion. They are very versatile and so don't be alarmed if your saxophone/acoustic guitar/bongo is mic'd up in the same way as the singer! ●

Useful info: The louder a vocalist can sing, the clearer and louder you can make them through the PA. If people tell you your voice is lost in the mix, it is worth taking a couple of voice-coaching sessions to learn how to project your voice.

Recommended purchase: Shure SM58 (usually about £70) is the industry-standard vocal mic. It has a great response and natural sound, and is very robust.

7b DRUM MICS

What they do: Drums in a live-band situation can be drowned out by overly loud guitars and bass. Drum mics fit onto the rims of the drums to save space and cover the large range of frequencies given out by each piece of a kit.

SAY WHAT?

"You've got a song you're singing from your gut, you want that audience to feel it in their gut. They've got to be able to relate to what you're doing."
– Johnny Cash

When you need them: Most small venues will need to mic-up drum kits to help them cut through loud guitars and screaming vocals. Even a bit of kick-drum and snare coming through the PA can make the sound punchier and fuller.

Useful info: Often, in small venues, no overhead mics will be set up on a drum kit. This is because the brash, high frequencies of cymbals tend to cut over everything in a small room. So when you're playing a shoebox-sized room at the back of a pub, don't be offended if you do not have an overhead mic. Your cymbals are deafening as it is!

Recommended purchase: Red 5 Audio (for seven-piece drum kit) – usually retails (new on eBay) about £150.

8 MICROPHONE STANDS

What they do: Hold the mic in place, either next to the instrument/amp or at the right height for the singer to sing into.

When you need them: Minor pieces of equipment, but, without them, you are in a very difficult situation if you need to play an instrument as well as sing.

Useful info: Mic stands come in many shapes and sizes, and all have their own way of collapsing and being clamped into position. During sound check, make a note of your stand's height and angle, and, just before you go on stage, make sure it's in the right position. It's annoying for the band and audience if you spend the first three songs adjusting your mic stand!

Recommended purchase: K&M Boom Arm – usually about £25.

9 MONITOR SPEAKERS

What they do: Send sound to the band on stage so they can hear what they're playing and singing.

When you need them: Monitors are possibly not essential in small venues, but they are useful and help artists to perform better. They are often most needed by the singer because it can be hard to hear your voice over the rest of the band – then you have no excuse for being out of tune!

Useful info: At a small venue, it's very hard to get monitors as loud as the band would like without causing a lot of feedback. Earplugs are useful to help you monitor your own voice and because of the way they attenuate sound, you will hear the rest of your band better too.

Recommended purchase: Elacin ER20 Earplugs – about £15

10 REVERB/DELAY

What they do: Add echo to the sound of the instruments coming out of the PA.

When would you need them: Adding a bit of reverb and delay to the mix can make it sound professional and help to bed sounds together. It can also make a vocalist sound stronger. But too much can spoil a good mix and make the band sound like they are playing in a cave. Tell the sound engineer if you want reverb and delay, but leave it up to them how much they use.

Useful info: Singers are starting to use their own effects pedals, which plug in line with their mic, giving them total control over their vocals. This is a very good idea in a small venue.

Recommended purchase: Digitech VX400 – usually about £200.

11 XLR LEADS

What they do: Connect mics (and other audio inputs) to the PA.

When you need them: Every mic has a three-pin cable coming out of it – these are XLR cables (mic leads). They attach to DI Boxes and are the main input connection to a PA. A good venue will have more than enough.

Useful info: XLR leads are quite fragile and, often, are the most common things to break in a live situation – usually because musicians mistreat them. If you like to swing your mic about or need a long lead so you can walk about the stage, buy and use your own. The sound engineer will be much happier knowing his equipment isn't being destroyed!

Recommended purchase: Neutriks 10m male/female XLR cables – usually about £15-£20 ★

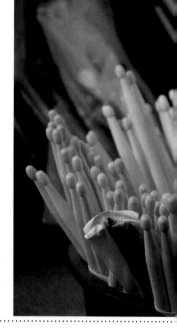

INTERVIEW

Tom Tom Club

GOOD KIT IS KEY, BUT IT AIN'T NOTHING WITHOUT RHYTHM

Tom Wilkinson – drummer and owner/manager of Tom's Drum Store, above Wunjo Guitars (see page 28) – has worked in music retail since 1963 and has sold instruments to Jimi Hendrix, Keith Richards, Paul McCartney, John Lennon and Mitch Mitchell.

What does a drummer need before they even pick up a set of sticks?

Percussion requires an inbuilt sense of rhythm, so go to a good teacher, who will be able to tell whether you've got a natural aptitude for drumming. If you have, he/she will let you know what you need to work on and advise you on finding kit that suits you. Your progress will depend on strengthening your wrist muscles and developing the skills to play three or four things at the same time without losing the beat.

What makes a good drum part and a great drummer?

A good drum part will sit comfortably with the other instruments and not distract from the main structure of the song. Similarly, a great drummer needs more than just the ability to play fast and loud; the most

---

DRUM UP TRADE

Among the artists to whom Tom has supplied kit are: Vinnie Colaiuta, Sean Moore (Manic Street Preachers), Mick Avory (The Kinks), Bob Henrit (Argent, The Kinks), Abe Laboriel Jnr (Paul McCartney, Sting), Steve Ferrone, Foo Fighters, Sex Pistols, The Police, Gnarls Barkley, Smashing Pumpkins, Hawkwind, The Strokes, The Cure, Franz Ferdinand and Lostprophets

---

respected are those who've built brilliant technique and instinctive understanding of which rhythmic patterns best suit a song.

Which sticks do drummers most commonly use?

The majority use 5As, but it depends on your personal preference and style. Sticks cost about £8 per set, with Vater and Vic Firth being the most popular brands.

How often would you recommend replacing sticks and other breakables?

If you play heavily and continually whack your drums, rather than stroke across the top of them, your sticks and the rest of the kit will suffer. You should expect to go through sticks pretty regularly, but breakables – clash, hi-hat, rides, splashes and pedals – shouldn't need replacing that often. A set of breakables ranges from £60 – which will get you what are known in the trade as 'dustbin lids' – to £900 for pro-quality equipment.

How much does a good quality, gigging drumkit cost?

A good Mapex kit costs £300-£400 new. You would have to buy any breakables separately,

"Drummers do the hardest physical work in the band, so fitness is important"

but most shops will do a deal if you're buying it all at the same time. You can pick up good second-hand kits for about half that price – they may need a few replacement drumheads and some TLC, but you'd be surprised at what you can find. Failing that, try eBay.

Most drummers can't play at home without annoying the neighbourhood, so how should they practise?

Leave the really heavy-duty stuff to a rehearsal space, where you can play as loud as you want. Get some practise pads if you plan to work at home. You can set up two pads as a snare and kick, which are the

pieces of kit used the most, and, even though you'll only be able to knock out dull thuds, you can still work on your technique. You can buy practise cymbals too, but they're not as good as the real thing, so I'd suggest dampening the sound of your regular set-up. Drum stores carry dampeners that sit on top of your cymbals and muffle noise, but you can achieve a similar effect by strapping the edge of each one in a band of two-inch elastic.

What advice would you give aspiring drummers?

Drummers do the hardest physical work in the band and a good level of fitness is important. Most professionals spend a few weeks in the gym before a tour to get in shape and to build upper-body strength. It's also not the best idea to get wasted before a gig. You'll suffer the most and discover a pounding head doesn't mix with pounding drums – and your playing will suffer. ★
www.myspace.com/tomsdrumstore

INTERVIEW

Guitar Man

SUPPLIER TO THE STARS TALKS STRINGS

W unjo Guitars' motto, borrowed from the film *Fear And Loathing In Las Vegas*, is 'We're not like the others, we're your friends'. Brian Rowe – founder, owner and manager of the store in Denmark Street, near Covent Garden, London – trained as a luthier (guitar builder) and has collected and dealt in vintage equipment for years. Here, he gives advice on buying the perfect 'axe' and getting the sound you always wanted.

Is there equipment you'd recommend to all artists, experienced or novice?
Most people who are just starting to play live go for Fenders – Stratocasters or Telecasters – or Gibson/Epiphone models such as Les Pauls or SGs. A good, basic electric guitar can be picked up for about £300-£400. Classic rock players looking for big, chunky riffs tend to go for the Les Paul because of its association with Jimmy Page, Keith Richards and Slash. In recent years, most popular bands have tended to play Fender Stratocasters, so these sell well to guitarists in their teens or early twenties. In terms of amps, the Fender Blues Junior and Hotrod Deluxe both sound great on stage and are available at a good price. The best mid-level acoustic guitars are made by Simon & Patrick, Guild, Takamine and

Tanglewood. You can expect to find one of these for about £400-£500.

Which are the best strings to use and how often should you change them?
The best strings are D'Addario's, Ernie Balls and Rotosound. About 80% of electric guitarists use medium-gauge strings (10-46), so these have become industry standard and most new guitars come with strings in this range. If you buy a new guitar and it has a lot of fret buzz, it may be because the strings are of a low quality, rather than the instrument needs 'wearing in' or 'setting up'. Replace them with a professional-standard set and this will probably clean up the sound.

The majority of acoustic guitar players use a light (12-54) set of strings and find these give them a good, balanced sound. Whether acoustic or electric, though, the heavier the gauge of string, the more 'bassy' your guitar will sound.

We often hear about the 'action' of a guitar – what exactly is this?
It is the distance between the fretboard and the string, and is measured at the 12th fret (the midpoint of the open string, between the nut and saddle of your guitar). This will usually be set at 3mm on the bass (low E) and 2mm on the treble (high E).

Action like this will cover most playing styles – lighter players can have it adjusted to 1mm at the treble end, while heavier players can go up to 8mm at the bass end.

If I wanted a pick-up installed into my acoustic guitar, how would I go about it and what are the best ones to buy?

You need a hole drilled through the side of your guitar and a jack-lead socket fitted. The pick-up is then mounted underneath the saddle and wired up. But get a professional to do this, not some drill-toting pal. Pick-ups start at £60, and I'd recommend Fishman Prefix and LR Baggs M1.A.

Is your business affected by music trends or are there always enough people interested in buying guitars?

Guitars never go out of fashion. Even in the mid-80s when synth bands were very much

in vogue, there was a massive heavy metal scene that kept guitar shops afloat. When I opened Wunjo's, in 1996, Brit-pop was at its height and there were hundreds of guitar bands forming. This trend has continued through the indie, EMO and metal scenes, and even though some of today's bands are more interested in vintage synths, there will always be a guitarist in the background.

What advice do you have for today's unsigned artists?

Don't come to London until you are ready and don't ignore your local scene. If you build up a following outside of the capital, record label A&R people will come to you. Don't underestimate the value of hard work and preparation; even if it takes six months, make sure you're well-rehearsed before your big showcase – the tighter you are, the bigger impact you'll make.

Lastly, what do you think of games like *Guitar Hero* and *Rockband*?

If these games encourage people to move on to real instruments, I'm all for them. ★

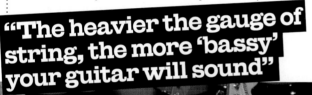

"The heavier the gauge of string, the more 'bassy' your guitar will sound"

TIPS ON

Sound Checks

THEY'RE VITAL, SO DON'T MAKE THEM TESTING, TESTING...

Live performance is the best possible promotion for you and your music – so don't risk sounding anything but your best. As a general rule when it comes to sound checks, don't turn up late and avoid winding up the engineer!

1 TURN UP ON TIME

It's crucial to use all of the time available for your sound check, which, generally, go in reverse order to ensure the headline artist gets a sound check. It also means the last band to sound check don't need to take off their gear before going on to play. So, have your equipment ready to put on stage when you are called.

2 SUPPLY A SPEC SHEET OF THE BAND

This will save time during sound check and can be used by the sound engineer as a guide when you are on stage. Give a basic description of how much equipment you'll need; for example, put your band name followed by '2 x vocals, 1 x drum kit, 2 x guitars, bass'. You could be more specific – '1 x lead vocal (centre stage), 2 x backing vocals (stage left and right), drum kit (1 kick, 1 snare, 2 rack toms, 1 floor tom), 1 guitar amp and 1 bass amp'. Whatever information you can provide will be useful.

3 BE POLITE BUT ASSERTIVE

Do not be afraid to ask for specifics and to suggest ideas with regards to levels, EQs and reverb/delays. The sound engineer should be responsive to this, as long as you know what you're talking about! There is nothing worse than a guitarist saying "can you make my guitar sound like it is in space?". If you have a specific request in mind, make sure you can describe how to achieve it, technically.

4 CHECK THE SOUND FRONT OF HOUSE

Try to walk out to the front of the stage while you are sound checking to hear for yourself what you sound like.

5 MONITORS

If the sound engineer tries to get you through your sound check without checking your monitor mix, don't be afraid to ask him or her to sort it out. In smaller venues, monitors can be a pain because they create feedback. Sometimes, there is only so far a monitor mix can go and, if the engineer says it can't go any louder, it's probably the truth.

6 REMEMBER SETTINGS

Having sound checked, there is nothing worse than another artist borrowing your equipment, changing the settings and then you forgetting where everything was for your own sound. So jot down at what number the dial on your guitar amp should be or the volume level for keyboards. ★

Hit the Highway

MAKE THOSE WEEKS IN A BEAT-UP FORD TRANSIT MORE BEARABLE

O rganising a tour can be a logistical nightmare – but use a booking agent and much of the stress will be removed. Blanket email companies and explain how long you have been playing, where you have already performed and when you are planning to tour. Look for agents who work within your musical genre; they may be able to help you out with a few dates and advise on which venues to approach. If you have to book the tour yourself, invest in a decent map of the UK, work out your route and book gigs city by city. Make sure you sort out any payment beforehand and double check all of the gigs before you head out on the road. ★

BOOKING AGENTS

HELP IS AT HAND TO EASE THE TENSION OF TOURING

www.

Indie/rock: myspace.com/fabagency
PsychoBilly/punk: myspace.com/hdp_group
Indie/rock: myspace.com/mixedtapeagency
Indie/rock: primary.uk.com/myspace.com/
primarytalent
Electro/indie/rock: codaagency.com/myspace.
com/codaagency
Electro/indie/rock: myspace.com/elasticartists/
elasticartists.net
Indie/rock/other: helterskelter.co.uk
Indie/rock/acoustic: myspace.com/
10xbetterbooking/10xbetter.com
Rock/metal/alternative: myspace.com/vortexlive/
vortexlive.net
Rock/metal/alternative: myspace.com/
blackoutbookinguk
Rock/indie/acoustic/other: theagencygroup.com

TOURING

The Sweat Smells of Success

THOSE EARLY DAYS ON THE ROAD ARE BADLY PAID AND OFTEN QUITE PONGY

E very band should hit the road and head out into the big wide world of touring. By breaking away from your local scene, you will widen your fanbase, play to people who have no knowledge – and, therefore, no expectations – of you, and play several nights in a row. Touring will help you to grow as an artist, strengthen the bonds between bandmates (or confirm that there aren't any) and add to your gigging experience.

But before heading off into the great unknown, there are several things to consider. As an unsigned artist, you won't make much, if any, money from a tour (see panel, *opposite*). At best, you'll break even. Your main concern will be transport for your equipment – transport that may double as your bedroom – food, drink and a washbag. Your first few tours may romanticise the rock 'n' roll lifestyle, but they probably won't be pretty – or pleasantly scented. ★

TOUR EXPENSES
PAYING THE PRICE FOR LIVING THE DREAM

You're a four-piece band about to break out of your local scene and hit the road for the first time. But how much will you have to fork out for a typical two-week tour of the UK?

Breakdown of costs

Rental of a standard
Diesel Transit Van: £600

Fuel: £350
(at summer 2008 prices)

Hostels: £20 a night,
£280 each

Food and drink (if not
included by promoter):
£20 a day, £280 each

Other costs (float in case
of emergencies): £100

Total: £3,290.00 total/
£822.50 per person

Another day, another
motorway service station

In for a Penny

BLUESMAN DAVE ARCARI ON KEEPING OUT OF THE RED

Slide guitarist and songwriter Dave Arcari's first full-length solo album, *Come With Me* (BRS032006), was released in 2007, while a series of shows with Seasick Steve, Alabama3, Son of Dave and Jon Spencer have established him as a formidable live performer. Arcari is also frontman of alt-blues band Radiotones.

How's life on the road?
Well, it needs a fair bit of planning. Playing the right sort of gigs is vital; it's no good one night playing a gig that's a tenner to get in to and, the next, doing a free-entry pub gig, especially if they're in the same area.

Tips for a successful tour
Touring is a valuable tool to generate press coverage and radio-play, which will bring longer-term benefits than those associated with the gig. Make sure every local and regional paper, magazine, gig guide, fanzine and website gets promo CDs, good pictures and a press release with your tour dates. The same goes for local, regional and national radio. It goes without saying that the gigs on any given trip should follow some sort of sensible geographical order – chasing up and down the country in an irregular fashion wastes time and costs a fortune. It can be a bit of a juggling act.

Balancing the books
I use a spreadsheet with details of fees (guarantees only) and costs. If you spend a lot of time on the road, it's not just fuel costs – use proper mileage estimates because you'll need tyres, services, road tax and insurance, and, eventually, you'll have to find the cash for a new vehicle. When I started out, we used a camper van to travel in. It was cool, but cost 70p a mile to run, campsites were £15 a night and, in the winter, things always seemed a bit damp. We also ate out most nights if the

> **"We used a camper van to travel in. It was cool, but we were haemorrhaging money'**

venue/promoter didn't supply a meal. We were haemorrhaging money. Now we travel in a Ford Focus estate that costs 30p a mile to run and have become adept at finding £19-a-night Travelodge-type places. We've got a coolbox that plugs into the car's lighter socket and also into the mains in a hotel room, so we shop in the supermarket and eat cheaper and better than before. ★

For more on Dave Arcari visit: www.myspace.com/davearcari and www.davearcari.com

WHAT ABOUT... the promoter who charged a Scottish band £180 to play a 'London venue with a 200-strong audience'? It was a run-down, empty pub in the arse-end of the city.

DOs & DON'Ts

Concerted Effort

LIVE GIGS ARE YOUR SHOP WINDOW, SO DON'T SMASH 'N' GRAB

laying live is not just about getting on stage, banging out a few songs, getting drunk and then heading home. Your general behaviour is important because you come across other artists, promoters, bar and door staff, the audience and the sound engineer. These people are there every night, making sure a venue runs smoothly, and the last thing they want to deal with is unnecessary stress created by a difficult musician.

BOTHERED

When looking to rebook artists, promoters will, of course, listen to your performance – with most asking the sound engineer's opinion because of the amount they hear during an evening. But they will also be noting whether you turn up on time, how you are with the other artists, if you have bothered to hang around after your set (this doesn't mean all night, but at least for an hour) or whether you have spent the night outside, smoking cigs with your mates and only turning up for your own slot.

By all means have fun – it's the reason you're there and the reason you started playing in the first place. But, if you really want to get somewhere with your music, retain a sense of professionalism when you play live, otherwise you will simply end up as another horror story for promoters to add to their (very long) list. ★

GETTING TO GRIPS WITH GIGS

A FEW COMMONSENSE GUIDELINES TO HELP YOU MAKE
FRIENDS AND INFLUENCE PEOPLE WHEN PLAYING LIVE

DO BE HONEST

When you contact a promoter, be truthful about your playing history. As long as the quality of the songs on your MySpace page/website is of a good standard, the music should speak for itself.

DO BE PREPARED

The day before a gig, make sure your stage equipment (guitars, amps, effects pedals) are in working order. Also make sure you have spare jack-to-jack leads and batteries if required.

DO ASK NICELY

If you need to share equipment, pre-arrange this with other acts (the promoter should provide contact details). Do not assume all acts will be fine with you borrowing their gear.

DO BE ON TIME

Arrive at the venue at the time specified by the promoter or you will end up with a short, or no, sound check. If you know in advance that you are going to be late, email the promoter the day before the gig so arrangements can be made.

DO SHOW MANNERS

Be polite. Don't storm in, have a sulk, dump your gear off, flop into a seat and wonder why you're not sound checking.

DO KNOW YOUR STUFF

Make sure everyone in the band is aware of which songs are included in the set and that you are all well rehearsed.

DON'T WASTE TIME

A sound check is not a rehearsal, so don't spend time teaching band members the chords of a new song, working on bits you're not sure of or pulling out material you haven't played for a while.

DON'T DIS THE CROWD

Respect your audience. Don't have a go at them because you're not getting the response you were aiming for. It's up to you to command respect and attention – you are not guaranteed silence simply by walking on stage.

DON'T BE UNSOCIABLE

It's not good to turn up, sound check, go for food, return for your set, then head upstairs – or hide at the back – before picking up your gear and going home.

DON'T PANIC

If you break a string, don't cry/whinge/sulk/stomp off stage or whimper 'does anyone have a guitar I can borrow?'. Play through it and, if you have the chance, swap guitars or replace the string as soon as possible.

DON'T GET SMASHED

The last thing people want to watch is someone off their face, falling about the stage, dropping microphones and slurring out songs in the mistaken belief they are Mick Jagger.

DON'T BIG YOURSELF UP

You are not playing Wembley, you have not had a platinum-selling record. You are unsigned – and an ego is a friend of no-one.

On the Spot

OPEN-MIC NIGHTS MAY NOT BE TRENDY, BUT THEY ARE CHARACTER BUILDING

DON'T FORGET... to arrive at the venue early if you are required to sign up on the night. It will save you panicking on the evening of the gig!

According to the Virtually Acoustic Club website (*www.thevac.co.uk*), there are 142 open-mic nights in London, but – as far as gigs go – they are the ones with the biggest stigma attached to them. Audiences tend to shun the nights for fear of poor-quality music and even someone with little live experience may think they're beyond the open mic. But no matter how good your gigging CV, the chance to play three songs to, mainly, other artists is still one of the steepest – but most productive – learning curves you can put yourself on.

The open mic remains the domain of the solo artist or the duo and it's one of the few places where you'll have up to 20 performers – each wildly different from the others – during the course of one evening. The show may leap from two members of a band testing new material in front of an unfamiliar audience to a dusty old blues singer who ambles up to the mic before letting loose with a rich, honeyed vocal or a guy in drag, who is under the mistaken belief he is the second coming of Judy Garland. As a performer, you don't know if the act before you will be amazing, forcing you to up your game, or really bad, making the audience grateful for

a guitar that is (hopefully, for your sake) in tune. In other words, the diversity of material will keep you on your toes.

No matter how long you've been playing, an open-mic session is still one of the best places to find an audience (the nights are all free entry, so you'll get a good mix of passing trade, locals and friends of performers), test out new material, build your confidence and make contact with promoters and other artists. ★

STAND UP AND BE COUNTED

LISTED ARE SOME OF THE UK'S MOST RENOWNED OPEN-MIC NIGHTS. VISIT THE WEBSITES TO GET A SAMPLER AND TO BOOK A SLOT

Hidden Away (London):
www.myspace.com/hiddenawaymusic
T-Birds (London):
www.myspace.com/acousticbirds
David Goo Variety Show (London):
www.myspace.com/davidgoo
Ear Music (London):
www.earmusic.co.uk
The Primrose Pub (Leeds):
www.myspace.com/theprimrosepub
Acoustic Lounge (Birmingham):
www.myspace.com/acousticloungebirmingham
Acousdeck (Glasgow):
www.myspace.com/acousdeck

A Boatload of Knees (Bristol):
www.myspace.com/aboatloadofknees
Sofa Sessions (Brighton):
www.myspace.com/sofasessions
The Castle Hotel (Manchester):
www.myspace.com/thecastleopenmic
Electro/indie/rock: www.elasticartists.net
Indie/rock/other: www.helterskelter.co.uk
Indie/rock/acoustic: www.10xbetter.com
Rock/metal/alternative: www.vortexlive.net
Rock/metal/alternative: www.myspace.com/
blackoutbookinguk

No Short Circuit to Success

INSTANT FAME IS RARE, BUT GOOD MUSIC WILL OUT, SAYS BARFLY PROMOTER MARK RICHARDS

Mark Richards was the main independent promoter at The Garage venue, in Islington, for many years. He now promotes at the Barfly/Mean Fiddler chain of venues, as well as booking for some London-based festivals.

How did you get into the business and what do you consider to be the role of a promoter?

When I was 14, we formed a band at school and wanted to do gigs. We were too young for the established venues, so we put on our own events, which were pretty successful. One of the band's parents owned a 1,500-capacity venue, so, from the age of 16, I worked there in my school holidays. It was not planned; I just did it because I enjoyed playing and listening to music. A promoter takes the risk in putting on a show. They need to choose the right bands for the gig and make sure the audience turns up. That means working closely with new bands to reach their friends and families, and, with established bands, reaching their fanbase through the media. It is important to remember that, while some shows will be profitable, others will lose money. Promoters are only as good as the bands they book.

What do you normally look for in an artist before you book them?

I have to really like their music. I watch every band I plan to put on and if I think 'I would not like to watch 30 minutes of this' I won't hire them. If I am going to ask the public to pay money to see a band, I have to really believe in them. Promoting gigs in venues with less than 500 people is not very financially rewarding – so the pay-off has to be hearing great music!

Is there too much pressure on artists to fulfill commitments to promoters, such as having to bring a guaranteed number of followers to a gig to get a rebooking?

In small venues, on week nights, I don't

SAY WHAT?

"...t cling to fame. You're borrowing it. It's like ...ey. You're going to die, ...nd somebody else is going to get it."
– Sonny Bono

"Bums on seats are the aim of any show. Numbers keep us in business"

believe there is that much pressure to bring a certain number of people. However, if a venue has three bands on at the weekend and fewer than 100 people are there, that venue will go under. So it's a pressure bands need to get used to. It is best to play small shows to build a fanbase and then approach venues with larger capacities, knowing you will easily take 30 or 40 fans along. Promoters don't help themselves sometimes by trying to fill venues that are too big for the quality of their acts. In the entertainment industry, getting bums on seats is the aim of any show. Numbers are really important for promoters and venues; they keep us in business.

Does good music always win out or are you seeing a lot of talented artists giving up because of the state of the industry?

Good music usually wins out. Being well organised, with good management, helps bands to reach fans. Getting recognised is sometimes a slow process, but most talented performers I have put on are prepared to work for a long time to achieve what they want. Overnight success stories do not happen very often.

Is more importance now attached to building a good reputation as a live act than on having a polished, professional-sounding demo?

The level of recording technology now means most reasonable musicians can sound great on a demo. But, in my view, a live performance is the most exciting part of what a band does. If a band can draw people to their shows and then engage that audience, it is a fantastic experience. Some bands have built their careers around the quality of their live performances. ●

What are the best ways for a band to get their name known and to pull punters though the door?

Start with friends. If you can get them backing the band, you have a ready-made 'street team' to spread the word to other people. Advertising is expensive and flyers end up in landfill. Word of mouth, backed up by a great live set, a fan-friendly MySpace page and a mailing list usually mean a band can do well – if they have the talent. Bands should not over-gig. Over-gigging is the fastest way to kill the group. Even large bands limit the number of times they play in certain areas. Each show should be a special event. In the early days, doing as many shows as possible is a good idea, but, once bands step onto the professional venue circuit – where they can be 'discovered' and where signed bands play – they need to make an impression. Having events everyone wants to attend is the way to make your gig a success.

Do you think there are too many bands and not enough venues now – or is it the other way around?

There can never be enough bands or venues. Music is one of the best things in life. It is positive and life-affirming. As long as enough fans are willing to go through the doors, I hope live music continues to grow in the UK.

ADVICE FOR GIGGING ARTISTS

Make sure you have rehearsed a great live show

Decide how you are going to get people to every gig – mailing lists, MySpace, street teams – and work closely with venues and promoters to achieve this

Be well organised when you play live and run a diary so you don't run the risk of over-gigging

Above all – enjoy it!

Has MySpace killed the posted demo; are you more likely to book artists via the internet or from following up a demo you have received?

MySpace has saved so much time and money for bands and promoters. Bands contact us to give us their links and we check out their music. We may ask for demos, but, generally, MySpace is a great way to discover a band. Experienced promoters know how to assess a MySpace profile, so bands need to be truthful.

What is the best way to gain gig experience?

Offer your services to the local community and local venues. If you become popular, think about touring or playing a London showcase. Organising a party for a friend and booking yourself as the entertainment is the easiest way to get a gig!

"The industry is in a state of flux, but live music is very vibrant and growing"

What has been the difference between acts that have passed though your venue and found success, and those who have thrown in the towel?

I'd say hard work is the basis of success, but you can't beat talent. Even when you see hundreds of bands a year, the ones with great talent always stand out.

How do you see the music industry in the future and what will be the promoter's role within it?

The music industry is currently in a state of flux, but live music is very vibrant and growing. Promoters and bookers will always have an important role to play in shaping great gigs and festivals. I would like to see the promoters of major festivals taking more risks on their main stages – the line-ups seem to lack any true identity and there's a lack of fresh talent being given a chance on the main stages. That, in turn, would help the major venue promoters to discover and break more new bands each year. ★

Enhance Your Stage Presence

DOING SOME BASIC RESEARCH MAY HELP YOU TO BAG A BOOKING

P ure talent is not the only thing promoters look for in an artist. Some may want a specific genre of music, others may just need musicians to help them to create a good, coherent line-up of artists for a particular event. Others, still, will just be looking to get punters though the door.

Before contacting a promoter, read thoroughly any information they have posted on their MySpace page/website; this will give you a good idea of what they are looking for – in terms of audience numbers or genre of music – and is the best way of contacting them. It's also worth checking what gigs they have coming up and analysing the artists they have already booked. If you're a four-piece rock band, you won't be booked for a singer-songwriter night. If the line-up is wildly incoherent, it's likely the promoter is just trying to get artists on and off the stage as quickly as possible while hoping the venue is filled to capacity with the 25 people they have asked each band to bring.

The information below – taken from a London-based promoter's MySpace blog – is a fair reflection of what a promoter may be looking for from an artist:

"*If you are interested in playing a gig for us, have a look at, and a listen to, the bands/ artists featured on our MySpace page. As a general guide, we don't promote indie/rock/ punk/metal bands or anything we think is cheesy, fluffy or corny. Other than that, we're pretty open-minded, but very particular, and we only book and promote the music we really like.*

"*We're easily impressed by Canadian banjo*

SAY WHAT?
"The things that come to those who wait may be the things left by those that got there first."
– Aerosmith's Steven Tyler

virtuosos, experimental laptop geniuses and brilliant eight-piece nu-folk collectives. If there's a saw or euphonium involved, we get pretty excited and when five-part harmonies or a kaos pad come into play, we might start whooping.

"On the flip side, we won't book you simply because you're an acoustic singer-songwriter who has played every other venue in London, no matter how many people you promise to bring along.

"If you haven't been to one of our shows before and you're in or around London, come along to get a better idea of what the club is all about – and say hello to us on the door or on the mixing desk. If you think we might be interested in your sound and your songs, send an email to (name)@ nameofpromoter.com and include your band/ artist name, MySpace page/website link, a

brief description and biog, your name and phone number, and your location (town/ country).

"We receive a lot of submissions to play and there are only one or two of us to sift through them in between all the other work we do. Because of this, it may take up to 60 days for us to get around to your email and, if you're unsuccessful, we may not even be able to reply.

"If we turn you down – or you don't hear from us after this time – please don't ask us for feedback because, unfortunately, we don't have enough time to do that. Thank you very much."

A promoter will want an artist to be professional, have a couple, at least, of listenable songs on there MySpace page and not be overly fussy – then you'll get off on the right foot. ★

INTERVIEW

The First Cut is the Deepest

CIRCUIT LEGENDS THE BUTCHER BLUES FOUNDATION TALK GIGS, TOURING AND ADVERTISING

The Butcher Blues Foundation are a hard-working, talented band, who are prepared to do whatever it takes to bring their music to the masses – even uprooting themselves and moving to the capital. Having swapped Bournemouth sunshine for London's neon lights, BBF know the gigging scene inside out - add to this a self-released album and a constant stream of new material, the band have plenty of advice for aspiring musicians.

How easy was it to make the move from Bournemouth to London and how do the two scenes differ?

London *has* a music scene! In Bournemouth, there are a few places to play, but they will never compete with the laminate-floored-white-walled wine bars springing up everywhere. Making the move did throw us a few curve balls, including the loss of our drummer. He lasted nine days; he'd been part of the band for years, but couldn't cope with London, so it's certainly not always the greatest idea. Then again, if you're hoping to find good people to work with, and good places to play, London's the place to be. If you want something badly enough, you have to

> **"We lost our drummer. He lasted nine days. He just couldn't cope with London"**

give it full blast and power your way through the hard times.

Who are your main influences and are they reflected in your work?
Your journey through music should keep revealing new influences and shedding new light on your heroes. Rather than ape those you aspire to, listen and learn from their music. Absorb style, ideas and form if you like, and explore how they effect what you play, but don't tie yourself into copying them.

Is there a main songwriter in the band or do you each bring something

to the table and work on the idea as a group?
The latter, mainly.

Do you find promoters' demands make the gigging scene hard?
Yeah. In London, the whole 'don't play for two or three weeks either side of our event; bring at least 30 people along; you get paid after 50 people; it's like this or you won't come back' routine that bands hear from promoters makes it tricky to build up a following. Starting from scratch here is a nightmare unless you bring some of your local loyals up to cheer you on while you establish yourself in the big city. There are some promoters who

WHAT ABOUT...
"People say we take things too seriously, but we're not going to sit around and wait and just be happy if something turns up. We are ambitious. You have to be." Thom Yorke

really need to look up what 'promote' means. Some take 80-100% of the ticket revenue. They have overheads to pay, of course, but some of them seriously exploit the acts they book. Having said that, we have come across really good promoters, who care about music and put a lot of effort into creating a great night for the bands and crowds.

The current system could clearly do with improvement. How would you like to see it change?
The music business is like other industries, in that the people at the bottom of the heap work the hardest and receive the

Grrrrrrrrrrr!

I'm not always serious

"cream rises to the top, but, in this game, you learn it's not the only thing that floats"

least reward. This isn't going to change. I firmly believe cream rises to the top, but, in this game, you soon learn it's not the only thing that floats. When you consider the rubbish pop-chart acts that have been put together over the years – one-hit wonders styled up as something fashionable, raking in cash for someone else behind the scenes – the respected route of 'paying your dues' as a bona fide artist can feel a little irritating. No one likes to work their backside off for the fat cat without getting a purr of recognition or a slurp of the milk they've conjured up. It's important to remember the huge music world that flourishes outside of the control of the big-name, high-street brands.

I'm sure you've been approached by loads of record labels, but do their A&R people always turn up? Can you trust them to show or do you have to constantly chase them?
Chase 'em boy – chase every last one. You

need them more than they need you and this week's unmissable 'in thing' soon turns into a disregarded 'out thing'.

Is every gig worth playing or have there been nights when you wished you'd never turned up?
We drove from Bournemouth to do a gig in Islington. The other two bands (one of which was providing the drum kit) didn't turn up and neither did the soundman. That grated.

How do you see the future of music? Is it still in the hands of record labels or can artists be self-sufficient?
The future lies in the power of advertising. If you're going to succeed, you need to tell people what you're doing and what you're about. The labels still hold all of the high-scoring cards and will usually win the fight for public attention. However, we don't have to join in their fight – we've got a scene they're not capable of taking away from us.

You have been playing for a while; what are the most important attributes an artist needs to have?
The desire to work hard, thick skin, that 'thing' and a load of luck. ★

Gigging venues and their promoters

THE DEFINITIVE HITLIST OF PLACES TO PLAY AND PROMOTERS TO APPROACH

12 BAR CLUB

Genres: Country/Acoustic/Punk/Indie/Rock
Venue: 12 Bar Club
Website: www.12barclub.com
www.myspace.com/12barclub
Contact: 12barclub@btconnect.com or send demos to: Andy Lowe, 12 Bar Club, Denmark Street, London, WC2H 8NL
Info: One of the best and famous venues in London, know for it's tall but small stage and spilt level venue the 12 Bar Club has an amazing and unquie atmosphere, also the t-shirts that are on sale behide the bar are very cool.

93 FEET EAST

Genres: Various
Venue: 93 Feet East
Website: www.myspace.com/93feeteast
Contact: sean@93feeteast.co.uk
Info: Live music venue and bar on Brick Lane, East London. Consisting of three main areas, a large main hall with stage, the intimate gallery bar, and the recently redecorated bar, 93 also utilizes its large cobbled courtyard with seating and BBQ and Thai Food.

ALL ABOARD THE MUDLARK

Genres: Folk /Acoustic /Experimental
Venue: Filthy McNasty's, The Social
Website: www.myspace.com/allaboardthemudlark
Contact: Simon, Martin or Dave at the myspace address
Info: Low key vibes and chilling, great 40s 50s 60s psych electro mountain music DJs, intimate atmosphere and great acts. FREE ENTRY!

ANOTHER MUSIC = ANOTHER KITCHEN

Genres: Indie/Electro/Rock
Venue: Proud Galleries & Bar
Website: www.myspace.com/amequalsak
Contact: Via MySpace
Info: Club night hosted at the newly moved Proud Galleries that features some of the hottest new signed and unsigned acts on the scene.

BARFLY

Genres: Rock/Alternative/Indie
Venue: Various throughout the country.
Website: www.barflyclub.com
Contact: See website for details
Info: Barfly works on an ethos of supporting the world's best new music by filling its 10 venues with the stars of tomorrow 7 days a week.

BEDFORD PARK

Genres: Indie/Rock/Country/Alternative
Venue: Bedford
Website: www.myspace.com/theoldkingsheadrocks
Contact: Via Myspace
Info: Rock, metal, country, southern rock venue on Streatham High Street, near Brixton tube.

BIG CITY REDNECK

Genres: Indie/Rock/Alternative

Venue: Various

Website: www.myspace.com/bcrpresentsbigbadlove

Contact: bigbadlove@gmail.com

Info: BCR Presents Big Bad Love is a monthly gig night at various venues around London.

BITTER END

Genres: Indie/Rock

Venue: Bitter End

Website: www.myspace.com/thebitterend

Contact: Via MySpace, include links and band bio

Info: This historic, and famous live music venue is right in the heart of thriving Romford, Essex, recently refurbished, and with a new pro PA system, the layout of the venue lends itself excellently to live performance.

BORDERLINE

Genres: Various

Venue: Boarderline

Website: www.myspace.com/borderlinevenue

Contact: cornford@barflyclub.com, include myspace address and details

Info: Right in the heart of the west end the boarderline cover everything from disco to country and is one of the priemer venues in London.

BONANZA

Genres: Avant-Country, Folk, Cajun, Bluegrass, Blues, Garage Punk, Rockabilly, Rock 'n' Roll

Venue: Powers Acoustic Bar, Lock Tavern, Bardens Boudoir

Website: www.myspace.com/Bonanzablues

Contact: Via MySpace

Info: Country, Rock, Blues promoter that offers a dip in the water of Americana with both the gig nights and weekly radio station on Resonance 104.4FM (Sundays at noon).

BUGBEAR BOOKINGS

Genres: Indie/Rock/Acoustic

Venue: Dublin Castle, Hope & Anchor, Constitution

Website: www.bugbearbookings.com

Contact: demo@bugbearbookings.com

Info: Bugbear Bookings have been providing a platform for up and coming musicians, young, old and somewhere in-between, since 1996, and are a well respected signpost on the route to success for many a band.

BULLET BAR PROMOTIONS

Genres: Indie/Rock

Venue: Bullet Bar

Website: www.myspace.com/bulletbarpromotions

Contact: Via MySpace

Info: Great looking and sounding venue in Kentish town/Camden, gigs are on almost every night of the week.

CAFÉ ROCKS

Genres: Indie/Rock/Acoustic/Soul

Venue: Café de Paris

Website: www.caferock.co.uk

Contact: mickyp@cafedeparis.com

Info: Club night run every Friday at the Café De Paris in the heart of the west end. Contact Micky P for further information.

COMMUNION

Genres: Alternative/Indie/Rock

Venue: Notting Hill Arts Club

Website: www.myspace.com/getcommunion

Contact: Via MySpace

Info: Run by ace London five-piece Hot Rocket (www.myspace.com/wearehotrocket) Communion is the first Sunday of every month. With a range of genres covered, DJs and special treats this club night is worth checking out.

CORRUPT EVENTS/ CASINO ROYAL

Genres: Alternative/Experimental/Imdie

Venue: Barfly. Bloomsbury Bowling Lanes

Website: www.myspace.com/corruptevents

Contact: genia@corruptmanagement.com

Info: Corrupt Events promotes and arranges bands for live music events, club nights & showcases.

CURIOUS GENERATION

Genres: Indie/Rock/Acoustic

Venue: Soho Revue Bar, Troubadour, 93 Feet East, Nambucca, Hoxton square bar & Kicthen, the Source Below, Pressure Point (Brighton)

Website: www.myspace.com/curiousgeneration / www.curiousgeneration.com

Contact: info@curiousgeneration

Info: Deals with every level of gigging on the unsigned scene while developing the most exciting cutting edge artists. They run around 25 nights a month across the UK and work on a number of media platforms.

DEAD OR ALIVE

Genres: Indie/Rock/Acoustic

Venue: The Metro Club, The Comedy, The Buffalo Bar, The Bullet Bar, The Dry Bar, The Old Queen's Head

Website: www.myspace.com/deadoralivepromotions / www.deadoralive.org

Contact: demo@deadoralive.com

Info: Hosts gigs on most week nights, books both acoustic and bands for a 3-4 artist line-up.

DICE CLUB

Genres: Rock/Indie

Venue: The Legion

Website: www.myspace.com/diceclublondon

Contact: Via MySpace

Info: The ethos of Dice Club is chance. Everyone attending dice club will be given a die on entry and encouraged to use it to make decisions during the evening, anything from which drink to have to which band to watch making this a unique night on the London scene.

DIRTY WATER CLUB

Genres: Garage/Blues/Punk

Venue: Boston

Website: www.myspace.com/dirtywaterclub / www.dirtywaterclub.com

Contact: info@dirtywaterclub.com

Info: Run every Friday at the Boston, Tufnell Park, North London. Check website for booking details but the Dirty Water Club mainly deal with Garage Rock/Blues/Punk acts.

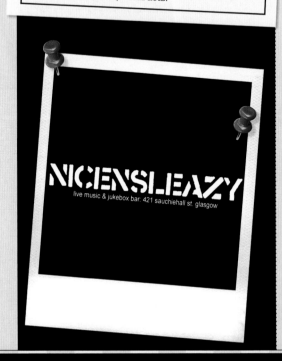

NICENSLEAZY

live music & jukebox bar. 421 sauchiehall st. glasgow

EAR MUSIC

Genres: Acoustic/Indie/Rock

Venue: Monkey Chews (Open mic and showcases), The Star (Open Mic and featured artists), Paradise

Website: www.earmusic.co.uk
www.myspace.com/earmusic

Contact: joel@earmusic.co.uk (in subject line put OPEN MIC for the open mic or GIG for a showcase featured artist slot)

Info: Put together by a collective of like-minded music loving souls Ear Music is not only a promoter but a resource of information/aid/help for the gigging artists, visit www.earmusic.co.uk for more information.

HALFMOON PUTNEY/ HALFMOON UNPLUGGED

Genres: Indie/Rock

Venue: Halfmoon

Website: www.halfmoon.co.uk

Contact: Via the website and click on 'Demos'

Info: The famous Halfmoon Putney is one of London's longest running, and most respected live music venues.

ELECTROACOUSTIC CLUB

Genres: Acoustic/Folk/Blues

Venue: Slaughted Lamb, Wimington Arms, Cavendish Arms, Gallery Cafe

Website: www.myspace.com/electroacousticclub
www.electroacousticclub.com

Contact: will@electroacousticclub.com

Info: The main focus for the Electroacoustic club is acoustic bands, duos and solo artists, but check the website for regular updates on a large variety of nights.

ILOVEGIGS.COM

Genres: Indie/Rock/Acoustic

Venue: The Troubadour

Website: www.ilovegigs.com

Contact: See website for details

Info: Co-run by uber-piano wonder Andrew Balkwill, Ilovegigs is all about great music at great venues.

FLAG PROMOTIONS

Genres: Electro/Alternative/Industrial

Venue: KoKo, Madame JoJo's, The Garage, Electrowerkz, Islington Academy, The Underworld, Academy III (Manchester)

Website: www.myspace.com/flagpromotions /
www.flagpromotions.com

Contact: info@flagpromotions.com / For gig's send demo's to : MYSPACE SUBMISSIONS, FLAG PROMOTIONS, P.O. BOX 181, WEMBLEY, LONDON HA0 4BE UK and mention myspace.

Info: One of the UK's leading Electro/Alternative promoters, running both gig nights and club events at a number of venues.

JERICHO ACOUSTIC

Genres: Acoustic

Venue: Macbeth

Website: www.myspace.com/wearejericho

Contact: Via myspace

Info: Regular acoustic night that's held at the Macbeth, east London.

KEBABYLON

Genres: Rock/Acoustic/Indie

Venue: Tommy Flynn's

Website: www.myspace.com/clubkebabylon

Contact: Via Myspace

Info: Run every Tuesday at Tommy Flynn's in Camden you'll find a range of genres within the 5-6 acts playing and a friendly atmosphere from both the promoters and the audience.

THE GOOD SHIP

Genres: Various but mainly Indie/Rock

Venue: he Good Ship

Website: www.thegoodship.co.uk /
www.myspace.com/thegoodship

Contact: john@thegoodship.co.uk

Info: A unique venue due with the stage known as 'the pit' due to the balconies that surround it. This adds a great atmosphere to the venue and makes you feel slightly like a Gladiator.

KAPARTE PROMOTIONS/ NOCTURNE FOLKS

Genres: alternative, dark folk, post-punk, progressive, neo folk, electronica, glam noir
Venue: The Half Moon (Herne Hill)
Website: www.kaparte.info
Contact: klarita@kaparte.info
Info: Nocturne Folks is a music/performance art showcase taking place the last Friday of the month at The Half Moon in Herne Hill, and putting on artists with a twist of darkness.

KBY ROCKS

Genres: Rock/Metal/Punk
Venue: Barfly, Water Rats, Bar Monsta, Lark in the Park
Website: www.myspace.com/kbyrocks
Contact: Send demos to: KBY, PO Box 14721, London, N7 6WD or e-mail : Keiths_backyard@yahoo.co.uk / Teria.lee@gmail.com or send a message Via Myspace, include a bio and where the band are based.
Info: KBY Rocks is most Sunday evenings at The Barfly, London. Also shows at, The Water Rats, Bar Monsta & Lark in the Park, plus other select venues.

KING MONKEY PROMOTIONS

Genres: Indie/Rock/Alternative
Venue: Basement Bar (The Venue)
Website: www.myspace.com/kingmonkeypromotions
Contact: Via MySpace
Info: New Cross based gig promoters.

LONDON UNPLUGGED

Genres: Acoustic
Venue: Blag club, Ballroom at the Cavendish arms, Viva Viva
Website: www.myspace.com/londonunplugged
Contact: Via MySpace
Info: London Unplugged prides itself in providing a platform for artists to be heard in a variety of wonderful venues

THE LUMINAIRE

Genres: Various
Venue: The Luminaire
Website: www.theluminaire.co.uk / www.myspace.com/theluminaire
Contact: bookings@theluminarie.co.uk
Info: Winner of both the Time Out and Music Week venue of the year the Luminaire is one of the best looking and sounding venues in London. Because of this they are one of the busiest in terms of artists contacting them but it's worth the email and the wait.

LIAR LIAR CLUB

Genres: Garage/Psych/Northern Soul/Mod/Beat (60s)
Venue: New Cross Inn
Website: www.myspace.com/liarliarclub
Contact: Danny Grave Via MySpace or on 07981556362
Info: A spectacular time warp of a night for the New Wave of Mods, Hippies, Soul Brothers, Psychos and Beatniks.

MONKEY BOY PROMOTIONS

Genres: Punk/Rock/Indie
Venue: The Flag, Watford
Website: www.myspace.com/monkeyboypromotions
Contact: Via MySpace
Info: Second and fourth Saturday of every month at the Flag, Watford. Always on the look out for new bands or bands that have played there before to come back.

MONSTER BAND NIGHTS

Genres: Indie/Rock
Venue: Ballroom at the Cavendish arms
Website: www.myspace.com/monsterbandnights
Contact: Via MySpace, include availability and band details
Info: Monster Band Nights are a monthly event showcasing the best breakthrough and emerging bands from London on the first Wednesday of every month.

MONTO WATER RATS
Genres: Indie/Rock/Acoustic
Venue: The Water Rats
Website: www.themonto.com
Contact: info@themonto.com included Myspace link, bio, contact number and e-mail
Info: Great venue and great location, just make sure that you can bring the punters through the door.

MUMDANCE
Genres: party music/grime /electro/indie
Venue: The Old Blue Last
Website: http://www.myspace.com/mumdance
Contact: Via MySpace
Info: MumDance parties are known for a forward thinking music policy and breaking new acts. Monthly parties are always free entry.

NAMBUCCA
Genres: Indie/Rock/Alternative
Venue: Nambucca
Website: www.myspace.com/nambucca
Contact: Via MySpace
Info: North London based venue, winner of the Indy Music Award 2008 for Pub of the year.

NORTH SOUTH DIVIDE
Genres: Indie/Rock
Venue: 333 Mother Bar, The 100 Club (London), The Ruby Lounge (Manchester)
Website: www.myspace.com/northsouthivide
Contact: NSDgigs@yahoo.co.uk
Info: Promotion company that puts on monthly gigs alternating between London and Manchester.

THE OLD BLUE LAST
Genres: Indie/Rock/Alternative
Website: www.theoldbluelast.com
www.myspace.com/oldbluelast
Contact: ben.s@viceuk.com
Info: Majority of nights are put on by outside promoters, so check the top friends list on the Old Blue Last's MySpace profile for further information and direct links to promoters who work out of the venue.

PLUM PROMOTIONS
Genres: Punk/Indie/Rock/Electronica/Pop/Acoustic/Folk/Lo-Fi/Alt-Country
Venue: Hoxton Bar & Kitchen/Besty Trotwood/Industry
Website: www.plummusic.com
www.myspace.com/plummusic
Contact: Via the online submission form which can be found at www.plummusic.com
Info: For the past ten years Plum Promotions have been putting on gigs at a number of venues throughout London. A well respected and established promoter, past acts have included Muse, Ash, The Hives, The Dears, Doves and The Kaiser Chiefs.

POWERS ACOUSTIC ROOM
Genres: Acoustic/Rock/Country
Venue: Powers Acoustic Room
Website: www.myspace.com/powersacousticroom
Contact: Via MySpace
Info: A great, young venue that is growing in stature within the London scene.

THE REDBRICKS
Genres: Folk/Psychedelic/Progressive
Venue: Albert Embankment, Black Gardendia, Dulcmer, Defectors Weld, Lock Tavern, Dulcmer (Manchester)
Website: www.myspace.com/downattheredbricks
Contact: Via MySpace or theredbricks@hotmail.co.uk
Info: Folk/country nights run throughout a number of venues in both London and Manchester.

ROUGH TRADE SHOP ROTA AFTERNOON
Genre: Indie/Rock
Venue: Notting Hill Arts Club
Website: www.myspace.com/rotaclub
Contact: Via MySpace
Info: Rough Trade Shops' RoTa afternoons have been running for 7 years. Saturdays 4-8pm and always free entry.

RSW CONCERTS

Genre: Rock/Indie
Venues: Barfly/Fly/Borderline/ULU/Forum
Website: www.myspace.com/rswconcerts
Contact: garagerocknights@aol.com / check myspace for details
Info: Concert and party promoters based in central London. Made their name at the Highbury Garage, now working with Barfly/Mean Fiddler and a number of other independent venues throughout London.

SKA BURLESQUE

Genres: Ska/Rock
Venues: Amersham Arms/Macbeth
Website: www.myspace.com/skaburlesque
Contact: Via MySpace
Info: Run by DJ Kleenex this is the event that Lewisham council tried to ban. The majority of bands will be Ska but they are open to just about every genre, all of this mixed in with burlesque.

SIXES AND SEVENS

Genre: Acoustic
Venue: The Cedar Room
Website: www.myspace.com/sixesandsevensmusic
Contact: Via MySpace or email sixesandsevensmusic@googlemail.com
Info: Free, weekly acoustic showcase at the Cedar rooms, North London.

SLWC

Genre: Punk/Psychobilly/Ska
Venue: Various
Website: www.myspace.com/southlondonpunks
Contact: Via myspace
Info: South London based promoter that puts on mainly PsychobillyRockabilly. nights at a number of venues throughout London.

THIS IS MUSIC

Genre: Various/Other
Venue: Macbeth
Website: www.myspace.com/thisismusiclondon
Contact: Via MySpace
Info: Once a month club night at the Macbeth with the occasional gig run via a number of other venues. Check their MySpace for details.

TURNING WORM

Genre: Indie/Rock
Venues: Bloomsbury Bowling lanes, 100 Club, Constitution, Worlds End Camden, Wilmington Arms, Tommy Flynn's, Bush Hall
Website: www.myspace.com/turningworm
Contact: info@turning-worm.co.uk
Info: Turning worm are a music promotion, event management and music production company.

UNHAPPY BIRTHDAY CLUB

Genre: Indie
Venue: Tommy Flynn's
Website: www.myspace.com/unhappybirthdayclub
Contact: Via MySpace
Info: Indie promoter that puts on a range of different genres of music.

UP ALL NIGHT PROMOTIONS

Genre: Alternative/Indie/Rock/Acoustic
Venues: The Miller, The Spice of Life, The Hard Rock Café
Websites: www.upallnightmusic.com / www.myspace.com/upallnightpromotions
Contact: Info@upallnightmusic.com
Info: Up All Night Music is a London based company working hard to promote live music across the city.

WHAT'S COOKIN

Genre: Country/Alt-Country/Folk
Venue: The Sheep Walk
Website: www.whatscookin.co.uk
Contact: ramblinsteve@whatscookin.co.uk
Info: One of the best looking stages in London and some of the best UK, and sometimes further a-field, Country/Alt-Country acts around. Free entry with all that's requested is a donation of your choosing which goes straight to the bands.

WINDMILL BRIXTON

Genre: Various
Venue: Windmill
Websites: www.windmillbrixton.co.uk
www.myspace.com/windmillbrixton
Contact: windmillbrixton@yahoo.co.uk , included band name in subject line
Info: Great venue in the heart of Brixton. There might be a wait for a slot but a venue that is well worth playing.

THE FLEECE

Genre: Indie/Rock
Venue: The Fleece
Website: www.myspace.com/thefleecebristol /
www.fleecegigs.co.uk
Contact: dave@dcbpromotions.com
Info: 350 capacity venue in the heart of Bristol

LOFI HIFI

Genres: Indie/Alternative
Venues: The Louisiana, The KLA
Website: www.myspace.com/lofihifi
Contact: tre_bailey@hotmail.com
Info: See MySpace for details.

MOLES CLUB/THE PORTER

Genres: Indie/Rock/Acoustic
Venues: Moles Club, The Porter
Website: www.moles.co.uk
Contact: Check the "Want to play" section of the website
Info: Both an acoustic (Moles) and full band venue (Porter).

OFF BEAT PROMOTIONS

Genres: Acoustic/Indie/Rock
Venues: St James Wine Vaults, The Louisiana
Website: www.myspace.com/offbeatpromotions
Contact: Via MySpace
Info: Bath and Bristol based promoter.

444 CLUB

Genres: Indie/Rock/Alternative/Rockabilly/Psychobilly
Venue: The Rainbow
Website: www.myspace.com/kamikazeevents []
Contact: Via MySpace
Info: Birmigham/Digbeth based rock promoter.

10 LIVES

Genres: Indie/Rock/Alternative
Venue: The Flapper
Website: www.myspace.com/10livesmusicvenue
Contact: flapper10lives@hotmail.co.uk
Info: Regular Saturday night promoter at the Flapper Birmingham.

THE CATAPULT CLUB

Genres: Indie/Rock/Alternative
Venues: Bar Academy, The Actress and Bishop, The Hare and Hound
Website: www.myspace.com/thecatapultclub
Contact: Via MySpace, include a mobile number
Info: The Catapult Club is a live music promotion company booking regular gigs into Bar Academy, The Actress and Bishop and The Hare and Hounds in Birmingham.

HUMBUCKER PRESENTS LIVE @ SOUND BAR

Genre: Indie
Venue: Sound bar
Website: www.myspace.com/theiconspresentssoundbar
Contact: Via MySpace
Info: Read the teams and conditions that can be found on MySpace

BRIGHTON

611 PROMOTIONS

Venue: Prince Albert
Venues: Ska, punk, metal, emo, indie, rock, pop, jazz
Website: www.myspace.com/onceover
Contact: Send a demo to: Ben Melmoth, 611 promotions, flat 3, 19 bedford place
Brighton, BN1 2PT
Info: South coast promoter putting on a number of gigs in the Worthing area.

THE BULB BASH

Genres: Art/Pop/Punk/Metal/Experimental/Electronic/Grind
Venue: The Hope
Website: www.myspace.com/thebulbbash
Contact: Via MySpace
Info: The Bulb Bash is a monthly club night based at The Hope in Brighton hosted by the writers of Bulb Bash Magazine.

CABLE CLUB

Genres: Indie/Rock/Alternative
Venue: Prince Albert
Website: www.myspace.com/cableclub
Contact: Via MySpace or email cableclub@hotmail.com
Info: Promoters of regular Tuesday night gigs at the Prince Albert.

EVIL BUDDHA PROMOTIONS

Genre: Punk/Ska/Metal (no emo/screamo)
Venues: The Junction Pub, Engine Rooms
Website: www.myspace.com/evilbuddhapromotions
Contact: Send an email via MySpace containing your name, contact number, genre and estimated crowd. Before you send a message read Evil Buddha's MySpace Blog regarding their booking policy.
Info: Punk/Ska/Metal promoter whose main focus is on local bands, but are open to gig swaps with other artists based throughout the UK.

GILDED PALACE OF SIN

Genre: Americana/Alt-Country
Venue: Prince Albert
Website: www.theguildedpalaceofsin.com
www.myspace.com/guildedpalace
Contact: Demos: demoposse@thegildedpalaceofsin.com
Gigs: info@thegildedpalaceofsin.com
Info: The Gilded Palace of Sin posse has been bringing the best in Americana and alt-country to the south coast town of Brighton for the past six years.

THE GREYS

Genre: Acoustic/Folk/Americana
Venue: The Grays
Website: www.myspace.com/thegrayspub
www.greyspub.com
Contact: chris@greyspub.com or via myspace
Info: The Greys pub in Southover Street, Brighton has built itself a persona that continues to grow far beyond its tiny interior and strange box-like shape.

HECTORS LIVE

Genre: Various
Venue: Hectors House
Website: www.myspace.com/hectorshouse
Contact: Via MySpace
Info: Hectors House is now getting a reputation as one of Brighton's best live music venues where you get to see the best bands from Brighton every week for free.

MELTING VINYL

Genre: Various (check website to see if you would fit one of there nights)
Venues: Various
Website: www.meltingvinyl.co.uk
www.myspace.com/meltingvinyl
Contact: general-enquiries@meltingvinyl.co.uk
Info: Melting Vinyl is committed to bringing the cream of live music (national and international) to Brighton.

THE HOPE

Genre: Various
Venue: The Hope
Website: www.myspace.com/thehopevenue
Contact: thehope@zelnet.com
Info: With a highly central position between the Clock Tower and Brighton station, the Hope is a bustling, music-led, watering hole popular with everyone from skinny, guitar-toting types to the after-work crowd, with the location guaranteeing a regular supply of fresh faces.

PORTLAND ROCK BAR

Genre: Rock/Indie
Venue: Portland Rock bar
Website: www.portlandrockbar.co.uk
www.msypace.com/portlandrockbar
Contact: Via MySpace
Info: A weekly Wednesday event dedicated to showcasing the exceptional amount of original talent in Brighton & Hove and the surrounding areas. However, bands from slightly further a-field with a dedicated following are also welcome to participate.

KONG PROMOTIONS

Genres: Indie/Rock/Alternative
Venues: Various
Website: www.myspace.com/kongpromo
Contact: Via MySpace or info@kongpromotions.co.uk
Info: Promoter throughout a number of venues in Brighton and beyond.

RANELAGH ARMS

Genre: Blues/Rock/Country
Venue: Ranelagh Arms
Website: www.myspace.com/theranelagh
Contact: Bulb Gash Magazine
Info: The Ranelagh has been presenting the best local, national and international Blues, Rock & Country acts for almost 20 years.

LOUT PROMOTIONS

Genre: Indie/Rock/Acoustic
Venue: Concorde 2, Corn Exchange
Website: www.loutpromotions.co.uk
www.myspace.com/loutpromotions
Contact: Info@loutpromotions, or via MySpace
Info: Lout Promotions is an independent live music and events company based in Brighton.

SANCTUARY

Genre: Acoustic
Venue: Sanctuary
Website: www.myspace.com/sandramcdonagh
www.myspace.com/sanctuary_hove
Contact: Via MySpace
Info: Seven nights-a-week live music and multi media showcase venue.

SOUND FACTORY

Genre: Rock/Factory/Indie
Venue: The Providence
Website: www.myspace.com/provuk
Contact: Via MySpace
Info: Promoters/venue putting on the best new bands from Brighton and beyond.

THE COUNTRY CLUB

Genre: Country/Alt-Country/Blues/Acoustic
Venues: The Bay Horse, The Ruby Lounge
Website: www.myspace.com/thecountryclubmanchester
Contact: Via MySpace
Info: Country/Blues promoter that runs bi-monthly club nights throughout Manchester.

WHITE NOISE

Genre: Indie/Rock/Alternative
Venue: Engine Room
Website: www.myspace.com/whitenoisebrighton
Contact: See www.rockbrighton.com/rules for details on how to book a gig.
Info: White Noise helps local bands get gigs and play to a larger audience.

DISCO APOCALYPSO

Genre: Rock/Garage/Punk
Venue: The Ruby Lounge
Website: www.myspace.com/discoapocalypso
Contact: Via MySpace
Info: Disco Apocalypso is held on the third Friday of each month at The Ruby Lounge, Northern Quarter, Manchester. Doors open at 10pm with a late bar until 4am.

MANCHESTER

THE AFTERSHOW

Genre: Indie
Venue: Moho
Website: www.theaftershow.net
www.myspace.com/theaftershow
Contact: Via MySpace
Info: Co-Run by Embrace frontman Danny McNamara, the Aftershow features some of the best unsigned and newly signed acts currently on the scene.

E.B.A. PROMOTIONS

Genre: Rock/Indie/Acoustic
Venues: Saki Bar, Whitworth, The Thirsty Scholar, The Attic, Fuel
Website: www.myspace.com/ebapromotions
Contact: Via MySpace
Info: E.B.A Promotions is an ever expanding project committed to bringing the best music in Manchester to as many venues as possible.

BOMB IBIZA
GENRES: PUNK/SKA

Venue: The Retro Bar
Website: www.myspace.com/bombibiza
Contact: Send any demos to 2 Agnes Street, Levenshulme, Manchester, M19 3AZ
Info: Established in 2003 as a Ska-punk clubnight, Bomb Ibiza has developed into Manchester's most thriving community for the Ska genre.

GET PUNK PROMOTIONS

Genre: Punk/Rock
Venue: The Retro Bar
Website: www.myspace.com/getpunk
Contact: Via MySpace
Info: Manchester-based Punk night happening on the third Monday of each month at the Retro Bar.

I'VE GOT A SEMI

Genre: Indie/Rock

Venues: The Ruby Lounge

Website: www.ivegotasemi.com
www.myspace.com/ivegotasemi

Contact: Via MySpace or click on the 'Contact Us" section of the website

Info: Bands with style and substance that vary in sound but not quality with admission prices that won't break the piggy bank.

JAMBOREE

Genre: Anti-Folk/Experimental/Indie-Pop/Lo-Fi

Venue: Klondyke Bowls Club

Website: www.myspace.com/jamboreemanchester

Contact: Via MySpace

Info: Jamboree happens every second Thursday of the month and are always looking for new and interesting people to perform.

LEAF PROMOTIONS

Genre: Rock/Indie/Ska/Blues/Folk/Pop/Latin/ Reggae/Metal

Venues: Arden Arms, The Crown, The Bakers Vaults

Website: www.leafpromotions.com
www.myspace.com/leafpromotions

Contact: leafpromotions@hotmail.co.uk

Or send demos to: The Arden Arms, c/o John @ Leaf, 23 Millgate, Stockport, Cheshire, SK1 2LX

Info: Leaf promotes the best of the north west's unsigned music talent.

LOST AND FOUND

Genre: Indie

Venue: The Ruby Lounge

Website: www.myspace.com/lostandfoundlive

Contact: Via MySpace

Info: Running on one night of each month at The Ruby Lounge with 3-4 live bands and then DJs until late.

RADIO FOREPLAY

Genres: Folk/Punk/Pop/Rock

Venue: Fuel Café Bar

Website: www.myspace.com/radioforeplay

Contact: Albaker@riseup.net

Info: Radio Foreplay is a monthly program of entertainment to be showcased at the Fuel Cafe Bar, Manchester on the second Saturday of each month.

RED@RETRO

Genre: Rock/Indie

Venue: The Retro Bar

Website: www.myspace.com/redatretro

Contact: Via MySpace

Info: Monthly night to promote the best unsigned acts in the Manchester area.

TRAGIC EYE PROMOTIONS

Genre: Metal/Rock/Alternative

Venue: The Retro Bar

Website: www.myspace.com/tragiceye

Contact: Via MySpace (check to make sure that they have slots avaible)

Info: Rock/Metal Promotions Company, booking gigs in and around Manchester for bands from all over the country.

VOODOO CLUB

Genre: Punk/Rockabilly/Garage

Venue: The Retro Bar

Website: www.myspace.com/voodooatretro

Contact: Via MySpace

Info: Voodoo club night held on the last Friday of every month in the basement of the Retro Bar, focusing on Punk, Rock n' Roll, Garage Rock and Rockabilly.

WHILE OTHER BANDS PARK THERE VANS

Genre: Acoustic/Alternative

Venue: Trof

Website: www.myspace.com/whileotherbandspacktherevans

Contact: nsdgigs@yahoo.co.uk

Info: Acoustic night brought to you by the same people who run the North/South Divide club nights.

WOT GOD FORGOT

Genre: Indie/Rock

Venues: Ruby Lounge, Café Suki, Retro Bar

Website: www.myspace.com/wotgodforgot

Contact: Via MySpace

Info: WOTGODFORGOT Promotions aims to bring the best in signed and unsigned music in Manchester and from around the world. If you are a touring band looking for a gig then get in touch.

ADVENTURES IN THE BACKROOM

Genre: Indie/Rock

Venue: Lamp

Website: www.myspace.com/undertheinfluence

Contact: Via MySpace

Info: Indie/Rock night featuring both newly signed and unsigned acts plus DJs.

YORKSHIRE

APOLLO 15 PROMOTIONS

Genre: Indie/Rock/Other

Venue: Basement

Website: www.myspace.com/apollo15promotions

Contact: Via MySpace

Info: Indie/Rock club, York.

BRAINWASH PROMOTIONS

Genres: Rock/Prog/Metal/Indie/Fold/Electronic

Venues: Upstairs @ the Library

Website: www.myspace.com/brainwashpromotions

Contact: brainwashpromotions@hotmail.com

Info: Promoter of a number of genres (basically anything that they like), also manage two acts and a record label, are open to both local and touring bands.

THE FENTON

Genre: Hardcore/Metal/Punk

Venue: The Fenton

Website: www.thefenton.com
www.myspace.com/thefentonhotel

Contact: playitloud666@yahoo.co.uk

Info: Situated between the two universities in Leeds, The Fenton hosts regular foreign touring bands and killer local bands, making The Fenton central to the DIY/punk/hardcore/metal underground scenes in Leeds.

THE GIG THAT EXPLODED

Genres: Alternative/Club/Other

Venue: Hull Adelphi

Website: www.myspace.com/thegigthatexploded

Contact: Via MySpace

Info: Non-profit music nights run by a collection of people who want you to dance, gasp in awe and have a good time.

JAGER TUESDAY

Genres: Indie/Rock

Venue: Trash

Website: www.myspace.com/jagertuesday

Contact: Via Myspace

Info: Jager Tuesday is a weekly night at Trash with 3-4 live bands per week and DJs 'til 2am.

JOSEPHS WELL

Genre: Indie/Rock

Venue: Josephs Well

Website: www.myspace.com/josephswell

Contact: booking@josephswell.com

Info: Live music venue with bands on 7 nights a week.

MOOG

Genre: Indie/Rock

Venues: Cardigan Arms, Brudenell Social Club

Website: www.myspace.com/moogpromotions

Contact: Via MySpace

Info: Moog is a Leeds-based company, which promotes live music and entertainment at The Cardigan Arms and The Brudenell Social Club. The bands/acts booked vary between rock, metal, punk, emo, indie and electro.

THE NEW ADELPHI CLUB

Genres: Rock/Indie

Venue: The New Adelphi Club

Website: www.myspace.com/adelphiclub

Contact: paul@theadelphiclub.karoo.co.uk

Info: Live music venue in Hull. Check MySpace for further details

THE REVOLUTIONARY FREAKED OUT FUZZ CLUB

Genre: Psychedelic/Garage/Blues

Venue: Upstairs in Dusk

Websites: www.myspace.com/fuzzclub

Contact: Via MySpace

Info: The only place you can get your groove on to Howlin' Wolf, Captain Beefheart, James Brown, Little Milton, The Sonics & Bobbie Gentry. Also Cult Movies like 'Hells Angels On Wheels' & 'The Trip', and also the best live bands this side of the Fillmore, east, or west!

RISE ABOVE PROMOTIONS

Genre: Rock/Metal

Venues: Various

Website: www.myspace.com/rise_above_promotions

Contact: Leave a comment at the Myspace blog intitled "Bands wanting show."

Info: Promoters in the Leeds/Bradford area, are also open to hearing from touring bands.

RUSTY HAT

Genre: Alternative

Venue: Beehive

Website: www.myspace.com/rustyhatpromo

Contact: rustyhat@btconnect.com

Info: A gig promoter for bands and solo acts in Bradford, now running a monthly night at the Beehive.

THE SESH

Genre: Indie/Rock

Venues: Various

Website: www.myspace.com/maks33onions

Contact: Via MySpace

Info: Free, weekly live music event now into its fifth year.

TRASH

Genre: Indie/Rock/Garage Rock

Venue: Trash

Website: www.myspace.com/trashleeds

Contact: info@vibrations.org.uk, send your MySspace link, when you want to play and how many people you expect to bring. Address the email to the attention of Jordan

Info: Great Venue in the heart of Leeds city centre.

WHERE ANGELS PLAY

Genres: Indie/Rock
Venue: Trash
Website: www.myspace.com/soundpeople
Contact: Via MySpace
Info: Indie based club night run every Saturday night at Trash.

YOUNG BRADFORD MUSIC

Genre: Indie/Pop Punk/Power Pop
Venues: Various
Website: www.myspace.com/youngbradfordmusic
Contact: N/A
Info: Resource for gigs and venues in Bradford who put on artists that are under 18. Check MySpace for further information.

LIVERPOOL

FUSE

Genres: Classic Rock/Experimental/Indie
Venue: The New Picket
Website: www.myspace.com/fuseliverpool
Contact: Via MySpace
Info: Rock and Indie promoter who put on monthly/bi-monthly gigs at the New Picket.

HAUNTED HOUSE

Genres: Indie/Rock/Pop
Venues: View Two Gallery / The New Picket
Website: www.myspace.com/hauntedhouseliverpool
Contact: hauntedhouse-liverpool@hotmail.com
Info: Acoustic nights at the New Picket run by a collection of promoters who are putting on nights for love not profit.

JUST ANOTHER BAND NIGHT

Genre: Indie/Rock
Venue: Liverpool Carling Academy
Website: www.myspace.com/justanotherbandnight
Contact: Via MySpace
Info: Just another band night is a regular night for local bands held on various Friday and Saturday nights at the Liverpool Carling Academy.

KOROVA

Genre: Indie/Rock/Electro/Other
Venue: Korova
Website: www.korova-liverpool.com
Contact: Via online booking form
Info: Korova is Liverpool's most insightful and creative venue. A joint venture between Rob Gutmann and Liverpool group Ladytron, the venue is an amalgamation of eating, drinking and playing.

LIVERPOOL CALLING

Genre: Alternative/Indie/Rock
Venue: Korova
Website: www.myspace.com/liverpoolcalling
Contact: Via MySpace
Info: Not belonging to any scene means that just about every genre is welcome at Liverpool Calling, making for a line up of great bands and DJs playing classic tunes.

SAMIZDAT

Genre: Indie/Rock
Venue: Korova
Website: www.myspace.com/samizdarpromotions
Contact: Via MySpace
Info: Samizdat is a DIY collective putting on shows in Liverpool. Their aims are to showcase the best in new (and old) music whilst keeping costs low for you, making sure everyone playing has the best time possible.

TAPE AND MIX PROMOTIONS
Genre: Alternative/electro/Indie/Acoustic
Venue: Korova
Website: www.myspace.com/tapeandmixpromotions
Contact: Via MySpace
Info: Go to tape and mix with a burning desire to play gigs, whether you're an up and coming band or hugely famous, and they shall cater to your needs.

FAB PROMOTIONS
Genres: Indie/Rock/Alternative
Venue: The Jericho Tavern
Websites: www.myspace.com/fabpromotions / www.fabpromotions.co.uk
Contact: Frank@fabpromotons.co.uk
Info: Fab Promotions was set up in 2004 to bring more activity to Oxford's entertainment scene.

ZANZIBAR CLUB
Genre: Indie/Rock
Venue: Zanzibar Ckub
Website: www.thezanzibarclub.com
Contact: info@thezanzibarclub.com
Info: Indie, Rock venue in the heart of Liverpool that plays host to a number of signed and unsigned artists.

THE WHEATSHEAF
Genres: Indie/Rock/Alternative
Venue: The Wheatsheaf
Website: www.myspace.com/wheatsheaf_music
Contact: Via MySpace for further information on promoters at the Wheatsheaf.
Info: 150 capacity live music venue that hosts live music 5 nights a week.

OXFORD

NEWCASTLE + SUNDERLAND

THE CELLAR
Genres: Indie/Rock/Alternative
Venue: The Cellar
Website: www.myspace.com/thecellaroxford / www.cellarmusic.co.uk
Contact: Via MySpace or info@cellarmusic.co.uk
Info: Regular Thursday night live music.

THE END BAR/TEO MUSIC
Genres: Indie/Rock
Venue: The End Bar
Website: www.myspace.com/theendbar
Contact: theend@teomusic.co.uk
Info: A fine venue with a great sound, The End is a hub of music in Newcastle.

CROSS TOWN TRAFFIC
Genres: Indie/Alt Folk/ Electronica
Venue: The Jericho Tavern
Website: www.myspace.com/crosstownjericho
Contact: Via MySpace
Info: Promoter of Thursday night gigs at the Jericho that aim to showcase emerging local talent, especially favouring anything unusual, quirky or just downright entertaining.

INDEPENDENT
Genres: Indie/Rock/Alternative
Venue: Independent
Websites: www.independentsunderland.com / www.myspace.com/independent_venue
Contact: ben@independentsunderland.com
Info: Independent is a Sunderland based music venue and club.

THE RIGGER

Genres: Indie/Rock

Venue: The Rigger

Website: www.riggermusic.com

Contact: riggermusic@btconnect.com

Info: Newcastle based rock venue that puts on both signed and unsigned artists.

TOO FAR NORTH

Genres: Indie/Rock/Alternative

Venues: Various

Website: www.toofarnorth.co.uk / www.myspace.com/toofarnorthmusic

Contact: info@toofarnorth.co.uk

Info: Record and gig promoter.

SHEFFIELD + NOTTINGHAM

ATTICUS PROMOTION

Genres: Rock/Metal/.Progressive

Venue: The Old Angel Inn

Website: www.myspace.com/atticuspromotion

Contact: Check Myspace for booking details and if they are currently looking for artists to book.

Info: A Nottingham based live music promotions company with a passion for Rock, Metal and all genres in between.

THE BOARDWALK

Genres: Rock/Indie/Pop

Venue: The Boardwalk

Website: www.myspace.com/theboardwalk

Contact: Via MySpace

Info: Quality live music seven days a week, with an acoustic night every fortnight, regular local unsigned acts during the week, as well as more established bands on tours across the country, variety is the key.

HALF A HAND SHAKE

Genre: Indie/Rock

Venues: Various

Website: www.myspace.com/halfahandshake

Contact: Via MySpace

Info: Promoter of a number of nights across Sheffield which features a range of genres.

JUNKTION 7

Genres: Indie/Rock/Heavy Rock/Metal

Venue: Junktion 7

Websites: www.myspace.com/junktion7 / www.junktion7.co.uk

Contact: Via demos section on website

Info: Junktion7 is an independent live music venue in Nottingham, England.

THE MAZE

Genres: Indie/Rock/Metal

Venue: The Maze

Website: www.myspace.com/themazerocks / www.themazerocks.com

Contact: info@themazerocks.com

Info: Underground music and live entertainment venue, supportive of artists on the local scene.

REDHOUSE

Genre: Rock/Indie

Venue: Redhouse

Website: www.myspace.com/redhousesheffield

Contact: Via MySpace

Info: Rock, Indie venue who book unsigned artists and the occasional small show for bigger named acts, visit the MySpace blog 'Booking policy and Info' for further information.

TEAM TALL PROMOTIONS

Genres: Alternative/Rock/Experimental
Venues: The Red House, The Casbah
Website: www.myspace.com/teamtallpromotions
Contact: Via MySpace
Info: Team Tall's ethos is to showcase quality bands, at quality shows, aiming to cater for as many musical tastes as possible and offer a varied range of talent to attract a varied group of like minded people.

UNEVEN BLONDE

Genre: Various
Venues: Various in Leeds and Sheffield
Website: www.myspace.com/unevenblonde
Contact: m.coop@unevenblonde.co.uk
Info: Promoter in both Sheffield and Leeds, have a read 'FAO band wanting to play' blog on MySpace before contacting.

13TH NOTE

Genres: Indie/Rock
Venue: 13th Note
Website: www.myspace.com/13thnote
Contact: notebookings@gmail.com
Info: An independent music venue, bar & vegetarian/vegan cafe in the centre of Glasgow that hosts gigs 7 nights a week.

GLASGOW

CAPITOL

Genres: Indie/Rock
Venue: Capitol
Website: www.myspace.com/capitolglasgow
Contact: capitol@g1group.com
Info: Open from Sept '06 the Capitol is continuing to build its reputation as a hot spot for both signed and unsigned bands.

KING TUTS WAH WAH HUT

Genres: Alternative/Rock/Indie
Venue: Kinsg Tuts Wah Wah Hut
Websites: www.myspace.com/kingtuts / www.kingtuts.co.uk
Contact: Send any demos to: King Tut's c/o DF Concerts, PO Box 25241, Glasgow, G2 5XS
Info: Quite possibly the finest small venue in the world.

KYL PROMOTIONS

Genres: Indie/Rock
Venues: Various
Website: www.myspace.com/kylpromotions
Contact: Via MySpace
Info: Promoter that puts on gigs in and around Glasgow.

INDIEVOUS

Genre: Indie
Venue: Capitol
Website: www.myspace.com/indievousgigs
Contact: Via MySpace or e-ail at: indievous@hotmail.co.uk
Info: For over three years Indievous has been dedicated to the rise of up and coming local and national Indie bands that would like to perform to an upbeat and vibrant Scottish crowd.

MAGGIE MAYS

Genres: Indie/Rock
Venue: Maggie Mays
Website: www.myspace.com/maggiemaysglasgow
Contact: Via MySpace
Info: Live music every Thursday, Friday and Saturday nights, plus DJs into the early hours, also host a Monday night open-mic.

NICE N' SLEAZY

Genres: Indie/Rock

Venue: Nice n Sleazy

Website: www.myspace.com/nicensleazyglasgow
www.nicensleazy.com

Contact: Send any demos to: Mig c/o nice'n'sleazy, 421 Sauchiehall St Glasgow G2 3LG

Info: Glasgow based music venue.

PIN-UP NIGHTS

Genres: Indie/Rock

Venue: The Winchester Club

Website: www.myspace.com/pinupnights

Contact: Send any demos, including a bio, to: Pinup Nights, Flat 2/R, 26 Norham Street, Shawlands, G41 3XQ

Info: Pin-up Nights is a Glasgow indie, punk, soul and electropop club night that takes place on the first Friday of every month at The Winchester Edinburgh.

EDINBURGH

CABARET VOLTAIRE

Genres: Indie/Electro

Venue: Cabaret Voltaire

Websites: www.myspace.com/cabaretvoltaire
www.cabaretvoltaire.com

Contact: Leave a comment on the MySpace blog 'Looking for a gig'.

Info: Open seven nights a week, Cabaret Voltaire is a thriving, twin-roomed venue that hosts some of the best-known club events in Edinburgh.

HENRY'S CELLAR BAR

Genres: Various

Venue: Henry's Cellar Bar

Website: www.myspace.com/henrysvenue

Contact: axis@mrw44.co.uk

Info: Established live music venue in Edinburgh.

THE HIVE

Genres: Indie/Rock/Alternative

Venue: The Hive

Website: www.myspace.com/thehivelive

Contact: For more information email at gigs@clubhive.co.uk, also send any demos to: Gigs, The Hive, 15-17 Niddry Street, Edinburgh, EH1 1LG

Info: A 250 capacity venue in Edinburgh

STUDIO 24

Genre: Alternative

Venue: Studio 24

Website: www.myspace.com/studio24edinburgh

Contact: Via Myspace or studio24@uk2.net , also check , Myspace for a list of all other promoters.

Info: Edinburgh's alternative music venue.

ABERDEEN

CAFÉ DRUMMOND

Genres: Indie/Rock

Venue: Café Drummond

Website: www.cafedrummonds.co.uk
www.myspace.com/cafedrummond

Contact: See website for details

Info: Aberdeen based venue.

FUDGE PROMOTIONS

Genres: Rock/Metal/Indie

Venues: Moorings, Snafu

Website: www.myspace.com/fudgefanzine
www.myspace.com/blacktoothrock

Contact: Via MySpace

Info: Based in Aberdeen, fudge's intention is to promote decent, new music with regular gigs on a Monday and Saturday nights.

THE TUNNELS

Genres: Indie/Rock/Alternative
Venue: The Tunnels
Website: www.myspace.com/tunnelsaberdeen
Contact: Via MySpace/info@thetunnels.co.uk
Info: One of Aberdeen's Premier Live Music Venues.

HORSE FACE MUSIC PROMOTIONS

Genres: Rock/Alternative
Venue: The Cellar Bar
Website: www.myspace.com/horsefacepromotions
Contact: Via MySpace
Info: Belfast based Rock/Classic Rock promoter.

VOCOUSTICS PROMOTIONS

Genres: Alternative/Acoustic/Folk
Venues: The Tunnels, Café Drummonds
Website: www.myspace.com/vocoustic
Contact: Via MySpace
Info: Music promotions organisation based in Aberdeen.

LAVERYS BUNKER

Genres: Indie/Rock
Venue: Laverys Bunker
Website: www.myspace.com/djgregz
Contact: Via MySpace
Info: Gig booker for Laverys Bunker.

BELFAST

BRUISED FRUIT PROMOTIONS

Genres: Indie/Alternative
Venues: Various
Website: www.myspace.com/bruisedfruitpromotions
www.bruisedfruitpromotions.com
Contact: mike@bruisedfruitpromotions.com
Info: Gig promoters at a number of venues throughout Belfast.

CLUB SANDWICH

Genres: Indie/Rock
Venue: Laverys Bunker
Website: www.myspace.com/laverysclubsandwich
www.bruisedfruitpromotions.co.uk
Contact: angie@bruisedfruitpromotions.co.uk
Info: Club Sandwich is held two Saturdays a month in Laverys Bunker.

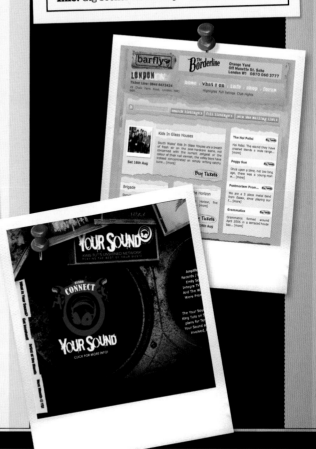

CHAPTER CONTENTS

A FIELD DAY

THERE'S MUCH TO LEARN FROM PLAYING THE LUNCH SHIFT AT A RAINY FESTIVAL

Nothing brings out the British public's celebrated resilience quite like Glastonbury. A stubborn refusal to be cowed means, even though it invariably rains every couple of days in June, the organisers will not reschedule the music festival to later in the summer, when the weather tends to be better. Resolute even when faced by the prospect of trench foot, hypothermia and toxic slurry – half rainwater, half by-products of cow farming – Glastonbury's hordes remain committed to consuming their music out of doors during the longest days of the year.

Not that other three-day events promise anything better – Reading, Leeds and the Isle of Wight can all contribute their own sagas; bitter tales of miserable conditions tempering the enjoyment of magnificent performances. ●

Stumbling around a field with your mind fried by cider and excitement – and your body battered by rain – coping with deep mud and invisible barbed-wire entanglements at twilight is now as British as fish 'n' chips.

While the main stages at Glastonbury, Reading or Leeds might still be out of your league, a growing number of the larger festivals have started to offer unsigned artists a shortcut to big crowds. Usually in the format of a competition, these promotions won't get you the headline on Saturday night; you're more likely to have the opening slot on the first day or the second stage at the end of the final day. Playing before lunch to a few hundred early risers and late revellers will feel weird to the traditionally nocturnal creatures that form heavy rock bands, but that's no reason to turn down the gig or cruise through the performance on automatic – such exposure can't be knocked. At a big festival, no matter when or where you play, you'll raise your profile, performing for an audience you may not otherwise have

Festival crowds are a very reliable guide to what you are doing right

reached, and have all the thrills that come with a new type of gig.

The smaller, regional – generally one-day only – festivals attract a lower turnout, showcase fewer musical genres and don't offer as many performance stages. But this means you'll get a greater share of the audience. Unsigned bands, especially if they're based in the area, often pick up desirable slots on the bill; they invariably bring their entire fanbase along to watch and, although they'll cheer loudest for the band they have paid to see, this kind of audience is hard to beat.

Less cynical than London crowds, well-disposed towards all kinds of entertainment, sober enough to pay attention, but drunk enough to forgive mistakes, festival crowds are a very reliable guide to what you're doing right and what parts of your set still need more work.

THE STUFF OF DREAMS – AND THE OCCASIONAL NIGHTMARE

FESTIVAL PERFORMANCES CAN LIVE LONG IN THE MEMORY, BUT NOT ALWAYS FOR THE RIGHT REASON

■ PULP, GLASTONBURY 1995:

Replacing The Stone Roses, who pulled out of a headline set, Pulp produced one of the all-time great Glastonbury performances. Striding through a magnificent rendition of the then unreleased *Different Class* album, they entranced the largest crowd of the weekend. *Common People* became an enduring festival anthem and, although Pulp had been together since 1980, this set broke them into the big-time.

■ THE STONE ROSES, READING 1996:

With two of the founder members having already quit, it was left to Mani and Ian Brown to nail the lid on The Stone Roses' coffin. Using

two session musicians, the band's set has gone down in history as one of the worst festival performances of all time. See for yourself on YouTube.

■ MY CHEMICAL ROMANCE & PANIC AT THE DISCO, READING 2006:

There's a cruel, but hilarious, tradition at Reading; at some point during the three-day binge of hard rock, heavy metal, strong beer and challenging food, an act will be sacrificed to the crowd. It may be a cheesy, female pop duo or school-age hip-hoppers. In 2006, it was 'emo' bands.

MCR and PATD encountered unprecedented hostility and both acts became targets for anything the crowd could throw at them. They played on through it all and PATD lead singer Brendon Urie was knocked out by a bottle a few seconds into their set, but earned grudging admiration on returning to the mic soon after.

The bands' preparedness to risk life, limb, hairstyle and makeup to finish the gig earned them a lot of respect and a much higher profile in the music press and mainstream media.

Opening out to a new audience away from your local venue will flood you with adrenaline

WHY PLAY A FESTIVAL?

The main appeal is the unique atmosphere each has. Nothing matches the feeling when thousands of people focus their attention on you and your performance – be it good or bad! Opening out to a completely new audience – without the safety net of loyal fans and away from your comfortable local venue – will flood you with adrenaline. This might propel you into giving the performance of your life, sending your confidence into orbit.

There are countless stories, however, of artists losing the battle of nerves, blowing the gig and taking months to recover. But with a spot of luck, reasonable weather and a competent sound engineer at the controls, the buzz around you will start as soon as everyone gets home – word will spread like wildfire and reviews of your performance will pop up online and in magazines.

HOW TO GET ON A FESTIVAL BILL

The application process usually involves filling in an online form or emailing a link to your MySpace page to the festival's website address. Even major festivals usually hold open one slot for unsigned artists and, to have a chance of playing, you'll probably have to win a Battle of the Bands contest.

GET CRACKING

On the opposite page, we provide a short list of music festivals and explain how unsigned bands should go about applying for a spot at each of them in 2009. It is also worth checking the websites of smaller festivals in the listings section, which start on page 80. However, you should be aware that festival billings are usually finalised by April, so don't hang around – start applying now! ★

SAY WHAT?
"Throw one more orange and we could make a fruit salad." – Member of Keanu Reeves' band Dogstar hits back after the Glastonbury crowd pelt the stage with missiles.

TOWN AND COUNTRY

WHETHER YOU FANCY PLAYING IN THE MIDDLE OF A FIELD OR AT A TRENDY CITY VENUE, GET THE BALL ROLLING NOW IF YOU WANT TO SECURE A 2009 SLOT

■ **BEACH BREAK LIVE, BATTLE FOR THE BEACH:**
Apply using the application form in the 'contact us' section of the website. There is also an online competition, the prize being a slot in the ACM (Academy of Contemporary Music) tent and two days in a recording studio with a top producer. Follow the link for 'Battle for the Beach' on *www.beachbreaklive.com*. This competition is only open to student bands.

■ **DOWNLOAD, GIBSON UNSIGNED:**
For the chance to play at Download Festival, upload a video to YouTube and email the link to *www.myspace.com/ gibsonolympus*. The winner will play the opening slot on the third stage and receive VIP passes.

■ **END OF THE ROAD FESTIVAL:**
Provides 10 unsigned acts with the chance to play longer sets than at most other festivals. Visit *www.endoftheroadfestival.com/ www.myspace.com/ endoftheroadfestival*.

■ **GLASTONBURY, NEW MUSIC:**
Run in conjunction with *Q* magazine, this competition offers the chance to play on The Other or Pyramid stages at Glastonbury. The judging panel includes festival organisers Michael and Emily Eavis and *Q* editor Paul Rees. Visit *www.q4music.com/ glastonburynewbands*

■ **LEEDS FESTIVAL:**
Apply to play the BBC Introducing/New Music stage via the Futuresound Competition, run by the Cockpit music venue (*www.thecockpit.co.uk*), BBC Raw Talent, broadcast on BBC Humberside on Sundays (send a demo and biog to Katy Noone, BBC, Queens Gardens, Hull, HU1 3RH or visit *www.bbc.co.uk/ rawtalent*) or *Sandman*, an online magazine for the Midlands/ Northern music scene (*www. sandmanmagazine.co.uk*), which runs a contest for local bands.

■ **ROCK NESS:**
Run in conjunction with Amazing Tunes and XFM, this online competition involves bands creating a homepage, on to which they upload songs, pictures and videos, which are then judged by experts. The winners will play an opening slot at the festival.

In-tent on having a good time!

■ **V FESTIVAL, ROAD TO V:**
Now in its fifth year, Road to V gives two artists the opportunity to open the festival. Entrants create a profile page containing pictures, songs and videos, and the public vote. A panel of experts then pick 14 from those with the most votes/profile views to play live in London and Liverpool before picking the winners. Visit *www.roadtov.com*.

■ **CITY SHOWCASE:**
Usually takes place in the first week of June. Visit *www. cityshowcase.co.uk*

■ **IN THE CITY:**
Started by the great, and sorely missed, Tony Wilson, In the City is a series of gigs, held over three days, that showcase the best unsigned talent in the UK. Visit *www.inthecity.co.uk* and follow the link 'Demo Submissions'.

■ **SUPERSONIC:**
This three-day event at the Custard Factory, Digbeth, finds room among more established acts for local, unsigned talent. Visit *www.capsule.org.uk* for more information.

Lazing on a sunny afternoon

DiSco ShEd

Shedloads of Opportunities

HE RUNS A FESTIVAL ACT FROM A SHED, BUT PATRICK BICKERTON'S NO TOOL WHEN IT COMES TO SUCCESS

estival nut Patrick Bickerton and his pal Aidan enjoyed festivals and partying in their shed so much they decided to mix the two. They converted an ordinary 8ft by 6ft garden shed into a Disco Shed, complete with light show and giant rooftop screen. They then invited DJs and other acts to help them to entertain the masses.

Patrick, what is the Disco Shed and why the move into your own festivals?
I've been a regular festival-goer and performer since attending the Big Chill in 2000 and was inspired to start my own club night, *Peepshow*, in Oxford. This was a success and I was asked to help book a small charity festival, Festinho, which I've done for four years now. I love partying in fields, so having the means to go to as many festivals as possible is a dream, hence the birth of the Disco Shed. In brief, it's a garden shed

mounted on wheels – with a sound system, light show, screen and kitschy décor – from which we DJ. The idea was conceived during a particularly euphoric moment as we DJ-ed in the shed at one of the many parties at Aidan's house in Oxford. Since then, it's developed something of a life and a character of it's own.

At what point do you start booking the artists for festivals?
Festinho is a year-round job, but booking starts about six to nine months beforehand. I start with the bands, trying to get the bigger names first, before working on the DJ and VJ line-ups. I've always got my eyes and ears open for decent acts

How do you pick the acts?
Because I work for a charity festival, our budgets are tiny, so – to avoid paying the agent their cut – I always tried to book an act

directly if possible or via their manager – so via email, MySpace or by meeting them in person. Having said that, I know plenty of the agents thanks to my club night, so I contact them as well – and as time has passed, I am more likely to go to the agent, to be honest. They get annoyed if you go directly to the artists and an agent usually looks after lots of acts, so you can kill a few birds with one stone, as it were. Despite the reputations they have, most agents I deal with are pretty decent and will drop the fee for a good cause.

What logistical challenges does a festival present?

Countless! Finding a site, getting a licence, funding and sponsorship, booking acts, programming multiple stages, building the stages and tents in a field, adhering to health & safety regulations, making sure there's enough toilets and water points, stewards,

SAY WHAT?
"Are you the fellow that started it all?" Festival founder Michael Eavis reveals what the Queen asked him when he received a CBE at Buckingham Palace

security, printing tickets, marketing and selling enough tickets. Unless you're one of the huge, well-established festivals, you can't guarantee you'll sell many tickets until a month before the event, so money is always tight. Then there's the weather…

Does a slot at a festival offer an artist more exposure than a standard gig?

Definitely. You'll be playing to a much bigger crowd than you're used to and, while you may have your fans at the front, there'll be a lot of people who have never heard of you before, so it's a good chance to win over a new audience. And don't forget how many people might be watching coverage of the festival on TV these days. Added to that is the fact a festival gets marketed a lot more – and to many more people than a normal pub or club gig – so, by just being on the line-up, a lot more people will see your name. ●

How do you draw in and retain an audience so they watch every act?

Good programming. Hopefully, the promoter has put a lot of thought into the flow of the stage and people will want to stay to watch. You do get people who stay at the main stage all weekend, regardless of who is playing, but, equally, you'll get people who wander around the whole festival trying to see everyone. There's not much you can do to stop them and there's often too much good stuff going on at once at festivals. Avoid putting the wrong act on at the wrong time or at the wrong festival is also a good tip – 50 Cent was bottled off at Reading a few years ago, but at least the crowd stayed long enough to throw stuff at him!

How important are festivals for labels and artists?

These days, they are more important than ever. There are plenty of examples of labels programming a stage at a festival, which is a sign of a good label getting recognition and a better profile. Equally, a summer of good festival performances can make a band and really consolidate their reputation as a live act. Good billing at a high-profile

> ## "50 Cent was bottled off, but at least the crowd stayed long enough to throw things"

festival is a definite sign a band has made it. Equally, messing it up can be the ruin of a band – the most obvious example being The Stone Roses' awful performance at Reading (see page 73), which pretty much signalled the end of their career.

How important is it for an unsigned artist to get on a festival bill, especially in their local area?

It's important for increasing their profile and, for organisers of a smaller festival, it's a good idea to book up-and-coming local bands in the hope their fans will come too!

Is it difficult to keep every act happy due to the time-scales involved with staging

a festival or is there lots of moving around to get the best spots?

It can be difficult, particularly if there are egos involved. Some people might want a better billing than others, but, above all else, you have to try to make the festival programming make sense. Most of the time, though, people are just happy to be playing, so it's not usually a major issue. The main thing is to make sure there's a big enough crowd for everyone who is performing – so don't over-programme on too many stages. You don't need all of the stages to be running all the time.

How different is the atmosphere at a festival compared to a normal gig?

This depends on the festival. Generally, people let themselves go more at festivals and aren't there just to see one act in particular, so you don't get the same hardcore fans at a festival as you might do at a gig. So while you're playing to more people, maybe not as many of those people are giving you their full attention. Having said that, festival crowds are usually more forgiving.

What advice do you have for people playing at a festival or setting up their own?

If you're playing – well, don't expect a sound check, but do just relax and enjoy it. If you're starting a festival, be patient and don't try to be too ambitious straight away unless you've buckets of cash – in which case you don't need my advice. Start small and expect to grow slowly and organically – most festivals don't break even for at least three years. Do your research because it's a saturated market from May to September and it's unlikely no-one else is trying to do what you're doing. Look after your suppliers; every year there are plenty of examples of promoters being escorted off of sites by the police for their own safety, so don't make promises you can't keep – to anyone! Most of all, be kind and respectful to everyone – you'll be calling in a lot of favours, so look after people and they will probably look after you! ★
www.discoshed.com

BEACH BREAK LIVE
UK'S BIGGEST STUDENT FESTIVAL IS FLOURISHING

Celia Norowzian and Ian Forshew founded Beach Break Live two years ago, with the aim of creating something unique for students. They took their idea to BBC television's *Dragons' Den* programme and walked off with the cash, but soon realised they'd need more than a cash injection and so rejected the offer, joining forces instead with Outgoing Travel, an event company that organises the Snowbombing festival in the Alps.

The pair shortlist acts for the festival and then approach their agents, and, in 2008, secured Mr Scruff, The Enemy and The Wombats. They also encourage unsigned bands to apply to play.

Creating the right ambience is key for the BBL team, so they use MCs and DJs to give the festival a personal, engaging feel.

New acts play a big part at the festivals and Celia's advice for them is simple: 'Persistence goes a long way.'

'Get in touch early or try to piggy back off another band who you have toured with to get some introductions.'
www.beachbreaklive.com

Festival fever: start applying now

A SELECTION OF SOME OF THE BEST FESTIVALS YOU COULD ACTUALLY PLAY AT

APPALACHIAN & BLUEGRASS MUSIC FESTIVAL

Where: Ulster American Folk Park, Omagh, County Tyrone, Northern Ireland

When: September

Website: www.bluegrassomagh.com

What: Thousands flock every year to this international bluegrass event set in the stunning Ulster American Folk Park.

BESTIVAL

Where: Robin Hill Countryside Adventure Park, Downend, nearr Arreton, Isle of Wight

When: September

Website: www.redfunnel.co.uk/bestival www.wightlink.co.uk/bestival

What: Family friendly festival which is organised by DJ Rob da Bank.

BIG SESSION FESTIVAL

Where: De Montfort Hall & Gardens, Leicester

When: June

Website: N/A

What: Founded by The Oysterband (who also perform), this friendly Midlands fest offers up folk stars young and old, homegrown and foreign.

BLISSFIELDS

Where: Matterley Bowl, nr Winchester, Hants

When: July

Website: www.blissfields.co.uk

What: Expect a carnival-like atmosphere at this family-friendly do which won the Best Small Festival 2007 category at the UK Festival Awards.

BORING BY THE SEA

Where: Various venues, Weymouth, Dorset

When: June

Website: www.wakestock.co.uk

What: New one-day event that features local talent playing along side established, signed acts.

BRIGHTON FESTIVAL

Where: Various venues, Brighton

When: May

Website: www.brightonfestival.org

What: The biggest mixed arts festival in England, now in its 42nd year and featuring no less than 12 premieres, 9 exclusives and 30 free events across the city.

BUSHY'S ISLE OF MAN BLUES FESTIVAL

Where: Laxey, Isle of Man
When: May
Website: www.bigwheelblues.com
What: Annual Manx blues fest.

CHIPPENHAM FOLK FESTIVAL

Where: Chippenham town centre, Wilts
When: May
Website: www.chippfolk.co.uk
What: Four days of folk song, dance and music by the riverside at this annual villagey knees-up now in its 37th year.

CAMBRIDGE FOLK FESTIVAL

Where: Cherry Hinton Hall, Cambridge
When: July/August
Website: www.cambridgefolkfestival.co.uk
What: Broadcast on Radio 2, this is the folk festival all other folk festivals look up to that always features a prestigious international line-up.

CAMP BESTIVAL

Where: Lulworth Castle, Dorset
When: July
Website: www.campbestival.co.uk
What: New sister shebang of Rob and Josie da Bank's Bestival which takes place on Dorset's dramatic Jurassic coast and features a strong family slant.

DOT TO DOT FESTIVAL

Where: Various venues in Bristol, London & Nottingham
When: May
Website: www.dottodotfestival.co.uk
What: Indie feastival run over different days in Bristol, London and Nottingham

CHELTENHAM JAZZ FESTIVAL

Where: Various venues, Cheltenham
When: May
Website: N/A
What: A yearly well-heeled jazz shindig.

END OF THE ROAD FESTIVAL

Where: Larmer Tree Gardens, Tollard Royal, Salisbury, Wilts
When: September
Website: www.endoftheroadfestival.com
What: Founded by two friends – one of whom sold his house to fund it – after an epiphany at the Green Man Festival, End Of The Road's basic idea is that bands are invited to play longer-than-usual sets.

EVOLUTION

Where: Spillers Wharf & Baltic Square, Newcastle

When: May

Website: www.evolutionfestival.co.uk

What: A one day festival run across two stages on the Newcastle Gateshead Quayside – huge value for money at only £3 per ticket.

FIELD DAY

Where: Victoria Park, London

When: August

Website: www.fielddayfestivals.com

What: New 'village fete'-style London one-dayer.

FOLK ON THE PIER

Where: Cromer Pier, Cromer, Norfolk

When: May

Website: www.folkonthepier.co.uk

What: Acoustic roots and mainstream electric acts.

FUTURESONIC

Where: Bridgewater Hall and various venues, Manchester

When: May

Website: N/A

What: A festival of digital culture and music with its roots in club culture.

GOWER FOLK FESTIVAL

Where: Gower Heritage Centre, Parkmill, Gower, nr Swansea

When: June

Website: www.halfpennyfolkclub.com/folkfestival.htm

What: Camping at the gorgeous Three Cliffs Bay campsite, this Gower Peninsula-based bash is full of real ale and craft stalls plus a children's programme with storytelling, magic and workshops, as well as sandpit and mini zoo.

GREEN MAN FESTIVAL

Where: Glanusk Park, Usk Valley, Brecon Beacons, Wales

When: Aug

Website: www.thegreenmanfestival.co.uk

What: Fantastic boutique festie for neo-wyrd and psych-folk types.

GUILDTOWN BLUEGRASS FESTIVAL

Where: Guildtown, Perthshire, Scotland

When: July

Website: www.scottishbluegrass.com

What: Founded in 1987 for and by local aficionados and practitioners of bluegrass, this is a real village affair sponsored by the village pub, with events in the village hall and camping on the village green.

HEART OF THE WORLD FESTIVAL

Where: Various venues, Cambridge

When: May

Website: www.heartoftheworld.co.uk

What: World music, film, dance, radio, workshops, family days and more, with artists drawn from everywhere from New York to Tokyo, Lhasa to Havana, London to Dakar.

HOLMFIRTH FESTIVAL OF FOLK

Where: Holmfirth, Huddersfield

When: May

Website: www.holmfirthfestivaloffolk.co.uk

What: Community folk festival, much of which is free.

HYDRO CONNECT FESTIVAL

Where: Inveraray Castle, Loch Fyne, Argyle, Scotland

When: August

Website: www.connectmusicfestival.com/content

What: The Duke Of Argyll hosts this upmarket newcomer in the grounds of his 18th-century castle on the banks of Loch Fyne.

INDIE TRACKS INDIEPOP FESTIVAL

Where: Butterley Station, Butterley Hill, Ripley, Derbyshire

When: July

Website: www.indietracks.co.uk

What: Old school C60-type indie flavours. Past acts have included The Wedding Present, Comet Gain, Darren Hayman, Milky Wimpshake and The Bobby McGees.

JERSEY LIVE

Where: Royal Jersey Showground, Trinity, Jersey, Channel Islands

When: August

Website: www.jerseylive.org.uk

What: The biggest little indie rock festival in Europe.

ORKNEY FOLK FESTIVAL

Where: Various venues, Orkney, Scotland

When: May

Website: www.orkneyfolkfestival.com

What: Concerts, ceilidhs, dances, sessions and more at this island-hopping shindig of homegrown and international folk talent.

PERFECT DAY FESTIVAL & GARDEN PARTY

Where: Bowood House, Calne, Wilts

When: July

Website: http://tinyurl.com/5pq25y

What: Live music, big Top cabaret, circus, comedy club, fun fair, green fayre, traditional English garden party antics, sideshows and hot air balloon rides.

SECRET GARDEN PARTY

Where: Secret location nr Huntingdon, East Anglia

When: August

Website: www.secretgardenparty.com

What: Relaxed four-day party where you're as likely to find Shakespeare being performed around a fire, a custard pie battle or an artist bidding you to make your own sculpture as you are a musical megastar of tomorrow.

SELLINDGE MUSIC FESTIVAL

Where: Hope Farm, Sellindge, Kent

When: June

Website: www.sellindgemusicfestival.co.uk

What: Kent-based indie, folk, dance and world music weekender.

SEVERNSIDE MUSIC FESTIVAL

Where: Plough Inn, Pilning, Bristol

When: August

Website: www.severnsidemusicfestival.co.uk

What: All-day music event showcasing local bands, covering rock, soul, blues, funk and reggae.

STRUMMERCAMP

Where: Macclesfield Rugby Club, Macclesfield

When: May

Website: www.strummercamp.co.uk

What: Charity event organised by friends and fans of the late Joe Strummer.

SUMMER SUNDAE WEEKENDER

Where: De Montfort Hall & Gardens, Leicester

When: August

Website: www.summersundae.com

What: Three-day, multi-award-winning affair that's set across five stages

THE BIG CHILL

Where: Eastnor Castle Deer Park, Malvern Hills, Herefordshire

When: August

Website: www.bigchill.net

What: Family-friendly, ridiculously laid-back and very friendly, The Big Chill is a little bit Ibiza, a little bit National Trust, a little bit village fête and a little bit your own back garden.

THE GREAT ESCAPE

Where: Various venues, Brighton

When: May

Website: www.escapegreat.com

What: 200 bands, 25 venues, three days boasts the UK's answer to South By South West. Launched in 2006, it has already earned a reputation as a place for fans and industry pros alike to spot new talent. Industry talks, panel debates and celebrity interviews for industry delegates too.

TWO THOUSAND TREES FESTIVAL

Where: Upcote Farm, Withington, Cheltenham, Glos

When: July

Website: www.twothousandtreesfestival.co.uk

What: This green, ethical Cotswold-based event keeps things intimate with a maximum capacity of just 2,500. Two stages and a disco tent host a motley crew of underground, with past feativals having featured artists such as Art Brut, Reuben, The Duke Spirit, Frank Turner, Future of the Left and Flipron.

TROWBRIDGE VILLAGE PUMP FESTIVAL

Where: Stowford Manor Farm, Wingfield, Trowbridge, Wilts

When: July

Website: www.trowbridgefestival.co.uk

What: One of the most picturesque festivals and a big hit with local families. Three stages, four tents and one of the best children's programmes.

UNDERAGE FESTIVAL

Where: Victoria Park, Hackney, London

When: August

Website: www.underagefestivals.com

What: Booze-free, music-savvy event for 14-18 year olds.

WAKESTOCK (BLENHEIM PALACE)

Where: Blenheim Palace, Oxford

When: June

Website: www.wakestock.co.uk

What: Europe's largest wakeboard music festival, past years has featured artists including The Streets, Supergrass, Hadouken and the Hoosiers.

WICKERMAN FESTIVAL

Where: East Kirkcarswell, Dundrennan, Scotland

When: July

Website: www.thewickermanfestival.co.uk

What: Inspired by the classic 1973 film, this cultish affair culminates in the spectacular burning of a 30ft willow and straw effigy at midnight.

WOOD

Where: Braziers Park, Oxford

When: May

Website: www.thisistruck.com

What: New festival celebrating music and nature from the people behind the Truck Festival.

Y-NOT FESTIVAL

Where: Pikehall, Matlock, Derbyshire

When: August

Website: www.ynotfestivals.com

What: An intimate, non-corporate event in the Peak District, features two stages and a dance tent.

CHAPTER #3

STEP THIS WAY

A MANAGER CAN OPEN DOORS FOR YOU, BUT WILL THEY TAKE YOU TO PLACES YOU WANT TO GO?

In the digital age, an experienced manager who understands the 360° model of promotion, who can offer reliable contacts and remain level-headed when it comes to negotiations is crucial to your success.

An experienced manager will open doors for you, bring your music to the attention of record label A&R people, publishers and promoters, and find you valuable support slots with established acts. They will also deal with the nitty-gritty of the business, acting as your booking agent, accountant, publicist and promoter.

A good manager will boost your band's motivation and help to drive you forward (in some cases literally, if they provide the transport to get you to the gig). Ultimately, your manager's role is to develop the band's identity and reputation. While you'll do much of this yourself on sites like MySpace, your manager will use his/her contacts to promote your act, sending out demos to labels and organising other promotional activities.

If you are approached by a manager or management company, it's tempting to just say 'yes' and sign the first thing stuck under your nose – but tread carefully because bad management can ruin a good reputation. Take time to do research: next week is soon enough to conquer the rock 'n' roll world. Check their background and management experience, find out what other acts they work with or have looked after in the past, and give some thought to what you, as an artist, will need from them.

Before you sign anything, have at least a three-month trial (any respectable company should offer you this without any problems) to see if you can work with them. During this period, establish whether you're both going in the same direction and whether your career has been helped by their management, and set up a schedule of what they expect to achieve with you during the term of your proposed contract. ●

Managers are not necessarily the gateway to instant success and you may go through several of them before you settle on someone suitable. A good manager will be a spokesperson, a diplomat, an authoritarian, a headmaster, an organiser and a mediator. You need someone tough, charming and ready to compromise, who'll allow you to focus on writing, recording and performing, secure in the knowledge that the rest of the business has been taken care of.

HOW TO GET A MANAGER

Finding a good manager is a difficult task; expect to have all sorts of people approaching you after a gig offering you their services. They'll give you a business card and promise you a phone call, but don't get your hopes up – it's standard music-biz practice. If you're going to find a worthwhile manager, do the groundwork.

What follows isn't directly about how to get a manager – it's about how to get noticed and maintaining hope.

EMAIL

Always do your research before approaching a management company. Check on the artists they already manage and find out how well those artists are doing. Look at the music genres they work in and whether they are currently adding names to their roster.

As with blanket emails to promoters and venues (see p17), keep the contents of this

SUITED OR BOOTED?

DON'T SAY 'YES' TO THE FIRST MANAGER WHO APPROACHES YOU – TAKE TIME TO CHECK THEM OUT

■ Ask about the artists they manage, the length of time they have been with them and where those artists are now.

■ Do they work solo or as part of a larger company? How would this affect how they manage you?

■ Do they have experience of playing live? Many of today's managers used to be artists and will be more likely to understand you and your ambitions.

■ Insist on a three-month trial period so you can figure out if a working relationship is possible.

■ Know what you want from a manager and make this clear when signing the trial-period contract. State your ambitions because it's their job to help you to achieve them.

■ If a manager approaches you, they obviously think you show promise. Listen to their suggestions regarding your music, but don't feel obliged to take on everything they say.

■ If you feel it isn't going to work out, don't be afraid to back away – it's much better to have no manager than a bad manager.

FIVE GO MAD FOR IT
THE MEN WHO MADE A SCENE BEHIND THE SCENES

DON ARDEN
A tough, unforgiving man, from the old school of management, Arden brought Bo Diddley, Chuck Berry and Gene Vincent to the UK, and built the foundations for long careers for the Small Faces, Black Sabbath and ELO. For a while, Arden was one of the most powerful men in British music.

PETER GRANT
A former professional wrestler and stuntman, Grant managed Led Zeppelin and pioneered the stadium tour. Zeppelin became one of the most profitable bands in history (it has been reported Grant got 90% of ticket sales' revenue paid directly to the band) and Grant helped to promote a closer relationship between managers and artists.

BRIAN EPSTEIN
Without Epstein, The Beatles would have been just another Merseybeat band playing at the Cavern Club. He changed their look, brought them to the attention of producer George Martin and signed them to EMI's Parlophone label, helping to bring them worldwide success.

MALCOLM McLAREN
Members of The Sex Pistols disagree about how much influence McLaren had over the group. But, while in no way the figurehead of the UK punk scene, he helped, through the Pistols, to create an enduring musical genre and the stereotypical 'punk rocker' image.

ANDREW LOOG-OLDHAM
At 19, Loog-Oldham began masterminding the career of the Rolling Stones. He influenced their anti-Beatles image and developed the Jagger/Richards songwriting partnership. He went on to manage the Small Faces and Humble Pie, and is still considered to be one of the great British music impresarios.

SAY WHAT?
"Rock and roll doesn't necessarily mean a band. It doesn't mean a singer, and it doesn't mean a lyric, really. It's that question of trying to be immortal." – Malcolm McLaren

message brief and to the point. If you receive a reply, it'll probably be no more than the standard response, something along the lines of 'we are currently busy with the acts we have on our books, but thank you for your interest and we wish you the best of luck for the future'. But you never know; your email may land in the right box at the right time. Send emails, mail demos when requested, be patient and hope for the best.

BUILDING A GOOD REPUTATION
In many ways, promoters are your gateway into the music world and building a good reputation is essential to getting through the gate. Be professional and put everything you can into every gig you play.

Promoters are in constant contact with managers and tend to know when they are looking to add to their rosters of artists. If you happen to be around at the right moment – or if you jump to the front of a promoter's mind because of your professional behaviour – they will pass on your details or mention your name at least.

BLIND LUCK
Your ideal manager might just show up at one of your gigs and approach you. Take their card and set up a meeting. You'll soon know if they are serious by the way they conduct themselves at this later encounter. ★

INTERVIEW

Fighting Chance

FORMER MTV HEAD HONCHO MALCOLM McKENZIE ON WHY YOU NEED SOMEONE TO FIGHT YOUR CORNER

aving been responsible for all of MTV Europe's commercial operations in Eastern Europe, Malcolm McKenzie is now a partner in The SuperVision Management Group and has much experience of the business to share.

What is the role of a manager?
Part wet nurse, part counsellor – only kidding. Actually, the job of managing a band is a complex one. Firstly, you are the primary adviser to the band and have a legal obligation to act in their best interests. The label doesn't, the booking agent doesn't, the PR doesn't, the publisher doesn't, the promoter doesn't... I could go on. The only people labels are beholden to are their shareholders. The manager is on your side for commercial reasons and because that is the nature of the legal agreement between you. Secondly, you are the guy all of those other people look to because you are engaged

MALCOLM McKENZIE'S TOP TIP

Speak to as many people who know the manager you are considering before you put pen to paper – and, if you get to that point, always seek advice from a music lawyer.

by the band to run their business. This means a manager has to have a good understanding of all areas of the entertainment business because he/she could be negotiating anything from a digital music licence to a sponsorship agreement.

How do unsigned bands choose a manager?
It is normally the other way around. Bands often start with a friend or family member helping out until they get some attention from the industry, at which point any number of managers may become aware of them. But they need to make sure whoever they talk to has enough experience to contribute to the process and that they will not be too busy to develop the band's career.

What do you look for when you take on an artist or a band?
Talent. It's not about haircuts, trends, scenes

"Bands increasingly hold the whip hand and having a knowledgeable adviser is key"

or fashions. I like bands who can write, sing and perform live, and who have a strong sense of who they are and what they want.

How important is it to have a manager?
More so than ever in this age, when music is 'used' rather than 'owned'. Bands increasingly hold the whip hand and having a committed, knowledgeable adviser is key to success.

How long should the contract period be?
This varies enormously. I prefer a rolling, fixed-term contract with an increasing notice period and a reasonable sunset clause.

Large management companies, such as Supervision and Big Life, seem to be very successful. Do you see management of bands moving away from the single manager?
Yes. It is very difficult for the old-fashioned, one-man-band operations these days, unless they already have a successful act.

When should a band approach companies like Supervision?
There is no right time, but – unless you honestly think your band is good enough to compete with comparable successful acts – it is probably going to be a waste of time. ★

Live Connection

FUSE WHITE-HOT GIGS WITH BURNING AMBITION TO STIR MANAGER PAUL HARVEY

Paul Harvey, of Madison Management, has worked with several up and coming artists such as John Watts and Anna Neale. He is a member of the Music Managers' Forum (MMF) and specialises in royalty collection and new-media marketing.

How would you describe what you do?
We sit down with the artists to define their goals and advise them. We help them to fill in any holes in their set-up; this can include creating a web presence, organising live performances and registering with royalties-collection agencies to improving the quality of their songs. Once these have been completed, we can start working to achieve the band's objectives. Our role is to provide industry knowledge and contacts, and to market the artist. We take care of the band's diary and co-ordinate their live work. The management is the main point of contact for band members and, most importantly, collects the money. We also build a team around the artist to cover things such as live work and recordings.

How do you find acts?
Bands will either contact me directly or I will hear about them through industry contacts, such as lawyers, promoters and labels.

How do you choose your acts?
I have to love them live. I need to connect with them and they have to have talent; most importantly, they have to have a work ethic. I look for bands with ambition and openness – I need to feel they'll work with me and that they're not just looking for a sub-contractor who'll just do their work and not add anything to the project.

Where is the music industry going and how will this affect the manager's role?
There is a growing digital-led approach in the industry, which has resulted in more revenue streams for bands. The traditional, record-company route will still exist, but bands at the start of their career will increasingly choose to release their music themselves or to license it via digital companies or through smaller, independent labels. The manager's job will evolve into one of trying to meet the artist's aspirations in the emerging digital industry. ★

> **"Bands have to have talent but, most importantly, they have to have a work ethic"**

Patience is a Virtue

PESTER-POWER HOLDS NO SWAY IN MANAGEMENT CIRCLES, SO CHILL OUT

Before you rush to send an email or post a demo to every address on this list, there are a few things you should consider. First of all, check the management companies' websites to see which ones cater for musicians of a similar style to you. Companies will never announce they are looking for artists, so, if you get a reply, expect it to be along the lines of 'our books are full at the moment'. Don't be disheartened – this is usually true. They are busy people, so don't phone them. The numbers given are for reference only, not for you to call every day/once a week to ask if they have listened to your demo – the chances are they haven't. Be patient. By all means get your name out to these people, just don't annoy them while you're waiting.

AIRE INTERNATIONAL
Director: Marc Connor
Address: 27 The Quadrangle, 49 Atalanta Street, London, SW6 6TU
T: 0207 386 1600
F: 0207 386 1619
W: www.airmtm.com
E: info@airmtm.com
Artists: I am Kloot, Jamie Cullum, Jason Mraz

BIGLIFE MANAGEMENT
MDs: Jazz Summers, Tim Perry, Tony Beard
Address: 67-69 Chalton Street, London, NW1 1HY
T: 0207 554 2100
F: 0207 554 2154
W: www.Biglifemanagement.com
E: Colin@biglifemanagement.com
Artists: The Verve, Richard Ashcroft, The Klaxons, The FutureHeads, Badly Drawn Boy

---

CEC MANAGEMENT
Managing director: Peter Felstead
Address: 65-69 White Lion Street, London, N1 9PP
T: 0207 837 2517
F: 0207 278 5915
W: www.myspace.com/cecmanagement
E: Rebecca@cecmanagement.com
Artists: 80's Matchbox B-Line Disaster, The Rakes

CITY ROCKERS ARTISTS LTD
MDs: Phil Howells, Charlie Lexton
Address: First Floor Rear, 3 Plough Yard, London, EC2A, 3LP
T: 0207 377 1210
F: 0207 655 4984
W: www.city-rockers.com
E: info@city-rockers.com
Artists: The Ghost Frequency, The Sunshine Underground

CMO MANAGEMENT INTERNATIONAL LIMITED

Managing director: Chris Morrison
Address: Studio 2.6, Shepherds East, Richmond Way, London, W14 0DQ
T: 0207 316 6969
F: 0207 316 6970
W: www.cmomanagement.co.uk
E: reception@cmomanagement.co.uk
Artists: Blur, Graham Coxon, Gorillaz

COALITION MANAGEMENT

Contacts: Tim Vigon, Tony Perrin
Address: Devonshire House, 12 Barley Mow Passage, London, W4 4PH
T: 0208 987 0123
F: 0208 987 0345
W: www.coalitiongroup.co.uk
E: management@coalitiongroup.co.uk
Artists: The Streets, The Music, Embrace, Adam Masterson, Witness

COURTYARD MANAGEMENT

Partners: Chris Hufford, Bryce Edge
Address: 21 The Nursery, Sutton Courtenay, Oxon, OX14 4UA
T: 01235 845 800
F: 0845 127 4663
W: www.courtyardmanagement.com
E: kate@cyard.com
Artists: Radiohead, Supergrass

CROWN MUSIC MANAGEMENT SERVICES

Managing director: Mark Hargreaves
Address: Matrix Complex, 91 Peterborough Road, London, SW6 3BU
T: 0207 371 5444
F: 0207 371 5454
W: www.crownmusic.co.uk
E: mark@crownmusic.co.uk
Artists: Get Cape Wear Cape Fly, Noisettes

CRUISIN MUSIC

Managing director: Sil Willcox
Address: PO Box 3187, Radstock, BA3 5WD
T: 01373 834 161
F: 01373 834 164
W: www.cruisin.co.uk
E: sil@cruisin.co.uk
Artists: The Stranglers, Bluetones, The Wurzels

EMPIRE ARTIST MANAGEMENT

Directors: Neale Easterby, Richard Ramsey
Address: 36 Uxbridge Street, Notting Hill, London, W8 7TN
T: 0207 221 1133
F: 0207 243 1585
W: www.Empire-management.co.uk
E: info@empire-management.co.uk
Artists: The Feeling, Estelle, Lucie Silvas

EMPEROR MANAGEMENT

Managing director: John Empson
Address: 2 Brayburne Avenue, London, SW4 6AA
T: 0207 720 0826
F: 0207 720 1869
W: www.myspace.com/Emperormanagement
E: john.empson@btopenworld.com
Artists: Sons & Daughters, Liam Frost, Lea Shores

FREDAG

MD: N/A
Address: (For demo submissions) Talent, Fredag Music Group, 39 Palmerstone Place, Edinburgh EH12 5AU
T: 0131 202 6236
F: 0131 202 6238
W: www.fredag.co.uk
E: talent@fredagartistgroup.com
Artists: Any Colour Black, Charlie Oxford

FRESHWATER HUGHES MANAGEMENT
Contact: Jackie Hughes, Brian Freshwater
Address: PO Box 54, Northaw, Herts, EN6 4PY
(Send demos to this address)
T: 01707 664 141
F: N/A
W: www.freshwaterhughes.com
E: info@freshwaterhughes.com
Artists: Foy Vance, Conner Reeves

FULL TIME HOBBY MANAGEMENT
Managing director: Wez
Address: 3rd Floor, 1A Adpar Street,
London, W2 1DE (Send demos to A&R at this address)
T: 0207 535 6740
F: 0207 563 7283
W: www.fulltimehobby.co.uk
E: info@fulltimehobby.co.uk
Artists: Autolux, Malcolm Middleton, Tunng

GRAHAM PEACOCK MANAGEMENT
Managing director: Graham Peacock
Address: PO Box 84, Hove,
West Sussex, BN3 6YP
T: 01273 777 409
F: 01273 777 809
W: www.gpmanagement.net
E: graham@gpmanagement.net
Artists: Moloko, Roisin Murphy

GR MANAGEMENT
MDs: Rab Andrew, Gerry McElhone
Address: 974 Pollokshaws Road, Shawlands,
Glasgow, Strathclyde, G41 2HA
T: 0141 632 1111
F: 0141 649 0042
W: n/a
E: info@grmanagement.co.uk
Artists: Primal Scream

GRAND UNION ARTIST MANAGEMENT
Managers: David Bianchi, Nick Ember
Address: 124 and 126 Buspace Studios,
Conlan Street, London, W10 5AP
T: 0208 968 7788
F: 0208 968 3377
W: www.granduniongroup.com
E: info@granduniongroup.com
Artists: The Enemy, Boy Kill Boy, Killing Joke

GRAPHITE MEDIA
Director: Ben Turner
Address: Graphite Media, PO Box 605,
Richmond, Surrey, TW9 2YE
T: 0208 948 8629
F: n/a
W: www.graphitemedia.net
E: duane@graphitemedia.net
Artists: Rob Da Bank, Sunday Best,
A Man Called Adam

HALL OR NOTHING
Managing director: Terri Hall
Address: Hall or Nothing Management,
3rd Floor, 19 Denmark Street,
London, WC2H 8NA (Send demos to this address)
T: n/a
F: n/a
W: www.myspace.com/
hallornothingmanagement
E: office@hallornothing.co.uk (Send MP3s to this address)
Artists: Manic Street Preachers, New Young
Pony Club, The Horrors, Kids In Glass Houses,
Ed Harcourt, Clocks, The Departure, Noah and
the Whale, The Script

IE MUSIC LTD
Managing directors: David Enthoven, Tim Clark
Address: 111 Frithville Gardens, London, W12 7JG
T: 0208 600 3400
F: 0208 600 3401
W: www.iemusic.co.uk
E: info@iemusic.co.uk
Artists: Archive, Craig Armstrong, Passenger, Robbie Williams, Sia, The Asteroids Galaxy Tour

IN PHASE MANAGEMENT
Manager: Fay Woolven
Address: 55a Ditton Road, Surbition, Surrey, KT6 6RF
T: 0208 390 4583
F: 0208 288 1597
W: www.Inphasemanagement.com
E: Info@inphasemanagement.com
Artists: Cradle Of Filth, Reef

JPR MANAGEMENT
Managing director: John Reid
Address: PO Box 3062, Brighton, East Sussex, BN50 9EA
T: 01273 779 944
F: 01273 779 967
W: www.jprmanagement.com
E: info@jprmanagement.co.uk
Artists: Justin Currie, Derek Meins, The Maccabees

KEY MUSIC MANAGEMENT
Artist Mgr: Richard Jones
Address: Edenhurst, 87 Station Rd, Marple, SK6 6NY
T: 0161 221 3681
F: N/A
W: www.keymusicgroup.com
E: Richard@kmmltd.com
Artists: The Breeders, The Kills, Pixies

LTM
Contact: Ed Millett
Address: Innit Studios, 33a Wadeson Street, London, E2 9DR
T: 0208 981 9210
F: 0208 981 9210
W: n/a
E: mail@lunchtm.co.uk
Artists: Guillemots

MANAGEMENT
Director: Timothy Leitch
Address: N/A
T: N/A
F: N/A
W: www.myspace.com/rumusicmanagement
E: Via Myspace
Artists: Sanjuro, Flying Space

MIDNIGHT TO SIX MANAGEMENT
Directors: Dave Haper, Tony Crean
Address: 4th Floor, 33 Newman Street, London, W1T 1PY
T: 0207 462 0026
F: 0207 462 0012
W: n/a
E: harper@midnighttosix.com
Artists: Goldfrapp, The Draytons, Candie Payne

MODERN WOOD MANAGEMENT
Managing director: n/a
Address: Cambridge House, Card Hill, Forest Row, East Sussex, RH18 5BA
T: 01342 822619
F: n/a
W: www.modernwoodmanagement.co.uk
E: info@modernwoodmanagment.co.uk
Artists: Imogen Heap, Nik Kershaw, The Deciphers, New Lost World, Froo Froo

MONDO MANAGEMENT

Contact: Rob Holden
Address: Unit 2D, Clapham North Arts Centre, 26-32 Voltaire Road, London, SW4 0DT
T: 0207 720 7411
F: 0207 720 8095
W: n/a
E: rob@ihtrecords.com
Artists: David Gray, Damien Rice

MYTHOPHONIS MUSIC MANAGEMENT

MD: n/a
Address: n/a
T: n/a
F: n/a
W: www.myspace.com/mythophonic
E: information@mythophonic.com
Artists: Enter Shikari, Saving Aimee

OUT THERE MANAGEMENT

Manager: Stephen Taverner
Address: Strongroom. 120-124 Curtain Road, London, EC2A 3SQ
T: 0207 739 6903
F: 0207 613 2715
W: www.outthere.co.uk
E: outthere@outthere.co.uk
Artists: Ash, The Ting Tings

POSITIVE MANAGEMENT

Managing director: Meira Shore
Address: 41 West Ella Road, London, NW10 9PT
T: 0208 967 6257
F: 0208 963 1974
W: www.positive-mgmt.co.uk
E: meira@positive-mgmt.co.uk
Artists: Terry Callier, Road, Lorna Brown

NATIVE MANAGEMENT

Managing director: Peter Evans
Address: 32 Ransomes Dock, 35-37 Parkgate Road, London, SW11 4NP
T: 0207 801 1919
F: 0207 738 1819
W: www.nativemanagement.com
E: info@nativemanagement.com
Artists: Howie B

NETTWERK MANAGEMENT UK

Contact: Sam Slattery
Address: Clearwater Yard, 35 Inverness Street, London, NW1 7HB
T: 0207 424 7500
F: 0207 424 7501
W: www.nettwerk.com
E: Eleanor@nettwerk.com
Artists: Dido, Gogol Bordello, The Pipettes, Stereophonics, Sum 41, Martha Wainwright

OUTSIDE MANAGEMENT

Director: Alan Edwards
Address: Butler House, 177-178 Tottenham Court Road, London, W1T 7NY
T: 0207 436 3633
F: 0207 436 3632
W: www.outside-org.co.uk
E: info@outside-org.co.uk
Artists: Amy Winehouse, David Bowie, Led Zeppelin, The Sex Pistols, The Who

PROBATION MANAGEMENT

Directors: Martin Bowen, Adam Stangroom
Address: 1st Floor, Warwick Hall, Off Banastre Avenue, Cardiff, CF14 3NR
T: 029 2069 4450
F: 029 2069 4455
W: www.myspace.com/probationmanagement
E: prodmgt@btconnect.com
Artists: The Automatic

PROLIFICA MANAGEMENT
Director: Colin Schaverien
Address: Unit 1, 32 Caxton Road, London, W12 8AJ
T: 0208 740 9920
F: 0208 743 2976
W: www.myspace.com/prolifica
E: colin@prolifica.co.uk
Artists: Blood Red Shoes, Maximo Park

QUEST MANAGEMENT
Managers: Scott Rodger, Stuart Green
Address: 36 Warple Way, Unit 1D, London, W3 0RG
T: 0208 749 0088
F: 0208 749 0080
W: www.quest-management.com
E: info@quest-management.com
Artists: Bjork

RIOT MANAGEMENT LTD
Managers: Matt Page, Ewan Grant
Address: 47 Hay's Mews, London, W1J 5QE
T: 0207 499 3993
F: 0207 499 0219
W: www.myspace.com/riot_management
E: info@riot-management.com
Artists: Feeder, SpiderSimpson

RIVERMAN MANAGEMENT
Director: David Mclean
Address: Top Floor, George House, Brecon Road, London, W6 8PY
T: 0207 381 4000
F: 0207 381 9666
W: www.riverman.co.uk
E: info@riverman.co.uk
Artists: Placebo, Martina Topley Bird, Red Organ Serpent Sound, The Officers, Hotel Persona

ROBERT MILLER MANAGEMENT/RUNNING MEDIA GROUP
Managing director: Bob Miller
Address: 14 Victoria Road, Douglas, Isle of Man, IM2 4ER (Send demos to this address, see website for further information)
T: 01624 677214
F: n/a
W: www.runningmedia.com
E: management@runningmedia.com
Artists: Corinne Bailey Rae, Back Door Slam

SB MANAGEMENT
Managing director: Simon Banks
Address: 2 Barb Mews, London, W6 7PA
T: 0207 078 9789
F: 0871 253 1584
W: www.sbman.co.uk
E: info@sbman.co.uk
Artists: KT Tunstall

SCRUFFY BIRD MANAGEMENT
Managing director: Duncan Ellis
Address: The Nest, 30-31 Shoreditch High Street, London, E1 6PG
T: 0207 247 4464
F: n/a
W: www.scruffybird.com
E: info@scruffybird.com
Artists: The Foals, The Rumble Stripes, Young Knives

SINCERE MANAGEMENT
Directors: Peter Jenner, Mushi Jenner
Address: 35 Bravington Road, London, W9 3AB
T: 0208 960 4438
F: 0208 968 8458
W: n/a
E: office@sinman.co.uk
Artists: Billy Bragg

SUPERVISION MANAGEMENT GROUP

Director: James Sandom

Address: 59-65 Worship Street, London, EC2A 2DU

T: 0207 688 9000

F: 0207 688 8999

W: www.myspace.com/supervisionmanagement

E: hazel@supervisionmgt.com (Direct all management enquires to this address)

Artists: Franz Ferdinand, Kaiser Chiefs, The Cribs, Late of the Pier

THE TCB GROUP

Managing director: Steven Howard

Address: 24 Kimberley Court, Kimberley Road, Queens Park, London, NW6 7SL

T: 0207 328 7272

F: 0207 372 0844

W: www.tcbgroup.co.uk

E: stevenhoward@tcbgroup.co.uk

Artists: Roxy Music, Unkle Jam, Bryan Ferry

UNDERDOGS MANAGEMENT

MD: Gemma Reilly/Faye Hunter

Address: N/A

T: N/A

W: www.myspace.com/underdogsmanagement

E: gemma@theunderdogsonline.com / faye@theunderdogsonline.com

Artists: Hella Cholla, Bop Social, High Rankin

WILDLIFE ENTERTAINMENT

Directors: Ian McAndrew, Colin Lester

Address: Unit F, 21 Heathmans Road, London, SW6 4TJ

T: 0207 371 7008

F: 0207 371 7708

W: n/a

E: Info@wildlife-entertainment.com

Artists: Arctic Monkeys, Stephen Fretwell

TRUST MANAGEMENT

MD: Dave Cronen

Address: 10-112 Disraeli Road, Putney, London, SW15 2DX

T: 0208 705 278

F: n/a

W: www.trustmanagement.co.uk / www.myspace.com/trustmanagement

E: Vdave@trustmanagement.co.uk

Artists: Air Traffic, Iain Archer, Zut Alors

TRC MANAGEMENT

Managing director: Phil Chadwick

Address: 10c Whitworth Court, Manor Park, Manor Farm Road, Cheshire, WA7 1TE (Send demos to this address)

T: 01928 571 111

F: 0871 247 4923

W: www.trcmanagement.com

E: mail@trcmanagement.com

Artists: Elbow, Thirteen Senses

WAR ZONES AND ASSOCIATES

Managing director: Richard Hermitage

Address: 33 Kersley Road, London, N16 0NT

T: 0207 249 2894

F: 0207 254 3729

W n/a

E: wz23@aol.com

Artists: Art Brut, Frank Black/Black Francis

XL TALENT LLP

Partners: Maggi Hickman, Mike Box

Address: Reverb House, Bennett Street, London, W4 2AH

T: 0208 747 0660

F: 0208 747 0880

W: www.Reverbxl.com

E: management@reverbxl.com

Artists: Apollo 440, Assembly Now

CHAPTER #4

I SOUGHT THE LAW

A LEGAL TEAM CAN DO A LOT MORE THAN JUST DOT THE Is AND CROSS THE Ts

The traditional role of lawyers within the UK music scene has changed. In the past, bands would only approach solicitors when there were contracts to read through or to draw up, or amendments to be made to existing ones. Nowadays, you're likely to see them scouting around the clubs and venues – much like record company A&R departments – in search of the next big thing.

Lawyers will often now offer their services for free, a practice that has existed in the United States for several years. They promise to take care of building the team around you – arranging management and locating a booking agent – while approaching record labels and weighing up contracts they might be offered on your behalf. Lawyers adopting ●

this stance are gambling their regular fee on the chance you'll sign a contract and the percentage they will receive will reimburse them for their time and effort.

Artists backed by well-heeled lawyers have the wherewithal to undertake nationwide tours and to secure favourable support slots on festival bills. This helps to build a strong fanbase and generate press support; in turn, this makes it easier to negotiate a publishing deal. Naturally, record labels prefer to sign a finished product than make a risky investment in 'the next big hope', so – by having everything in place (thanks to your lawyer) – you'll be in a strong position when it comes to approaching labels, agreeing your marketing budgets and deciding on recording costs.

Of course, music lawyers will happily read through contracts and negotiate on your behalf for an hourly fee; but this can be costly and doesn't necessarily safeguard your interests. You only have to look to the past decade to see examples of apparently lucrative and favourable contracts signed by artists (The Stones Roses, Prince and

If possible, choose a lawyer via personal recommendation

George Michael to name but a few) that have come back to haunt them. Where possible, choose a music lawyer through personal recommendation – otherwise, look for someone who has a fearsome reputation.

Today's unsigned musician is more than just a performer. You're a manager, booking agent, record-label producer, artwork designer, distributor and accountant. However, unless you happen to be a law student too, it's probably best to leave legal documents to those who understand them. It's easy to get over-excited when a contract is thrust under your nose and it's always flattering to hear that someone likes your music – just don't let your enthusiasm get the better of you. ★

PITFALLS TO WATCH OUT FOR
TAKE A STEP BACK TO AVOID LEGAL MINEFIELDS

1 UP-FRONT FEES
Managers and agents should never ask for a fee up front. Watch out for companies with badly designed websites, especially if they guarantee you a record deal within a year or promise support slots with major artists – in reality, they'll take your money and run.

2 THEY FOUND YOU ON MYSPACE
Be careful if you get a 'friend request' from a lawyer or management company who 'heard you on MySpace'. This doesn't happen, despite the legends. The Arctic Monkeys achieved success once they had built a reputation as a great live act and Lily Allen already had a team in place when the MySpace propaganda exploded around her. MySpace is a great promotional tool, but always check those who contact you.

3 PERCENTAGES
Make sure you, as the artist, keep a reasonable percentage of earnings. Standard management fees vary between 10% and 20%. On top of that, you will have to reimburse the record label, pay the booking agent and retain a lawyer – all this chips away at your earnings, so make sure, at the outset, you'll be making something for the amount of work you are putting in.

4 RENEWAL OF CONTRACTS
Look for 'get out' clauses in your management contract. Be aware that these may be worded to give your manager the option to renew the contract at expiry or to pull out of involvement at any point. Either of these options might not fit in with your plans, so read the terms carefully.

5 IS IT TOO GOOD TO BE TRUE?
If it seems too good to be true, it probably is. If someone offers to take you from saloon bar to stadium gig, it's best to say 'thanks, but no' and walk away – unless that person is representing a major record label, in which case you should grab the opportunity with both hands. But don't hold your breath; the odds on you being that lucky are roughly the same as those for winning the lottery.

6 YOU ARE NOT ALLOWED TO GET ADVICE
If someone offers you a contract, but says they won't be offering advice as part of the deal, forget it – you should be looking for transparency in any contracts you sign. Don't fall for them suggesting they put you in touch with their own lawyer either. Always get independent advice on contracts. That's the only way to ensure you will be receiving an unbiased opinion.

Copper-bottomed Contracts

INVESTIGATE THE SMALL-PRINT TO SEAL A DEAL THAT'S WATERTIGHT AND WORTH IT

Creative types are, traditionally, reluctant to deal with business things, but you don't want to lose out because of ignorance. You must have a basic understanding of the law and how it relates to the music business or you'll be shark food. Chuck Berry once said, if he could start his career again, he'd do a business studies course before he even picked up a guitar. You certainly don't want to be ripped off or exploited like those poor musical heroes who sold millions of records, but ended up with little more than a handful of bitter stories to show for it. The material below should mean you're not so easily misled by weasel words.

Dean Marsh is a solicitor specialising in the music industry (*www.deanmarsh.com; dean@deanmarsh.com*). Aware that bohemian, artistic creatures like yourselves don't really relate to the nuts and bolts of making a living from your music, we asked him to sketch out the essentials and clarify some of the jargon you'll have to deal with (but only when your legal people are around to consult with, of course). ●

What follows is a very simplified version of two areas of law applicable to you as an artist – Intellectual Property (what we amateurs know as copyright) and Contract Law (what you and 'The Man' promise to do for one another). You need to understand everything you put your name to, so always get your lawyers to clarify any complex phrasing before you sign on the dotted line.

INTELLECTUAL PROPERTY

The main rights are copyright and performer's rights; however, as an artist working within the 360°/DIY model, you should be aware of data protection as it relates to your mailing lists and have an understanding of trade marks.

Copyright essentials

There are two separate and distinct copyrights in music:

■ Copyright in the song (contract documents may refer to this as 'the work' or 'composition'), which is both the lyrics and the melody. This lasts for 70 years after the composer's death.

■ Copyright in the recording of the song. This lasts for 50 years from the date the recording was made. Sound recording copyright is owned by the person who made the 'necessary arrangements' for the recording to be made.

Copyright does not require registration in the UK. It automatically comes into being at the moment an original work is written or a recording is made. As owner of the copyright, you have the legal right to stop others from doing certain things with your music, including copying it or broadcasting it without your permission.

You can sell your copyright (in what is termed 'an assignment') or you can give permission for certain usages ('a licence'). Licences will either cover a fixed, specified period or extend for the life of the copyright, and will be defined as being exclusive or non-exclusive.

The collection society MCPS acts on behalf of songwriters (see page 157). It grants licences to reproduce (i.e. record) songs and

There are strict rules about how you can collect and store data, and the way you use it

acts according to a 'blanket licence' (i.e. it applies to all). Songwriters are entitled to royalties – CDs and vinyl records earn 8.5% of the dealer price, downloads generate 8%. The PRS deals – on behalf of songwriters – with the licensing of performance income earned from such arenas as radio-play, bars, gigs and clubs.

Performers' rights essentials

Artists have the right to stop others from reproducing their performance without their permission. This is why you will be required to assign or license those rights to allow the recording to be released. The collection society Phonographic Performance Limited (PPL) deals with the collection of airplay and

Registry helps to protect it (costs start at £200 for UK registration). With a registered brand, it is easier to enforce cases of infringement, but the common-law charge of 'passing off' may help if someone is using the same band name as you.

CUSTOMARY DEALS

The music business is going through all sorts of unpredictable changes, but the basic terms of certain types of deal are known as 'customary' and, as such, rarely change. You're likely to come up against any of the following in your career and, even though they are customary, you must always get your lawyer to check them before you sign.

Management deal

■ **Remember:** The manager works for the artist and not vice versa.

■ **Term:** Normally between 18 months and three years, although you will often see a get-out clause if the manager does not procure a 'major deal' within a reasonable time, say a year to 18 months.

■ **Commission:** Usually 20% of what is earned. For live income, it is based on the net amount (i.e. after costs, including booking agent's fee), but, otherwise, it's based on gross income (i.e. with no deductions). However, it is not normal for a manager to commission recording costs or other recoupable expenditure by third parties and certain other costs.

■ **Territory:** Normally, this is worldwide, but sometimes the US is excluded so a separate American manager can be appointed.

other income on behalf of registered performers. Compared with that generated by record sales, performance income is increasing yearly, so you should consider registering with the PPL as soon as appropriate.

Database rights essentials

There are strict rules, under the Data Protection Act 1998, about how you can collect and store data, and the way you can use it. Databases should be protected by encryption – not only are they valuable, there are harsh penalties for non-compliance with the rules. For more information visit *www.legislation.org.uk* or check with your legal team.

Trade mark essentials

Registering your 'brand' at the Trade Mark

SAY WHAT?

"We know Sony completely own us. They can do anything they want with us. They can drop us."
– Richey James Edwards, Manic Street Preachers

Record Deal (Major)

They acquire rights in the recorded music.

■ Artist signs for an initial period, during which they will, generally, be required to deliver an album.

■ Label has options to extend the deal for subsequent recordings (contracts are normally for three to five albums).

■ Invariably, the deal will be worldwide.

■ Label will generally own the copyright in the recordings for the life of the copyright.

■ The label will generally pay an advance to the artist (to be negotiated). ●

MUSIC LAWYERS

■ Label will also pay a royalty of about 20% of the dealer price. For a CD, the full dealer price is about £8, so the artist will receive approximately £1.60 (plus mechanicals if they write their own music). However, there are other deductions and reductions', which means, in reality, the artist will receive significantly less, probably about £1 per album and, shockingly, only about 4p per individual download. The label will receive significantly more. The artist will not receive a royalty unless and until they 'recoup' (i.e. the royalty exceeds the advance and other recoupable costs the label has paid). Be aware, approximately 95% of artists never recoup. Few artists get to make a second album because of this.

All recording costs and half of video costs are recoupable from the royalty. However, marketing and promotional costs are not recoupable under this model.

Record Deal (Independent Label)

Independent labels also generally sign artists for an initial period, with a 'commitment' to deliver a certain number of recordings, plus options, although it's likely they may play a safer game and make a commitment for just

> Indies may play a safer game and make a commitment for an initial single or an EP

an initial single or EP, with the option for subsequent album(s) written into the terms of the contract.
■ They may be willing to do a UK-only deal, leaving the artist with the ability to do separate deals internationally.
They will want to own the recordings, but if you have already made these yourself, you can often do a deal in which the label licences them for a fixed period, after which they will revert to you and you can deal again.
■ Advances are rare and, invariably, low.
■ Profits are split 50/50. From the income generated, all costs are deducted. The profits are then split down the middle.
■ Under an indie deal, an artist will stand to

earn significantly more (perhaps £2 per album as opposed to £1). However, the recoupment process is different – some costs under a major label are not recoupable, whereas, with a 50/50 deal, they all are). It may take longer to recoup, but, once you do, it will be worth it.

Publishing deal

A publishing company looks to acquire an interest in your work. It may be for a single song, but will more probably be on an album-by-album basis, much like a record deal. They will agree to register the works, take care of administration and try to maximise revenue.
■ They may pay a recoupable advance.
■ They will own or license the works for a fixed term ('the retention period'), normally between 10 and 20 years.
■ There are various publishing income streams. The percentages that are paid after recoupment of advances are usually:
A. Mechanical income (see above)   **70-75%**
You should consider the basis on which it is

being calculated; 'at source' (i.e. with no deductions) if it's a major or 'receipts' (based on a percentage of what the publisher receives after costs) if it's an indie. If the latter, make sure the deductions are capped at about 20%.

B. Synch income 50-75%

This is when your music is used in conjunction with visual images (e.g. in adverts, films, games and on TV). Rates vary depending on who procures the synch.

C. Performance income 70-75%

Half of this will be paid directly to the artist by PRS (see page 106), but the above figure is the effective split.

D. Other income 60–70%

This covers things like ring-tone income.

Production Deal

This is similar to an independent record deal, but a production company is really operating as a middle man, looking to develop artists and then sell them on to another label.

■ Artists will normally receive 50% of the net profits if the production company releases the music, but they may see 60% (or more) if a third-party label comes on board.

■ Normally, you can negotiate a get-out clause in the event of the production company not procuring a major deal within a reasonable time – say a year to 18 months.

Producer Deal

A producer will produce the record in return for assigning all rights and will normally receive an advance for each track against a royalty. The advance is subject to negotiation, depending on the producer's status and who is paying.

■ After recoupment of any advances and recording costs, the producer will typically receive a royalty of between 2% and 5% of the dealer price. If the artist is signed to a major label, they will deduct it from the royalty. If you are operating on a net-profit deal, the producer royalty equates to between 10% and 25% of the artist's share of the profits.

Booking agent agreement

They will be engaged to get live gigs.

TERMS & CONDITIONS
CUT THROUGH THE JARGON TO PROTECT YOURSELF

A contract doesn't need to be in writing, but it's recommended you get everything on paper, just so there is no confusion later on about what has or hasn't been agreed. A deal that looks too good to be true probably is and signing the wrong deal can have awful results.

The music business is unique in that it is expected that every contract will be reviewed by a specialist lawyer. Therefore, you should not sign anything until you get expert advice. If you are being asked to sign a contract and cannot afford to hire a lawyer, ask the other side to pay your legal fees. They may agree to do so if they can recoup the costs from your royalties. The Musicians' Union also offers a limited amount of free advice for their members.

Most music-related contracts have the same basic structure and will cover similar points, using the same basic terms:

■ **Parties**
Who the agreement is between. Typically, it'll be between you and a manager, publisher, record label or promoter

■ **Term**
How long the agreement will last

■ **Territory**
Defines whether the contract applies world wide or only in certain parts of the globe

■ **Rights granted**
This specifies what the other party is allowed to do with your intellectual property. Depending on the type of agreement you're making, you'll give them 'exclusive rights' or 'non-exclusive rights' to exploit your work. Again, speak to your legal people for the best advice

■ **Obligations**
What each side agrees to do. The details will vary depending on the type of deal you're making

■ **Payment**
How do you earn? How is it calculated? When do you get paid?

■ **Termination**
Normally, a party can terminate the agreement if the other side goes bust or with 30 days' notice if the other party is in breach (i.e. if they're breaking the terms of the agreement, you can sack them after a month). Upon termination, make sure you negotiate to get back the rights to your work

■ **Warranties**
The promises each party makes to the other to induce them to enter into the agreement. This is where you agree to show up at the venue to play and they promise to give you money in exchange

■ **Indemnity**
This clause will specify that a party is allowed to take action for all of their losses against a defaulting party – for example, if you fail to play the gig after the tickets have been sold, the town's been plastered in posters and a security firm has been booked to look after crowd management, the promoter's going to be annoyed and out of pocket. This section lets you know in advance that there will be comeback

■ **Jurisdiction**
What law applies? What courts? If things do go wrong and you need to get the lawyers in, you'll presumably want proceedings to happen fairly locally and in a language you can understand

■ Normally, they will require exclusive rights for at least a year.
■ Typically, they will take between 10% and 15% of gross revenue (i.e. before deductions).

These are the main types of deals everyone has been doing for as long as we can remember. However, the industry is going through big changes and new types of deal are developing under what is being termed Music Business 2.0.

All the talk now is of 360° deals (see page 192), whereby artists are required to assign all rights (recording, publishing, live, merchandising. sponsorship) to one third-party rather than in separate deals, as was once the norm. Major labels are now pushing for 360° deals from all of the artists they sign. In this period of rapidly declining record sales, it is not surprising they are looking to maximise their revenue streams. However, artists should be cautious about granting valuable rights – such as merchandising, live or publishing – to a record label when it cannot demonstrate a proficiency in those areas.

There are different types of 360° deal that cover different structures, so, as always, you

Power is beginning to shift a bit towards the artist and away from the major labels

need to get expert advice: that said, 360° deals can work well if they are fair and balanced, and the parties are able to deliver what they promise.

Other types of deal are emerging as new players enter the market with novel ideas and different objectives. Music's increasing convergence with other forms of media is also having an effect. For example:
■ Artists setting up their own independent music businesses and obtaining funding from a variety of sources, such as friends, family, fans and brands, and then going it alone (see *www.independentlabelscheme.com*).
■ Sponsorship deals where brands become involved with an artist.

■ Joint ventures between managers and artists.
■ Digital deals and agreements regarding new technology.
■ Funding deals, either with investment companies or with patrons of the arts.

These new types of deal are often more egalitarian than those normally associated with the business and are generally based on a degree of co-operation between the artist and the funder.

This is a crucial and fascinating time in the development of music law. The music business will probably continue to change over the next few years and it's fair to say the law is finding it difficult to keep up. We are all facing a very challenging future, but there are currently unprecedented opportunities for artists to develop their careers in traditional

and new ways. The balance of power is beginning to shift a little towards the artist and away from the powerful major labels. This means artists need to construct an innovative business model, as well as making great music and playing fantastic live shows.

If you're talented and dedicated enough to get all of this right, you will join those artists who are making it happen on their own terms. Bands like these generate decent income, can develop at their own pace, retain creative control and keep ownership of their musical output.

You may not relish having to get to grips with all of this. However, if you're going to be part of the music business, you have to remember it is a business and the business side is as important as the creative stuff. It has never been more essential for you to

SAY WHAT?

"The best way to kill your music is to sit down every day and work at it. You got to sneak up on it and catch it when it's not looking." – Iggy Pop.

obtain specialist professional help when making deals and drafting and negotiating contracts. The law is technical and complex, and is evolving very fast, with digital technology making music available in increasingly different formats.

Remember, you don't need to sign the first deal that comes your way; you have got to look out for yourself and your future, so keep hold of as many of your rights as you possibly can.

Imagination – and the ability to see beyond what has been done before – will free you from traditional constraints and let you cross the demarcation between performer, creator and entrepreneur. Try to come up with a way of doing business that works well for you. Deal-wise, anything is now acceptable – as long as it's legal. ★

Signing on the Dotted Line

'LAWYER UP' TO GET A FAIR DEAL WHEN IT COMES TO CONTRACTS

ADDLESHAW GODDARD

Partner: Paddy Grafton Green
Address: 150 Aldersgate Street, London, EC1A 4EJ
T: 0207 606 8855
F: 0207 606 4390
W: www.addleshawgoddard.com
E: paddy.graftongreen@addleshawgoddard.com

COBBETTS

Partner: Frances Anderson
Address: 1 Colmore Square, Birmingham, B4 6AJ
T: 0845 404 2404
F: 0845 166 6279
W: www.cobbetts.com
E: frances.anderson@cobbetts.com

CHARLES RUSSELL LLP

Partner: Michael Cover
Address: 8-10 New Fetter Lane, London, EC4A 1RS
T: 0207 203 5134
F: 0207 203 5002
W: www.cr-law.co.uk
E: London@charlesrussell.co.uk

COLLYER BRISTOW LLP SOLICITORS

Partner: Howard Ricklow
Music Consultant: Nick Kanaar
Address: 4 Bedford Row, London, WC1R 4DF
T: 0207 242 7363
F: 0207 405 0555
W: www.collyerbristow.com
E: cblaw@collyerbristow.com

CLINTONS

Contact: Andrew Myers, Peter Button
Address: 55 Drury Lane, London, WC2B 5RZ
T: 0207 379 6080
F: 0207 240 9310
W: www.clintons.co.uk
E: info@clintons.co.uk

DAVENPORT LYONS

Partner: Rupert Sprawson
Address: 30 Old Burlington Street, London, W1S 3NL
T: 0207 468 2600
F: 0207 437 0613
W: www.davenportlyons.com
E: Via 'contact us' section of website

DAVID WINEMAN

Contact: Irving David
Address: Craven House, 121 Kingsway,
London, WC2B 6NX
T: 0207 400 7800
F: 0207 400 7890
W: www.davidwineman.co.uk
E: law@davidwineman.co.uk

ENTERTAINMENT ADVICE LTD

Consultants: Len Bendel, Anthony Hall
Address: 31 Penrose Street,
London, SE17 3DW
T: 0207 708 8822
F: 0207 703 1239
W: www.entertainmentadvice.co.uk
E: Anthony@entertainmentadvice.co.uk

DEAN MARSH & CO

Principal: Dean Marsh
Addresses: 73a Middle Street,
Brighton, BN1 1AL
54 Kingsway Place, Sans Walk, Clerkenwell,
London, EC1R 0LU
T: 01273 823 770 (Bri), 0207 553 4400 (Lon)
F: 01273 823 771 (Bri), 0207 553 4414 (Lon)
W: www.deanmarsh.com
E: dean@deanmarsh.com

ENTERTAINMENT LAW ASSOCIATES

Managing director: John Giacobbi
Address: Argentum, 2 Queen Caroline Street,
London, W6 9DX
T: 0208 323 8013
F: 0208 323 8080
W: www.ela.co.uk
E: ela@ela.co.uk

FINERS STEPHENS INNOCENT

Partner: Robert Lands
Address: 179 Great Portland Street,
London, W1W 5LF
T: 0207 323 4000
F: 0207 580 7069
W: www.fsilaw.com
E: Via 'contact us' section of website

ENGELMONJACK

Contact: Jonathan Monjack,
Lawrence Engel
Address: 16-18 Berners Street,
London, W1T 3LN
T: 0207 291 3838
F: 0207 291 3839
W: www.engelmonjack.com
E: info@engelmonjack.com

FORTE LAW

Solicitor: Pamela Forte
Address: The Cottage, Penmark,
Bro Morgannwg, CF62 3BP
T: 01446 713 599
F: n/a
W: www.fortelaw.co.uk
E: law@fortelaw.co.uk

HAMLINS

Managing partner: Laurence Gilmore
Address: Roxburghe House,
273-287 Regent Street,
London, W1B 2AD
T: 0207 355 6000
F: 0207 518 9100
W: www.hamlins.co.uk
E: enquiries@hamlins.co.uk

HOWARD LIVINGSTONE

Contact: Howard Livingstone
Address: 37 Trinity Road, East Finchley, London,
N2 8JJ
T: 0208 365 2962
F: 0208 365 2484
W: www.musicattorney.co.uk
E: howard@hlivingstone.fsnet.co.uk

HARRISONS ENTERTAINMENT LAW LTD

Principal: Ann Harrison
Address: Suite 4, 19-21 Crawford Street,
London, W1H 1PJ
T: 0207 486 2586
F: 0207 486 2786
W: www.annharrison.co.uk
E: info@annharrison.co.uk

JAYES & PAGE

Partners: Anthony Jayes, Bob Page
Address: Universal House,
251 Tottenham Court Road,
London, W1T 7JY
T: 0207 291 9111
F: 0207 291 9119
W: www.jayesandpage.com
E: enquiries@jayesandpage.com

lazarus media

OLSWANG

KIRKPATRICK & LOCKHART PRESTON GATES ELLIS LLP

Partner: Nigel Davis
Address: 110 Cannon Street,
London, EC4N 6AR
T: 0207 490 8140
F: 0207 648 9001
W: www.klgates.com
E: Via 'contact us' section of website

LAZARUS MEDIA

Managing director: Steve Lazarus
Address: Cydale House, 249a West End Lane,
London, NW6 1XN
T: 0207 794 1666
F: 0207 794 1666
W: www.lazarusmedia.co.uk
E: steve@lazarusmedia.co.uk,
clare@lazarusmedia.co.uk

HARBOTTLE AND LEWIS

Head of music group: Paul Jones
Address: Hanover House, 14 Hanover Square,
London, W1S 1HP
T: 0207 667 5000
F: 0207 667 5100
W: www.harbottle.com
E: Via 'contact us' section of website

LEA & COMPANY SOLICITORS
Partner: Stephen Lea
Address: Bank Chambers, Market Place,
Stockport, Cheshire, SK1 1UN
T: 0161 480 6691
F: 0161 480 0904
W: www.lealaw.com
E: mail@lealaw.com

MARRIOTT HARRISON
Partner & head of media: Tony Morris
Address: 12 Great James Street,
London, WC1N 3DR
T: 0207 209 2000
F: 0207 209 2001
W: www.marriottharrison.co.uk
E: tony.morris@marriottharrison.co.uk

LEE & THOMPSON
Contact: Robert Lee
Address: Greengarden House,
15-22 St Christopher's Place,
London, W1U 1NL
T: 0207 935 4665
F: 0207 563 4949
W: www.leeandthompson.com
E: robertlee@leeandthompson.com

MICHAEL SIMKINS
Contact: Paddy Grafton Green
Address: 45-51 Whitfield Street,
London, W1T 4HB
T: 0207 907 3000
F: 0207 907 3111
W: www.simkins.com
E: paddy.graftongreen@simkins.com

LEONARD LOWY & CO
Principal: Leonard Lowy
Address: 500 Chiswick High Road,
London, W4 5RG
T: 0208 956 2785
F: 0208 956 2786
W: www.leonardlowy.co.uk
E: lowy@leonardlowy.co.uk

MULTIPLAY MUSIC CONSULTANTS
Managing director: Kevin White
Address: PO Box 1323, Harrold,
Bedford, MK43 7WT
T: 01234 720 785
F: 01234 720 785
E: info@multiplaymusic.com

MAGRATH AND CO.
Consultant: Alexis Grower
Address: 66-67 Newman Street,
London, W1T 3EQ
T: 0207 495 3003
F: 0207 317 6766
W: www.magrath.co.uk
E: admin@magrath.co.uk

MURRAY BUCHANAN & CO
Senior partner: Murray Buchanan
Address: Regent House, 113 West Regent Street,
Glasgow, G2 2RU
T: 0141 221 9395
F: n/a
W: www.murraybuchanan.com
E: Via 'contact us' section of website

NORTHROP McNAUGHTAN DELLER

Partners: Tim Northrop, Christy McNaughtan, Martin Deller

Address: 18c Pindock Mews, Little Venice, London, W9 2PY

T: 0207 289 7300

F: 0207 286 9555

W: www.nmdsolicitors.com

E: nmd@nmdsolicitors.com

ROHAN & CO SOLICITORS

Contact: Rupert Rohan

Address: Aviation House, 1-7 Sussex Road, Haywards Heath, West Sussex, RH16 4DZ

T: 01444 450 901

F: 01444 440 437

W: www.rohansolicitors.co.uk

E: info@rohansolicitors.co.uk

OLSWANG

Partner: John Enser

Address: 90 High Holborn, London, WC1V 6XX

T: 0207 067 3000

F: 0207 067 3999

W: www.olswang.com

E: olsmail@olswang.com

RUSSELLS

Senior partner: Brian Howard

Address: Regency House, 1-4 Warwick Street, London, W1B 5LJ

T: 0207 439 8692

F: 0207 494 3582

W: www.russellslaw.co.uk

E: media@russells.co.uk

SHERIDANS

Partner: Stephen Luckman

Address: Whittington House, Alfred Place, London, WC1E 7EA

T: 0207 079 0100

F: 0207 079 0200

W: www.sheridans.co.uk

E: info@sheridans.co.uk

RANDALL HARPER – SOLICITOR

Consulting Solicitor: Randall Harper

Address: Harper-Strategic, 2nd Floor, 145-157 St John Street, London, EC1V 4PY

T: 0207 788 7417

F: n/a

W: www.randall-harper-solicitor.com

E: randall@harper-strategic.com or via 'contact us' section of website

SMITHS

Partners: Andrew Lewis, Liam McNeive

Address: 17 Shorts Gardens, Covent Garden, London, WC2H 9AT

T: 0207 395 8631/0207 395 8633

F: n/a

W: www.smiths-law.com

E: lewis@smiths-law.com/ mcneive@smiths-law.com

SSB SOLICITORS

Partners: Paul Spraggon, Sarah Stennett
Address: The Matrix Complex,
91 Peterborough Road, London, SW6 3BU
T: 0207 348 7630
F: 0207 348 7631
W: www.ssb.co.uk
E: legal@ssb.co.uk

STEELES LAW LLP

Contact: Simon Conroy
Address: Bedford House, 21a John Street,
London, WC1N 2BF
T: 0207 421 1720
F: 0207 421 1749
W: www.steeleslaw.co.uk
E: Via 'contact us' section of website

SWAN TURTON

Contact: Julian Bentley
Address: 68a Neal Street, Covent Garden,
London, WC2H 9PA
T: 0207 520 9555
F: 0207 520 9556
W: www.swanturton.com
E: info@swanturton.com

TODS MURRAY LLP

Contact: Andy Harris, Richard Findlay
Address: Edinburgh Quay, 133 Fountainbridge,
Edinburgh, EH3 9AG
T: 0131 656 2000
F: 0131 656 2020
W: www.todsmurray.com
E: maildesk@todsmurray.com

TURNER PARKINSON LLP

Partner: Andy Booth
Address: Hollins Chambers, 64a Bridge Street,
Manchester, M3 3BA
T: 0161 833 1212
F: 0161 834 9098
W: www.tp.co.uk
E: tp@tp.co.uk

THE WATERFRONT PARTNERSHIP

Solicitor: Alison Berryman
Address: 5 The Leathermarket, Weston Street,
London, SE1 3ER
T: 0207 234 0200
F: 0207 234 0600
W: www.waterfrontpartnership.com
E: info@waterfrontpartnership.com

WIGGIN LLP

Contact: Simon Baggs, Alexander Ross
Address: 10th Floor, Met Building,
22 Percy Street,
London, W1T 2BU
T: 0207 612 9612
F: n/a
W: www.wiggin.co.uk
E: law@wiggin.co.uk

ZIMMERS SOLICITORS RECHTSANWAELTE

Contact: n/a
Address: 32 Corringham Road,
London, NW11 7BU
T: 0208 457 8850
F: 0208 457 8860
W: www.zimmerslaw.com
E: info@zimmerslaw.com

CHAPTER #5

ON TRACK

YOU'RE SPLASHING CASH ON STUDIO TIME SO BEST TO GET YOUR MONEY'S WORTH

S tudio time is expensive and managing a recording session difficult, so it pays to be prepared before stepping through the soundproof doors. Your main aim is to make the best recording you can in the time available and within budget, so – before hitting the studio – decide what it is that you want to achieve.

You'll also need to establish how many songs you plan to record. Agreeing a realistic time-frame for accomplishing this will probably be the hardest thing because everything takes longer in the studio than you'd imagine. You'll need to decide whether to do a live recording or make individual recordings to layer at a later stage (this approach will, obviously, require more time).

Whether it's your first time in the studio or you're making that difficult fifth album, 'red-light fever' will cause you to make silly mistakes. You're unlikely to get it right on the first take, perhaps because the studio environment is new, exciting and worlds away from the dark pubs and clubs that you're used to. When you do find your feet, and assuming your songs have been well rehearsed, the actual recording process should be relatively pain free.

RECORDING COSTS

On average, studio hire costs £200 a day. This will usually include the sound engineer's costs and use of the live room, but most studios offer a deal if you book several consecutive days. When trying to work out how long you will need, allow for at least half an hour at the end of the session for your recorded tracks to be mixed down – this will be a temporary rough mix, but you will ►

Your aim is the best recording in the time and budget available

receive a CD with every track separated, allowing you to mix and master the recording yourself.

When you get in touch with a studio, let them know your plans and budget, and they will use this to calculate a realistic recording schedule. Before committing, establish whether a recording day is six, seven or eight hours long, and how the rates will be affected if you go over your allocated time. Also clarify whether there will be additional charges; for example, will you be expected to pay extra for equipment loan or for the CD-R that your final tracks are recorded onto? ★

GETTING THE MOST FROM YOUR SESSION
PLAN AHEAD AND BE PROFESSIONAL

Having booked your recording time, get the sound engineer's contact details. It's important to give him or her an idea of the set-up and mics you'll need, how many people to expect, any specialist equipment you have and how many tracks you are aiming to record.

Don't be afraid to ask questions or tell them of any worries you have – it's your time, your money and your project, and the better prepared everyone is, the more you will get out of the session.

When recording, you may find songs that worked in rehearsal or at a gig sound off-key or out of time. Rehearsal studio monitors and most venue PAs don't give a definite sound to every instrument, so you'll only hear the details of your song once it's been recorded, with every section separated into its own channel. This could lead to time being wasted in the studio as you rework parts or restructure a song. So go through every track acoustically to weed out any wavering notes. If you do this before you get to the studio, so much the better.

Lastly, ensure your equipment is in working order. Fit new guitar strings (and carry spares), change the drum heads, pack spare drumsticks, be well rehearsed and try not to be hung over. Studio work can be stressful and physically demanding, so be rested, clear headed and well prepared.

Our first studio session! Take one...

Overdub Be Good To Me

LAYERED OR LIVE, YOU JUST WANT TO SOUND YOUR BEST

A s soon as you get into the studio, talk everything over with the sound engineer again, set up your gear and start work on the recording levels. Everything in the studio will take a bit longer than usual because the surroundings will be unfamiliar and you'll be trying to get the best equipment set-up, check vocal lines, make sure the drums are in time and that you're getting the highest-quality sound possible.

The drummer should arrive first because the drum kit takes the longest time to set up. If you're making a live recording, the band will sound check individually before you play through the songs as you would on stage. It's typical to go through a few takes before everyone is happy with the recording and minor mistakes can often be overdubbed at a later stage. But, if the song has fallen apart, you'll have to re-record from scratch.

It's best to keep to five or six takes for each song – repetition can lead to tedium and, by the time you reach take 20, everyone will be bored. Live recording means you have to accept mistakes, but, if you're well rehearsed, these will only be minor.

RECORDING

ON A TIP
Don't celebrate too loudly after finally nailing that guitar solo because the sound engineer may find it difficult to edit out and you'll find yourself back to square one

Rather than recording everything live, you may want to overdub (or layer) each instrument. Usually starting with the drums and finishing with the vocals, this is a slower, but more precise, method of recording.

It's worth having to hand any previous recordings of the songs you plan to work on because they'll be useful reminders to you and will help the sound engineer to hear the song structure, note its tempo and look out for when the various parts come in. You may finish with fewer completed songs with layered recording, but the tracks you do record will probably be closer to what you want to achieve.

Don't be afraid to ask the sound engineer questions. If you're not happy with the headphone mix – whereby you hear everyone else playing (this is also what the engineer listens to) – ask for it to be changed. If you don't like any of the effects that are being used, say so. It's always worth listening to the engineer's advice, but don't be coerced into doing everything he/she says – the studio may be their environment, but it's your cash that is being used.

But, remember, while all of this is happening, the clock will be ticking away on your studio time, so don't spend hours in deep discussion with your band, arguing with the engineer or getting that unnecessarily complicated guitar part right or a drumroll perfect. The important thing is to finish the song – if you have the time to overdub a few extra lead parts and correct a few mistakes, see that as a bonus. ★

POST RECORDING

The engineer will mix down the recordings and the tracks will be balanced, equalised, bounced down to two tracks and burned onto a master CD. The final mix will be mastered, with every track levelled and equalised so the quality will be good enough to play on most stereo systems.

Mix & Max

GOOD MIXING WILL HELP YOUR SONGS TO STAND OUT

I t's worth spending at least a day mixing each song you record. No matter how good your material is, if it's poorly mixed the song will sound muddy, with all of the dynamics lost. A little extra time and money on mixing will improve the final sound.

What you want is a sound that will reproduce through any type of speaker. Studio monitors are of a much higher standard than your home stereo, but your songs have to sound great through iPod headphones, home-stereo systems and car speakers. It's worth listening to each mix you do through different speakers so you can address problems before they are finalised.

The initial rough mix will give you an idea of each track's final shape and will allow you to tell the engineer of any changes you want. As the songwriter, you will know how you want the tracks to sound, but it's a good idea to bring any recordings you like to help the engineer to understand what you are after.

When you start work on your final mix, the engineer will begin with the rhythm section – drums, bass, rhythm guitar and keyboards – then deal with any lead instrumental parts before finishing with the vocals. Drums tend to take the longest time to mix; with each section of a kit spread across separate channels, a balance has to be found that allows any fills to be heard while emphasising the beat.

Next, your engineer will mesh the bass and rhythm instruments with the drum sound so they stand out enough to propel the song forward. These instruments form the structure of any recording, so it's worth spending the time to get them right.

The lead instruments and vocals will be at the front of the mix, with the vocals sitting on top of all the other instrumentation. At this stage, any effects (delay, reverb) and overdubs you've recorded will be introduced to the mix. When all of these elements have been balanced, it will be a matter of making changes until everyone is happy with the final structure of the mix. ★

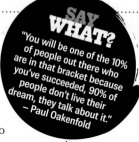

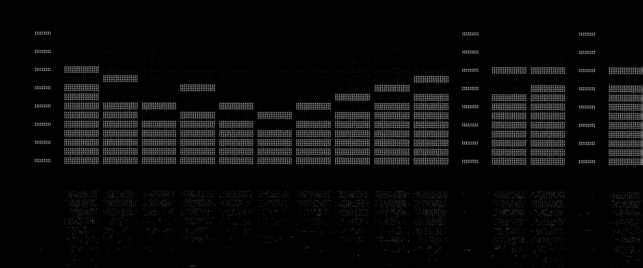

Master Mind
IF IT'S A QUESTION OF CLARITY, HOLD THE OVER-COMPRESSION

Mastering is the last stage of the recording process; a stage when engineers prepare and transfer your recorded audio from the source containing the final mix to a data storage device (the master), from which all future copies will be taken. During mastering, the final mixes are equalised, compressed and sequenced (the technical name for putting spaces between the songs). At its most basic level, mastering is about making the music sound loud and bright. Most record companies these days have everything mastered as loud as possible (see The Loudness War boxout, *right*) even though this comes at the expense of dynamic range and risks over-compression. If mastering is done incorrectly, your song could be robbed of its finer details, but, when executed properly, it will definitely improve the overall quality of your recordings.

MASTERING PROCESSES

1 EQ

One of the most fundamental steps of mixing and mastering audio is the balancing of the EQ (equalisation) levels of a recording. The EQ is the frequency spectrum of a recording, which can be displayed as a visual representation, or waveform, of the lowest troughs and the highest peaks of a voice or an instrument. The purpose of EQing is to achieve a tonal balance between different frequencies, to enhance any frequencies that add to the recording and to remove those that distract.

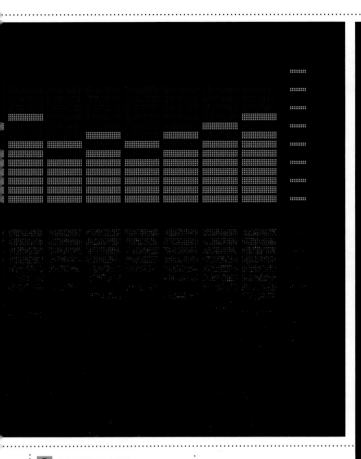

THE LOUDNESS WAR
SUBTLETY A CASUALTY OF COMPRESSION

Since the mid-1990s, record labels have competed with each other to release increasingly loud albums, following the theory that turning everything up will grab and retain a listener's attention.

You control the level at which you listen to music, but over-compressing an album during mastering means the songs are flattened to one level, creating a smaller dynamic range and removing the impact of instruments at a higher or lower peak of the recording – for example, drums that crash in or plucked lead notes on a guitar (search 'Loudness War' on YouTube for examples).

Producers and mastering engineers are not to blame; in fact, they are the most vocal opponents. Fingers should be pointed at the record labels, which are in desperate competition. Listen to a CD issued in the 1980s or early 1990s and you can hear the depth, range and clarity of the recording, while most recent releases sound almost like loud static.

HEAR FOR YOURSELF

CLEAR ▶

Modern Times,
Bob Dylan
Raising Sand,
Robert Plant & Alison Krauss

LOUD ▶

Alright Still, Lily Allen
Californication,
Red Hot Chilli Peppers

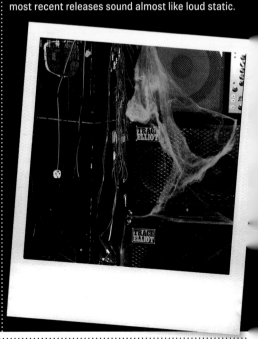

2 COMPRESSION

This process is used by mastering engineers to create a consistency in the dynamic range of a recording, so the instrumentation sits more comfortably in the mix while maintaining the attention of the listener. Compressing will also remove any instrumental peaks and level out the overall sound of the track.

3 DITHERING

This is the means by which engineers get the final master copy into the right format for burning onto a CD. Dithering takes the master – which will be at 96KHz/24-bit – and converts it to 44.1KHz/16-bit while retaining the quality of the original mastered recording.

4 OTHER PROCESSES

Other processes that may take place during the mastering stage are:
1. Editing minor flaws
2. Adjusting the stereo width
3. Eliminating hum and hiss
4. Adjusting volume
5. Peak-limiting tracks

If you have the funds, mastering is certainly worth the investment. Levelling out the sounds of a recording, while improving the overall quality, will help you to produce a professional-sounding demo that could make the difference when trying to get noticed. ★

INTERVIEW

Loud & Clear

ENGINEER STREAKY GEE EXPLAINS HOW MASTERING HELPS YOU TO BE HEARD

A fter long days, and hard cash, spent in the studio, you may be tempted to skimp on mastering. But engineer Streaky Gee (see interview, page 142) believes that could be a costly error.

Is mastering necessary?
Almost all tracks need mastering, from basic levelling to extreme compression and anything in between. All major releases have been mastered and, if your track hasn't had similar treatment, it probably won't have sufficient presence to compete against other tracks on the radio or MP3 players.

What does it add to a recording?
Balance, dynamics, space and clarity. You're unlikely to achieve these things by a simple recording and mixing process – to boost the whole mix, you need an experienced mastering engineer. But the effect will vary depending on the quality of the studio mix you start with.

Most recordings are over-compressed to the point that subtleties are lost. Does an unsigned artist have to do the same to get attention?
A good mastering engineer can get a track loud enough to compete without the need to compress the dynamics out of it. It's EQ that makes the difference to the perceived loudness, not compression and limiting.

How much does mastering cost?
A professional studio will charge between £100 and £250 per hour for an attended session. Each track will usually take about 30 minutes, depending on the mix you begin with. Most high-end studios have online services that allow unattended sessions for prices ranging from £50 to £125 per track. There are places online that will master tracks for £10 to £20 per track, but these are best avoided – you may as well do it yourself!

What advice would you give to artists about to enter the mastering process?
Make sure you are happy with the engineer you choose; look at their past clients and make sure they have experience in the same musical genre as yours. Do not compress your mix – that is a decision for the mastering engineer. Get your mix sounding as good as you can without trying to do their job for them. Then you can leave with a finished record and never have to think about tweaking it again. ★

WHAT ABOUT...
"Music is the only thing that engages me totally: emotionally, psychologically, intellectually, spiritually, physically." – Bob Geldof

INTERVIEW

Relax, Just Do It

ENGINEER DYLAN JONES ON WHY TEA AND TALK ARE THE BEST CURES FOR RED-LIGHT FEVER

Dylan Jones is an audio engineer and operations manager for the Songmaker Group, which provides packages for artists looking to achieve professional-sounding recordings. Here, he talks about preparing for going into the studio.

When a band enters the studio, what expectations do you have of them; in other words, how well prepared should they be?
It's important you show up well rehearsed and prepared for the session; you should go into the studio expecting to deliver the best performance of your career. Bringing an open mind will help you to add that vital creative touch to the recording – you'll get the most out of it by accepting input from people outside of the band, such as the producer or the engineer.

What essential equipment should they bring?
Make sure your equipment is in good working order – there's no point coming into the studio with an instrument that's going to fail after the first couple of takes and you don't want to waste expensive recording time attempting repairs. Make sure you have all the right power adapters and remember that you might need spare strings or reeds. If your set-up requires special tuning equipment, or you rely on effects pedals to

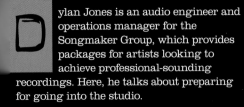

"Singers should be vocally prepared - no smoking, no screaming - and bring lyri

create your particular sound, make sure it comes with you to the recording studio. Guitarists, in particular, tend to write parts that can only be replicated with specific pieces of vintage equipment, then forget to bring it along. But anyone with responsibility for playing an instrument needs to double-check their kitbag. Singers should be vocally prepared for the session – no smoking, no screaming arguments – and should always ●

SAY WHAT?

"Somebody was trying to tell me that CDs are better than vinyl because they don't have any surface noise. I said, 'Listen, mate, life has surface noise.'"
– John Peel

RECORDING

bring their lyrics, especially if there are tricky parts in a song that they'll need to perfect over numerous takes.

What's a realistic time-frame for a band to lay down three songs, each with a full set-up and mix down – and what is it likely to cost?
Assuming the band is well rehearsed and the members are reasonably proficient, it should take about three or four days to complete a good recording of three songs. This allows a full day to lay down the drums and percussion, with the second spent on the bass, rhythm and lead guitar parts. The main and backing vocals will occupy most of the third day, with the remaining time spent on additional elements of the songs. If you're planning to do three songs, you should allow a full fourth day to mix them down. Costs vary quite a lot depending on where you record and the equipment the studio can offer, plus who's twiddling the knobs and who's paying for the session (the engineer and producer respectively). Generally, bands just starting out can get an entry-level studio package for between £600 and £1,200.

How long should bands allow for mixing and mastering?
Good engineers mix as they go along – building the sound they are trying to capture while you're playing is part of the process. Bringing your song to life by adding things like automation and effects comes later. You're looking at anything from a four-hour, half-day session to two days, depending on the complexity of the mix.

'Red-light fever' is said to strike every artist sooner or later. What is it and what's the best way to fight it off?
It's a common enough syndrome – a kind of studio-induced freezing. The best remedy is to make a conscious attempt to relax and just enjoy the studio experience. Half an hour spent wandering around asking questions, while drinking a cup of tea, is rarely time wasted. The best studios, such as those provided by the Songmaker Group, are those in which artists can relax in a welcoming environment throughout the whole session.

A BIT ABOUT SONGMAKER

The SongMaker Group caters for musicians of all levels and offers budget to high-end recording packages nationwide. It is also one of the largest suppliers of gift recording experiences in the UK (for those who want just a taste of being a star). For more information call 0871 7 505 555 or go to www. songmaker.co.uk

Is it helpful for an artist to have some basic knowledge of the studio before they start recording?
It can be helpful, but it's certainly not essential; in fact, a little knowledge can sometimes slow the session down. If artists become too involved with the recording, instead of concentrating on their performance, they can easily lose focus. That can be frustrating for engineers. They usually have an idea of how the finished product should sound and this can be sidetracked if there's too much artistic input.

Artists sometimes wonder if you and your fellow sound engineers really care about the recordings you make with them. How can they tell if their session is just another job for you? How do you give your best to each band?
You're only as good as your last recording and your future work will depend on how well you did last time. More importantly, though, every engineer is an artist and they try to achieve the best possible result with

every recording they make. Recording is an art in its own right and self-respecting engineers take it very seriously. They should see every session as a performance; it has to be as important to them as a stage show would be to the artists they work with.

Can an artist realistically expect to achieve a professional sound from a basic studio set-up?

These days, instruments capable of producing pro-quality recordings are within the budget of anyone serious about making music. Some studios will have a trusty old Gibson or rusty old Moog that you can hire for a small fee if your own kit isn't up to scratch. But, if you can't play your instruments, no amount of studio wizardry is going to make you sound better. Most entry-level studios run Pro Tools software (the industry-standard studio management application) and offer a range of outboard gear similar to that available in the main recording studios. In theory, this gives them the same professional digital recording quality, but using a Neve or SSL desk makes a difference. Top-quality gear might give your tune that indefinable, but vital, extra edge; that's why most major artists use them and why you might consider doing the same.

Is it always a good idea to spend a lot of the budgeted time and money on mixing and mastering?

BASIC DOs AND DON'Ts

RECORDING STUDIOS ARE COSTLY, OFTEN STRESSFUL, PLACES, SO TRY TO BE NICE – AND FOLLOW THE RULES

DON'T
mistreat the studio's equipment. If you're not sure what a knob does, ask before you start to twiddle it.

DON'T
yell at anyone if they screw up. It'll be your mess soon enough.

DON'T
expect to get everything right at the first attempt. You're not The Beatles and even they took a few attempts before perfecting their best tunes.

DON'T
waste time; time really is money. The recording studio is definitely not the place to start rewriting your guitar solo.

DON'T
be too wasted to play or sing. A buzz might be okay, but make sure you really want to capture that buzz – because you will.

DO
bring back-up instruments.

DO
be nice to the engineer.

DO
bring snacks and water.

DO
avoid dehydrating drinks, such as beer, coffee or fizzy pop, in the studio. If you're singing, bring plenty of water and an emergency throat spray.

DO
observe the rules of the studio. Most are non-smoking, so you'll just have to smoke outside on breaks. If there's a big sign in the control booth that says 'No Drinks on the Console', pay attention. Mixing consoles are expensive and you don't want to have to pay for that too. Drugs are a no-no, whether or not there's an explicit rule in place.

"Half an hour spent wandering around drinking tea is rarely time wasted"

I worked at Whitfield Street studios during the early days of my career and I witnessed just how important mixing and mastering is. We had tracks coming in from major artists; they usually sounded great already, but I was able to see how three hours in the mastering suite could totally transform them. These tunes were brought to life by the dynamics we were able to pull out and the importance of mastering and mixing showed up in the crystal clear, enhanced definition and

additional force of the final product when compared with the raw studio mix that we had at the start of the process.

With your experience of working with studio novices and professional musicians alike, is there any advice you would like to pass on to artists going into the studio?

Treat every recording like a performance and try to make it the best one of your career. Remember, it is important to document your work. Aim to enjoy every minute you spend making music just as much as your fans will enjoy listening to it. Be well prepared and give it your all. ★

Contact dylan@inspiredproductions.co.uk

Solar System

AN ECO-FRIENDLY STUDIO WHERE STARS ARE GREEN

T he Premises, in London's East End, is one of the capital's top recording studios – and now it is leading the way in helping to reduce the music industry's carbon footprint. It has become Europe's first solar-powered studio, built using mainly recycled material and featuring 18 solar panels that generate enough energy to run all of the equipment in the 14 high-spec studios. Friends of the Earth has endorsed the initiative – saying it demonstrates how businesses can reduce their carbon footprint and save money in the process – while acts such as Bloc Party, Klaxons and Johnny Borrell, all of whom have recorded here, have praised the example set by The Premises.

Why did you decide to go eco-friendly?
The music industry is becoming more aware of the issues of climate change and, yet, often struggles to keep its carbon footprint low. Choosing to go green was a natural progression of our work here; we have always had a sustainable ethos and aim to provide more than just a run-of-the-mill commercial studio set-up. We wanted a high-spec studio with a zero carbon footprint so the musicians could record at the highest level while keeping their fingers green!

Have there been any teething problems in switching to solar power?
None. The installation took one morning, the panels are self-cleaning and they run even on rainy days because they operate on light rather than sunshine. The supply is 100% stable. On a long, bright day, we produce more energy than we use and feed this back to the National Grid. During the night, we take our supply from the grid, but, over a year, we feed more in than we take out, so our panels supply green energy to everybody, not just those who use the studios.

ON THE PREMISES

Artists who have recorded at the studios include: Suede, Nina Simone, Bloc Party, Arctic Monkeys, Blur, Kate Nash, Nick Cave, Johnny Borrell, Al Green, Primal Scream, Franz Ferdinand and Jarvis Cocker

Has the cost involved in moving to solar power been reflected in increased prices for studio time?
Not at all.

Do you think other studios will follow your example and go green?
The set-up costs of solar power are pretty high, so it is a big investment and it's still difficult for a lot of businesses to go green. This is something we are currently leading a campaign on with Friends of the Earth and Lily Allen [who has recorded here].

Has having a solar-powered studio meant an increase in the number of clients wanting to use your facilities?
It is hard to say. Our solar studio got a lot of

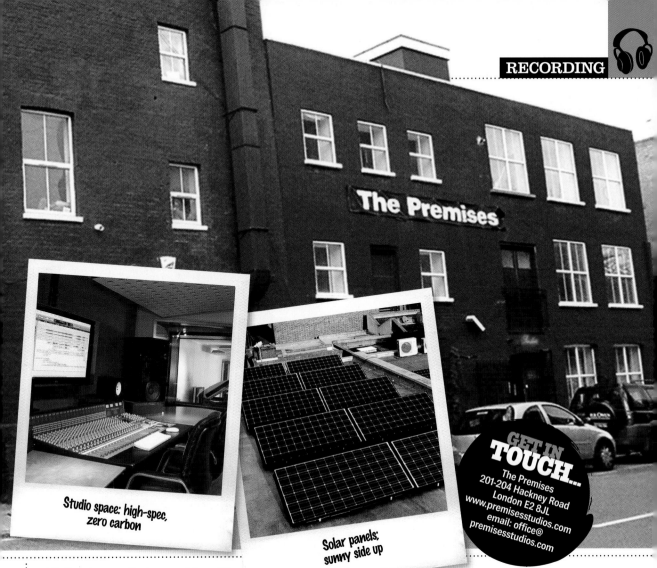

The Premises

Studio space: high-spec,
zero carbon

Solar panels;
sunny side up

GET IN TOUCH...
The Premises
201-204 Hackney Road
London E2 8JL
www.premisesstudios.com
email: office@
premisesstudios.com

publicity when we first opened it and I expect some people do come simply because of this. But we also have to be totally professional.

Does the fact you also run a café boost your profile?

Musicians love the café here – so many other studios don't provide decent food. If you are in a studio for days on end, you need good food, all day, right there.

If an unsigned musician wanted to use your studios, could you work around their budget?

We do what we can to work with musicians at every level to provide a recording package that fits.

Do you promote unsigned music in your local area?

We have a charity that has run the most successful New Deal training course in the country. We regularly take students for an apprentice course we run and provide access courses for local people. Working at a community level, as well as at a commercial level, is very important to us.

What advice would you give to an unsigned artist going into a studio?

Prepare, prepare, prepare! Studio time is expensive, so you need to be ready to work hard. The people who really make a career in the music industry are the hardworking ones who see music as a job, as well as a passion. ★

Making Music in the Bedroom

A HOME STUDIO MEANS NEVER HAVING TO SAY YOU'RE SORRY

T he conventional image of the home-recording artist is someone who hides away with a computer and hacks out electronics-heavy tunes from tweaked beats, trusty breaks and samples 'lifted' from somebody else's copyrighted material. However, today's process is adaptable to any musical genre, with the space to set up and play being the only real requirement; a drummer working at the kit, for example, will occupy more floorspace than all but the most extravagant saxophone player. Most instruments – together with amplifier, mic stand and cables – will fit into a good-sized (sound-proofed) bedroom, as long as the room isn't also being used for its intended purpose!

Maintaining good relations with your neighbours is going to be important, so you might want to farm out the heavy percussion recordings to a professional studio (at least until you can afford to convert one of the barns on your country estate into a sound-proofed playroom).

Unless you're rich or have been saving up for years (either of which will spoil your story if you're aiming for 'street cred'), you're facing months of frustration as you accumulate the funds to buy the equipment you need to make a start. That's not necessarily a bad thing because much of the gear you buy will come with useful instruction books since much of the kit is often less user-friendly than it could be. You'll need time to get your head ●

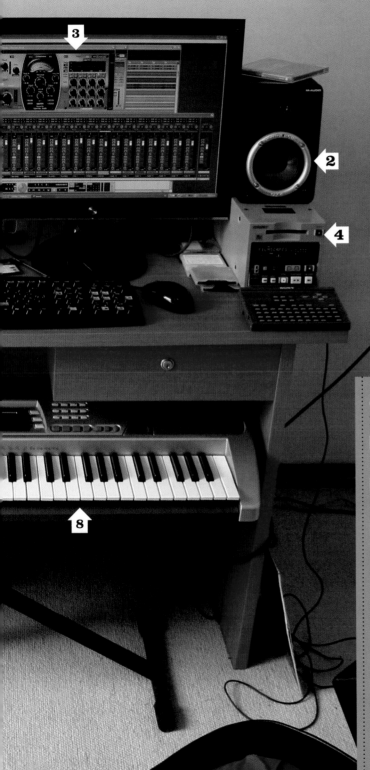

ANNOTATED BEDROOM
A TYPICAL HOME-STUDIO SET-UP

1 Main studio monitors for mixing

2 Near-field monitors for reference

3 Software for recording, mixing and sequencing

4 Mini-disc recorder/ player, digital in/out, 44KHz/24bits, for master archival and reference

5 USB 2 audio midi interface, 96KHz/ 24bits, 16 ins, 16 outs, S/PDIF and coaxial I/O, eight mics in, six mics out

6 Portable disk for projects, audio, samples, transport (buy the biggest capacity you can afford)

7 Custom-made PC/ audio workstation

8 Midi keyboard and stand

ALSO consider a portable midi/audio workstation/laptop for on-the-road recording, composing and mixing

around the peculiarities of your recording software (see Sequencers, *below*).

It might be worth investing in some training – when you learn to produce good-quality recordings, you're, effectively, learning to play an entirely new instrument (the studio) and expert tuition can make the process seem more logical. A patient friend who is fluent in home recording and prepared to share their skills will save you time by making things even easier to follow. There's bound to be a certain amount of stress and frustration as you put together your first few tracks, so anything that helps you to navigate the technology should be welcomed.

Once you're familiar with the equipment, though, you can use home technology to work on ideas, map out demos or even record an album. Producing professional-quality sounds without the expense or discomfort of an unfamiliar environment makes the home studio a positive choice for all but the most well-heeled of new acts.

BASIC EQUIPMENT

When it comes to computers, the Mac-versus-PC argument is growing less important because today's software applications generally come in

both flavours. Modern operating systems also tend to be more understanding of one another's quirks. Entry-level PCs are cheap, widely available and easily upgradeable. Macs generally have more built-in gadgetry and a higher build specification, but can be tricky to upgrade.

A software sequencer stores and manages the sounds you load into it, allowing you to cut and paste them, add effects, overlay them, drop them out and generally mess them about. You can load up your sequencer with conventionally recorded, acoustic tracks, vocals, electronically generated waveforms, stuff you picked up on your mobile phone, amplified guitars, violin – anything that makes a sound, really – and then edit and mix it until it matches the noises in your head.

The sequencer is the hub of professional and home-recording studios alike. The days of reel-to-reel recording onto magnetic tape are nearly over; the tapes themselves are expensive and unwieldy, while mechanical edits – when the tapes are cut and stuck back together – are inaccurate, slow and complicated. Digital technology allows you to be very precise (although ultra-accurate timing will soak the 'soul' from your

SEQUENCER PROGRAMS

CUBASE
RRP: £239
www.steinberg.net

SONAR
RRP: £219
www.cakewalk.com

LOGIC STUDIO:
RRP: £319
www.apple.com

PRO TOOLS:
RRP: £164
www.digidesign.com

music and you might want to add a bit of dirt and imprecision if you're aiming for realism).

Understanding the essentials is vital, but by reading the manual and punching buttons in a process of trial of error you should soon be putting together basic tracks. However, it's worth remembering sequencer programs are sophisticated suites of software engineering, mainly used by trained sound engineers with years of experience, so following the tutorials in the manual will help you to get the best out of your recordings.

Budget, suitability to your type of music and ease of use are the most obvious factors that will influence your choice of computer program; even standard-issue home-recording sequencers have their advantages.

MONITORS

Home-stereo speakers are engineered to enhance the sound of a mixed, edited recording and make it attractive to the ear in a domestic environment; in short, they lie to you. Monitors, on the other hand, are designed to tell the raw, unvarnished truth about the tracks you record and deliver it to you unaltered. So you will have to buy a set of active monitors (powered speakers) for your home studio. Expect to pay a minimum of £200 – but, if you're serious about your recordings and mixes, there's no way to avoid spending the money. On the plus side, if a mix sounds good through the monitors, it will generally sound fantastic when played through stereo speakers.

MICROPHONES

SHURE SM58
RRP: £70
General-purpose mic (right) that captures vocals and instrumentation to a high standard.
www.shure.co.uk

SHURE SM81LC
RRP: £280
Ideal for recording acoustic instruments.
www.shure.co.uk

RODENT 1A
RRP: £119
A great all-rounder for making high-quality, detailed recordings.
www.dolphinmusic.co.uk

When you plan the layout of your studio, your starting point should be the most convenient position for the two monitors. Ideally, the distance between them should be the same as the distance between each speaker and your head; that is, you and the mounted monitors should make up the three points of an equilateral triangle. This arrangement creates a stable stereo image and allows the speakers to fully project the sound.

Once you have suitable speaker placement, you're ready to build in the rest of your equipment. You'll want the items you use the most to be easily

Home-stereo speakers lie to you, but monitors are designed to tell the truth

accessible and the least important, rarely used, gear out of the way, on shelves or under a desk. Creating a comfortable environment to work in will let you concentrate on creativity; having to cope with awkward access and switches hidden in the shadows will distract you from doing your job. If you have everything you need close at hand – and you feel you could turn out tracks you're pleased with – everything important is in place. The messy, chaotic look of your compact studio might not impress your family and friends, but it'll be a more productive environment to work in.

CONDENSER MICROPHONES

The Shure SM58 microphone is a design classic, as much a part of the music scene as warm lager, battered tambourines and curly guitar leads. It's the one that looks like a short section of pipe with a wire golf ball stuck on the end and you'll come across it everywhere, from stages to studios. It's ●

GETTING SOUNDS INTO THE COMPUTER

THE FIVE MOST BASIC METHODS OF RECORDING LIVE INSTRUMENTATION

1 ONBOARD SOUND DEVICE

The cheapest, but most problematic method. An onboard sound device has one low-quality input, the mic pre-amps are hissy and, when you change instruments, you have to swap the leads at the back of the computer. As you become more comfortable with home recording, you will want to invest in better equipment.

RECOMMENDED SOUNDCARDS:
You can use the one installed in your computer, but it may not have the inputs you require.
M-AUDIO AUDIOPHILE 2496 *RRP: £48*
M-Audio Delta 1010LT *RRP: £116*
M-Audio Delta 44 *RRP: £85*
www.dolphinmusic.co.uk

2 MIXER/SOUNDCARD

The classic solution to home-recording hell, it involves plugging a small mixer into the input of your soundcard. This allows you to record several instruments at once and to use higher-quality, XLR mic leads, which plug straight into the mixer. You can also adjust the levels of the instruments so, for example, you can use guitar effects pedals without the signal peaking and distorting.
RECOMMENDED MIXERS:
YAMAHA MG166C *RRP: £199 (analogue)*
MACKIE DFX-6 *RRP £185 (Six channels)*
MACKIE DFX-12 *RRP £220 (12 channels)*
www.dolphinmusic.co.uk

3 MIXERLESS APPROACH

You can get all of the functions of a soundcard and mixer by using an audio interface, which contains mixer-quality pre-amps and line inputs/outputs. If you pick one with mic pre-amps, you'll bypass the need for a soundcard and a mixer – the level controls built into a sequencer can replace those on a mixer – with everything needed to start recording live instruments built into the audio interface.
RECOMMENDED AUDIO INTERFACE:
PRESONUS FIREBOX *RRP £199*

4 FIREWIRE/MIXER WITH BUILT IN AUDIO-INTERFACE

This also lets you bypass the soundcard and audio interface on your computer. By using a firewire-compatible analogue mixer you can record directly into your computer/sequencer.
RECOMMENDED FIREWIRE MIXERS:
M-AUDIO NRV10 FIREWIRE
MIXER *RRP £339*
www.gear4music.com
MACKIE U.420 FIREWIRE 4 CHANNEL PRODUCTION MIXER *RRP £199, www.dv247.com*
ALESIS MULTIMIX 12 CHANNEL FIREWIRE MIXER *RRP £349*
www.ebdj.com

5 MULTI-TRACK RECORDER

Record directly into the multi-track unit and then use the built-in interface (usually USB) to port material to your computer. You will still need a good soundcard to retain the quality of your recorded material, but these have everything you need to record and mix your tracks within one unit.
RECOMMENDED MULTI-TRACK RECORDERS:
YAMAHA AW1600 *RRP £669*
www.GAK.co.uk
TASCAM 2488 MK11 *RRP £559*
www.gear4music.com
ZOOM HD8CD DIGITAL MULTI-TRACK RECORDER *RRP £340*
www.nevadamusic.co.uk

HOME ADVANTAGE

If you fancy the challenge, and you have the cash, home recording offers the means of creating professional-quality material from the comfort of your own home. While converting your bedroom might not be very convenient, it will save you money in the long run and allow you to work in a familiar environment whenever the mood takes you.

Open the door every half hour so you don't suffocate – or purchase ventilation

robust and, at £69.99, the most reasonably priced high-end mic on the market. A great, all-purpose tool that will produce a good-quality, professional recording, the SM58 can be used to record vocals, amplified electric guitars, drums and just about every other acoustic instrument – and it is resistant to breaking up at high volume.

The many models of microphone on sale have been designed to respond in different ways, with some more suited to the subtleties of delicate acoustic stringed instruments, some built to capture the human voice and others constructed more like medieval weapons, to withstand the industrial levels of noise in more boisterous environments. You'll notice – particularly when recording live performances – that certain mics deal better with certain instruments, while other configurations add interesting (or annoying) 'colour' to the pure sounds they collect.

If your budget permits, buying several different mics to match the specific set of instruments you're working with would be best. It will also give you the opportunity to experiment with various mic/ instrument combinations. However, a set of SM58s will probably fulfill your initial requirements and different makes and models can be put on the wishlist for a later date.

QUIET ROOM/SOUNDPROOFING

If you're just creating beats or simple demos, all you need is a basic computer set-up and you can work without the worries of sound isolation. But if you're serious about putting together professional-quality

SOUND-PROOFING

AURALEX PROJECT 2 ACOUSTIC SOUND CONTROL KIT (contains 24 studio-foam wedge panels, eight LENRD bass traps and five Tubetak pro adhesives) RRP: £487

AURALEX 4 INCH STUDIOFOAM-22 WEDGE RRP: £135

AURALEX TUBETAK PRO LIQUID ADHESIVE/ AURALEX FOAMTAK SPRAY ADHESIVE RRP: £7-£16

For more information on all of these products visit www. dolphinmusic.co.uk

material – and if you have the space – it is essential to quieten the recording area.

If you've been collecting egg boxes for months in preparation for this stage, you can start dusting them off. There's no reason not to line your studio walls with egg boxes (it'll improve the acoustics in the room by dampening reflected sounds), but it takes more than a few millimetres of cardboard to stop the music you make from leaking into the outside world. When constructing a quiet room, it's just as important to minimise sound that leaks into the studio as it is to avoid bugging your neighbours with late-night rehearsals at full, gig volume. Having said that, soundproofing is nearly impossible; you won't be able to get rid of every bit of interference from the outside world, but you can cut down on leakage by sound-insulating the studio.

The most basic method of insulation is to create a layer of thick plasterboard with a layer of acoustic foam between the two walls, with all windows double-glazed and heavy rubber lining around the door (you'll have to open the door every half an hour so you don't suffocate or purchase ventilation that won't compromise the soundproofing).

To keep sound interference to a minimum, you can also set up a quiet room – using the entire studio or by building a separate booth, which need be nothing more than an empty cupboard – for recording vocals and instruments that require a microphone (mic-ing up). This will insulate against any low-level background noise, such as that created by the base unit of a computer.

To do this, keep as much equipment as you can outside of your main recording area and thread the connections through a small hole in the wall, keeping only essential items, such as a computer monitor or microphones, within the room. ★

For more information visit www.tweakheadz.com

INTERVIEW

The Sofa Sessions

FATBOY SLIM'S MASTERING ENGINEER'S MUSICAL ROOTS (AND AFFECTIONS) LIE IN HOME RECORDING

S treaky Gee started his music career as a DJ, specialising in chillout and Balearic house, and was also a singer in a band. He began creating tracks in Cubase on his Atari (yes, Atari!) and, eventually, produced tracks for film and TV. He also started remixing, under the guises of Elephant and The Merry Wives, for artists such as Groove Armada, The Stone Roses and Penguin Café Orchestra.

In 1994, Streaky began working in the CD mastering department of Battery Studios and worked on tracks by A Tribe Called Quest, KRS-1, Mystikal, R Kelly, Backstreet Boys, Aaliyah, Fatboy Slim, Britney Spears and numerous releases on Jive & Zomba Records He moved to The Soundmasters in 2000 and there he developed a reputation as a talented drum 'n' bass engineer. In 2004, The Soundmasters launched eMasters, an online mastering service, with Streaky as chief mastering engineer.

What are the advantages of home recording over working in the studio?
Familiarity with your surroundings. It's very difficult to develop a feel for the sound of the studio in the time available to you, unless you work there. Different rooms will make subtle differences to the results you get from your equipment; you need to be comfortable with your kit, to understand the best ways of chaining the pieces together and how different layouts will alter the sounds you get. Working from home, you can minimise the time it takes to record a track – this is important when you have a live band trying to get the most from a first run through.

Is the technology now at the point where a home-recording artist can produce studio-quality recordings?
Without doubt you can achieve a very high-quality recording using nothing more than some decent mics, standard pre-amps and a

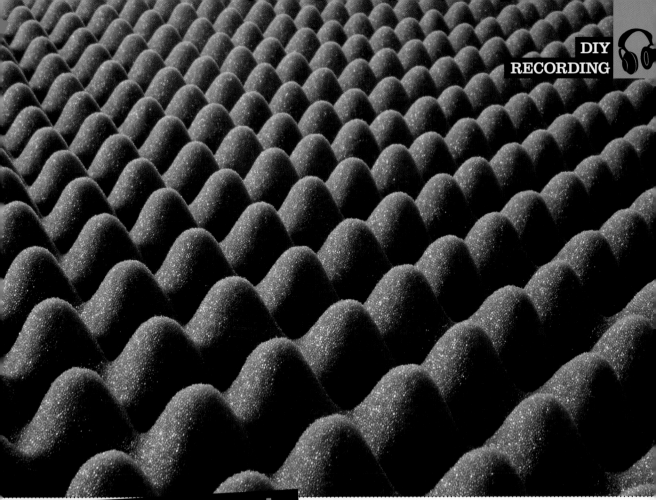

"On some 70s soul tracks you'll hear bum notes aplenty, but they have natural groove"

laptop. It all got a lot simpler when studio specialists learned more about mic positioning and setting up a band's equipment – suddenly, there was less need to process the individual instruments and it led to a natural 'live' feeling to studio recordings that is missing from most of today's top pop productions. If you listen to some 70s soul tracks, things are moving about all over the place. You'll hear bum notes aplenty, but they have such natural groove. These days, everything is Pro-Tooled to precision and perfection. We programme everything to digital tightness and most of us would agree the sound quality of yesteryear was amateurish by comparison with what we can

achieve now. I had the privilege of watching the older recording process in action while being involved with Joe Strummer's later albums. Bill Price, balance engineer for The Sex Pistols and The Clash during their 70s' heyday, would come in after the recording, set up a couple of NS10s, zero the faders and spend a couple of hours on each track, carefully nudging the channels into shape with only the smallest amount of EQ and reverb until he was satisfied.

What current software would you recommend for a home-recording artist and would this change depending upon the genre of music?
It's really down to what software the engineer feels comfortable with. Many home-studio users waste time trying to be the plug-in king instead of getting down to the business of producing music – I've been guilty of it myself. Get hold of the core basics, programs

that work for you and your sound, learn what they do, play around with them, understand them and then add more as you need them.

How easy is it to set up a home studio and what are the costs?

You just need a laptop and a program, such as Reason, and you'll have a track done in 10 minutes. What you'll spend depends on how high-tech you want to go and the kind of sound you want to produce; a basic set-up for dance music can be assembled for a few hundred pounds, but, if you want to record live instruments in high-quality studio sound, you could be looking at anything from £1k to £100k.

SAY WHAT?

"A studio recording is perfection, but emotion and passion come only when you turn on the machine and go for the groove." – Chuck Mangione

Is it now possible to record a whole band with a home-studio set-up?

Yes, but what you can achieve depends on the space available and how good your sound insulation is. You could fit a band into a good-sized living room, forget about sound-proofing, ignore the acoustics and record a decent, garage-quality demo. The one-man-band option is easier to manage, but a real band should produce more energy and a 'jamming' feel.

Can everything – recording, mixing and mastering – be done to a high standard on a home set-up?

It can. There are loads of software plug-ins that will help you to do a reasonable job. Most artists or producers in dance or hip-hop will record and mix in their home studios, but master their tracks with a professional to give them a final check on balance and the detail in the low end. Most bands will use external recording engineers and, if they have the budget, call in a mix engineer to add a fresh dimension to the recording. This engineer will usually then get a mastering engineer to perform the final checks.

What sound-proofing do you recommend for home recording? How easy and costly is it to set up a vocal booth?

There are a lot of options, from lining your bedroom with egg boxes and foam sheets to

"The best training is to get stuck in. Read everything you can and listen a lot"

fitting out the garage with professional baffles, bass traps and rock wool. What you decide to do will depend on space, the money you're willing to spend and the end result you're after. Sound-proofing helps to smooth out discrepancies caused by the shape of the room and, to some extent, helps the acoustics. A little research will show you what you can expect for your budget, while audio forums, such as *MyBedroomStudio* and *Gearslutz*, are great places to find out from the horse's mouth about home-studio building.

What basic equipment and training would someone need before they began?

The best training is to get stuck in; read everything you can and listen a lot. Start with a laptop and go from there. My fast-track to learning was to sit with other engineers and watch how they approached things; they gave me a million tips and tricks without even realising.

What is the future for home-recording?

It's here already; you can buy stripped-down versions of equipment and software used in major studios for your home set-up. The kit is widely available, but it can be expensive. Songs can be made entirely on your laptop,

but they'll usually lack the vibe and sound you'd harness by using real instruments, outboard gear and musicians. It all depends on your budget; even a basic set-up can cost a lot of money. Programs such as Garageband have opened up recording to amateur users and it's great that people who would never have had the chance to record their music now have something easy to use. There will always be wildly varying levels of quality and expertise, but with talent, sensitivity and skill you'll make interesting recordings.

What advice do you have for anyone who wants to set up their own studio?

Find out what other people working in your genre use and go with that. Pick out gear you feel comfortable using and, initially at least, keep what you do with it fairly simple. Write and record as much as you can to hone your skills. Learn your basic kit inside and out, and forget about adding to it until you have. The basics are most important, everything else is detail. For a proper studio, you need space. Everything has to be laid out and plugged in, ready to be picked up. If you spend hours unpacking your kit every time you want to record, you'll lose the spark and everything will take twice as long as it should. You want to be able to walk in, switch on and jam away. ★

And just for the record...

RECORDING AND REHEARSAL STUDIOS FOR LAYING DOWN YOUR MASTERPIECES

ALASKA STUDIOS

Address: 127-129 Alaska Street, London, SE1 8XE
T: 0207 928 7440
F: 0207 928 8070
E: blodge_uk@yahoo.com
W: www.alaskastudio.co.uk
Rates: Weekdays 10am-6pm – £7.50 per hour / Weekday evenings – £50 per 4 hour slot / Weekends – £50 per 4 hour slot

ARTISAN AUDIO

Address: 46a Woodbridge Road, Moseley, Birmingham, B13 8EJ
T: 0121 249 0598
F: 0709 214 8920
E: enquiries@artisanaudio.com
W: www.artisanaudio.com
Rates: £29 per hour including engineer

ASCAPE STUDIOS

Address: The Clan Works, 1a Howard Road, Bromley, BR1 3QS
T: 0208 460 0048
F: n/a
E: info@ascapestudios.com
W: www.ascapestudios.com
Rates: £350 for a 10-hour day, include engineer and use of instruments/amps

BACKFEED

Address: Black Dyke Mills, Queensbury, Bradford, West Yorkshire, BD13 1QA
T: 01274 817 817
F: n/a
E: n/a
W: www.backfeed.co.uk
Rates: Phone to enquire

BALLY STUDIOS

Address: 16-18 Millmead Business Centre, Millmead Road, Tottenham Hale, London, N17 9QU
T: 0208 808 0472
F: n/a
E: info@ballystudios.co.uk
W: www.ballystudios.co.uk
Rates: Check website for details

BANANA ROW REHEARSAL STUDIOS

Address: 47 Eyre Place, Edinburgh, EH3 5EY
T: 0131 557 2088
F: 0131 558 9848
E: info@bananarow.com
W: www.bananarow.com
Rates: Phone/email to enquire

BARK STUDIO

Address: 1a Blenheim Road, London, E17 6HS
T: 0208 523 0110
F: 0208 523 0110
E: brian@barkstudio.co.uk
W: www.barkstudio.co.uk
Rates: Phone to enquire

BERKELEY 2

Address: 93 Lancefield Street, Glasgow, G3 8HZ
T: 0141 248 7290
F: 0141 204 1138
E: n/a
W: www.berkeley2.co.uk
Rates: From £5 per hour, phone to enquire

BERRY STREET STUDIO

Address: 1 Berry Street, London, EC1V OAA
T: 0207 253 5885
F: 0207 635 8293
E: info@berrystreetstudio.com
W: www.berrystreetstudio.com
Rates: Phone/email to enquire

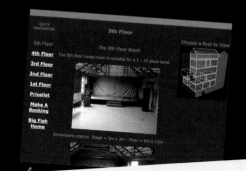

THE BIG FISH CORPORATION BOOM BOOM ROOMS

Address: Beehive Mill, Jersey Street, Ancoats, Manchester, M4 6JG
T: 0161 950 4250
F: 0161 228 0357
E: n/a
W: www.bigfishcorporation.com
Rates: Fill in the online booking form or phone to make bookings and for further information.

BIGTONE

Address: Bridgewater Mill, Eccles, Manchester
T: 0777 643 682
F: n/a
E: time@bigtonerecordings.co.uk
W: www.bigtonerecordings.co.uk
Rates: Phone/email to enquire

BLUEPRINT STUDIOS

Address: Elizabeth House, 39 Queen Street, Salford, Manchester, M3 7DQ
T: 0161 817 2520
F: n/a
E: time@blueprint-studios.com
W: www.blueprint-studios.com
Rates: Phone/email to enquire

CAFÉ STUDIO

Address: 18 Ordell Raod, Bow, London, E3 2DS

T: 0208 891 2588

F: n/a

E: cafemusicstudio@yahoo.co.uk

W: www.cafestudio.co.uk

Rates: E-mail to enquire.

BONAFIDESTUDIO

Address: Valetta Road, London, W3 7TG

T: 0207 684 5350

F: 0207 613 1185

E: info@bonafidestudio.co.uk

W: www.bonafidestudio.co.uk

Rates: 10 hour day – £12.50 per hour/ 5-9 hour day – £16.00 per hour / 4 hours or less – £20, check website for further deals and information, all prices include an engineer.

CARBON STUDIOS

Address: Unit 6 107 Parkview Trading Estate, Kings Norton, Birmingham, B30 3JX

T: 0121 486 1141

F: n/a

E: info@carbon-studios.com

W: www.carbon-studios.com

Rates: £5.50 – £10, phone/email with any enquiries

BRITANNIA ROW STUDIOS

Address: 3 Bridge Studios, 318-326 Wandsworth Bridge Road, London, SW6 2TZ

T: 0207 371 5872

F: 0207 371 8641

E: bookings@britanniarowstudios.co.uk

W: www.britanniarowstudios.co.uk

Rates: Phone/email to enquire

CHESTNUT STUDIOS

Address: 17 Barons Court Road, West Kensington, London, W14 9DP

T: 0207 384 5960

F: n/a

E: info@chestnutstudios.com

W: www.chestnutstudios.com

Rates: Phone/email to enquire

CABIN STUDIO

Address: 82 London Road, Coventry, West Midlands, CV1 2JT

T: 024 7622 0749

F: n/a

E: office@sonar-records.demon.co.uk

W: www.cabinstudio.co.uk

Rates: Phone/email to enquire

chestnut studios
an SSL studio has landed.

CHURCH ROAD RECORDING COMPANY

Address: 197-201 Church Road, Hove, East Sussex, BN3 2AH

T: 01273 327 889

F: n/a

E: info@churchroad.net

W: www.churchroad.net

Rates: Mon-Fri £26 per hour / Sat –Sun £30 per hour / 10 hour week-day rate £230 / Student discount (see website for details on information required) 10 hour day £180, all prices include an engineer

COURTYARD RECORDING STUDIOS

Address: Gorsey Mount Street

T: 0161 477 6531

F: n/a

E: crs@wwsrs.co.uk

W: www.wwsrs.co.uk

Rates: Phone/E-mail to enquire

CREEKSIDE STUDIOS

Address: Units C102 & C104, Faircharm Trading Estate, 8-12 Creekside, London

T: 0208 694 9484

F: 0208 694 9466

E: info@creeksidestudios.co.uk

W: www.creeksidestudios.co.uk

Rates: Check website for further information

THE DAIRY

Address: 43-45 Tunstall Road, London, SW9 8BZ

T: 0207 738 7777

F: 0207 738 7007

E: info@thedairy.co.uk

W: www.thedairy.co.uk

Rates: Phone/email to enquire

DIAMOND STUDIOS

Address: Suite A, Moor Park Business Centre, Thornes Moore Rd, Wakefield, WF2 8NZ

T: 01924 20 11 69 (Phone after 6pm)

F: N/A

E: enquiries@diamondstudios.co.uk

W: www.diamondstudios.co.uk

Rates: £6.50-£8.50 per hour, phone/email for further information

EARTH PRODUCTIONS

Address: 163 Gerrard Street, Birmingham, West Midlands, B19 2AP

T: 0121 554 7424

F: n/a

E: info@earthproductions.co.uk

W: www.earthproductions.co.uk

Rates: Studio One: £15 per hour (3 hours min), £12.50 per hour (20 hours or more) / Studio two: £25 per hour (3 hour min), £20 per hour (20 hours or more)/ Mastering £35 per hour, all prices include an engineer

FORTRESS STUDIOS

Address: 34-38 Provost Street, London, N1 7NG

T: 0207 251 6200

F: 0207 251 5892

E: info@fortessstudios.co.uk

W: www.fortessstudios.co.uk

Rates: Phone/email to enquire

HELL FIRE STUDIOS

Address: 90 Hoodgate Street, Unit A2, Digbeth, Birmingham, B5 5SR
T: 0121 772 7544
F: n/a
E: ajeet@hellfireproductions.com
W: www.hellfireproductions.com
Rates: Phone/email to enquire

IGUANA STUDIOS

Address: Unit 1, 88a Acre Lane, London, SW2 5QN
T: 0207 924 0496
F: n/a
E: info@iguanastudio.co.uk
W: www.iguanastudio.co.uk
Rates: Phone/email to enquire

THE JOINT

Address: 1-6 Field Street, London WC1X 9DG
T: 0207 833 3375
F: 0207 833 1178
E: info@thejoint.org.uk
W: www.thejoint.org.uk
Rates: Check website for details

LONDON RECORDING STUDIOS

Address: 9-13 Osborn Street, London, E1 6TD
T: 0207 247 5862
F: n/a
E: info@tims.co.uk
W: www.thelondonrecordingstudios.com
Rates: Studio 1: £210 Studio 2: £160, all prices are based on a 7 hour day and includes the cost of an engineer

MADHOUSE REHEARSALS

Address: 41 Hampton Street, Hockley, Birmingham, B19 3LS
T: 0121 233 1109
F: 0121 233 1286
E: n/a
W: www.madhouserehearsals.com
Rates: Phone to enquire

MILOCO

Address: Various locations throughout London
T: 0207 232 0008
F: n/a
E: Vicki@miloco.co.uk
W: www.miloco.co.uk
Rates: Phone/email to enquire

THE MUSIC COMPLEX

Address: 20 Tanners Hill, Deptford, London, SE8 4PJ
T: 0208 691 6666
F: 0208 692 9999
E: info@musiccomplex.co.uk
W: www.musiccomplex.co.uk
Rates: Check website for details

THE MUSICIANS HOUSE

Address: OJ Music, Golders Green, 516 Finchley Road, London, NW11 8DD

T: 0208 458 1332

F: n/a

E: studiobookings@ojmusic.com

W: www.themusicianshouse.com

Rates: Recording: £10 per hour, £100 per day off peak / £15 per hour, £120 per day peak (weekends) / Rehearsal: £6 per hour off peak, £10 per hour peak (evenings and weekends).

NIGHTFLY STUDIOS

Address: 24 Wallis Avenue, Southend-on Sea, Essex, SS2 6GS

T: 01702 337 048

F: n/a

E: info@nightflystudios.co.uk

W: www.nightflystudios.co.uk

Rates: Complete the online booking form or phone/email for further information

ONE LIFE PRODUCTIONS

Address: n/a (London)

T: n/a

F: n/a

E: n/a

W: www.onnelife-productions.co.uk

Rates: £200 for 8 hour day, £360 for two days, £750 for five days (which can be split); weekend, £250 for one day, £450 for two days, check website for contact information

THE OXYGEN ROOMS

Address: 122 Barr Street, Hockley, Birmingham, B19 3DE

T: 0121 551 7001

F: n/a

E: n/a

W: www.theoxygenrooms.com

Rates: £27 per hour / £159 for a 8 hour day; phone for further details

PARR STREET STUDIOS

Address: 33-45 Parr Street, Liverpool, L1 4JN

T: 0151 707 1050

F: 0151 709 4090

E: info@parrstreet.co.uk

W: www.parrstreet.co.uk

Rates: Phone/email to enquire

THE PREMISES (SEE PAGE 134)

Address: 201-204 Hackney Road, London E2 8JL

T: n/a

F: n/a

E: office@premisesstudios.com

W: www.premisesstudios.com

Rates: Phone/email to enquire

PINNA STUDIOS

Address: 34-38 Provost Street, London, N1 7NG

T: 0207 490 8719

F: n/a

E: lise@pinnaproductions.com

F: n/a

W: www.pinnaproductions.com

Info: £350 for a day / £50 for 2 hours, includes engineer, backline; phone/email for further information

THE ROCK N'ROLL CIRCUS

Address: 44-46 Canal Road, Leeds, LS12 2PL

T: 0113 231 9326 (if phoning to make a booking try to call after 6pm)

F: n/a

E: info@therockandrollcircus.co.uk

W: www.therockandrollcircus.co.uk

Rates: Massive Room £35 (5+ piece), Large Room £30 (4/5 piece), Small Room £25 (2/3 piece), all prices are for a 4 hour session and includes PA, drums, bass amp and guitar amp

ROGUE STUDIOS

Address: Railway Arch 4, Bermondsey Trading Estate, Rotherhithe New Road, London, SE16 3LL

T: 0207 231 3257

F: n/a

E: info@roguestudios.co.uk

W: www.roguestudios.co.uk

Rates: Fill in the online form or phone/email for further information

ROUNDHOUSE

Address: 91 Saffon hill, London, EC1N 8PT

T: 0207 404 3333

F: 0207 404 2947

E: roundhouse@stardiamond.com

W: www.stardiamond.com/roundhouse

Rates: Check website for details

SILENT CITY

Address: Central Leeds

T: 07759 592 887

F: n/a

E: robsilentcity@hotmail.co.uk

W: www.silentcity.co.uk

Rates: Check website for details

SOUND INC

Address: Factory Road, Blaydon, Tyne & Wear, NE21 5RU

T: 0191 414 5574

F: n/a

E: martin@soundinc.co.uk

W: www.soundinc.co.uk

Rates: Phone/email to enquire

SOUTHERN STUDIOS

Address: 10 Myddleton Road, London, N22 8NS

T: 0208 888 8949

F: 0208 889 6166

E: studio@southern.com

W: www.southern.com/studio

Rates: Phone/email to enquire

Steelworks Studios

◄ back

Studio One - Control room

TURTLE STUDIOS
Address: Wood Green, North London.
T: 01273 606978
F: n/a
E: info@turtlestudios.co.uk
W: www.turtlestudios.co.uk
Info: Phone/email to enquire

UPTOWN STUDIOS
Address: 22 Denmark Street, London, WC2H 8NG
T: 0207 379 0003
F: n/a
E: info@uptownstudios.co.uk
W: www.uptownstudios.co.uk
Rates: £320 for a 8 hour day, £40 per hour, includes programming, recording, editing, mixing

STEELWORKS STUDIO
Address: Unit D, 3 Brown Street, Sheffield, S1 2BS
T: 0114 272 0300
F: 0114 272 0303
E: steelworksmusic@mac.com
W: www.steelworks-studios.com
Rates: Phone/email to enquire

STAKEOUT STUDIOS
Address: Unit 503, Platts Eyot, Lower Sunbury Road, Hampton, Middlesex, TW12 2HF
T: n/a
F: n/a
E: simon@covertmusic.co.uk
W: www.stakeoutstudios.com
Rates: Follow the link 'Make a booking' which can be found on the top right hand corner of the website

WORLDS END SOUND
Address: Orpington, South East London
T: 07813 357774
F: n/a
E: info@worldsendsound.com
W: www.worldsendsound.com
Rates: Weekdays, £25 per hour / £170 8 hour day; weekends, £28 per hour,/£195 8 hour day, 5 days £700, 7 days £1,000, Saturday & Sunday offer £360; phone/email for further information

TERMINAL STUDIOS
Address: 4-10 Lamb Walk, London Bridge, London, SE1 3TT
T: 0207 403 3050
F: 0207 407 6123
E: info@theterminal.co.uk
W: www.terminal.co.uk
Rates: Check website for details

ZED ONE STUDIOS
Address: Camden
T: 0207 482 3500
F: n/a
E: info@zed-one-studios.co.uk
W: www.zed-one-studios.co.uk
Rates: Recording: £175 per day, 3 days £160 per day, 7 days £150, includes engineer / Rehearsal: between £27-36 for a 4 hour session, check website for further details

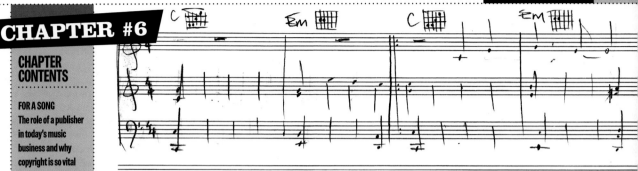

CHAPTER #6

FOR A SONG

PUBLISHERS CAN BE KEY TO BREAKING A NEW BAND, SO LEARN TO LOVE 'THE MAN'

Publishing used to refer, mainly, to the business of collecting income generated by sheet-music sales. But, these days, the primary functions of music publishing companies are to ensure the generation of royalties, fund the development of new talent and secure the protection of copyright. In today's rapidly changing music business, the publisher is more vital than ever. By syndicating your original music to films or adverts (also known as 'synching', see below), they can break your act to a worldwide audience, creating a buzz around you before a record contract has even been signed.

With the continual downturn in conventional album sales, major and independent labels see synching as a necessity for survival, and the stigma that was once associated with flogging your

fee. After all, the more exposure your work gets, the more chance there is of it being picked up. But it is important to understand how copyright works.

Once a piece of music has been created and documented – in writing (sheet music) or another physical format, including any kind of sound recording – it is automatically copyrighted, with the copyright owned by the composer(s). Copyright on material that has been physically recorded is owned by the producer of the recording. Technically, everything you have written is copyrighted and protected by law, to ensure no-one steals your material and uses it without your permission for their own gain.

Copyright is held by the composer for 70 years, after which it moves into the public domain and anyone can freely sample, cover or synch a musical work without the need for clearance or arrangement of royalties.

Music copyright only applies to the melody; the lyrics are protected by literary copyright (this is also automatically created once an original piece is written), while the physical recording is protected under mechanical copyright. As copyright holder, you have the sole authority to copy, issue, lend, perform, rent or communicate the music to the public (for example, broadcasting it via TV, radio and the internet).

Music copyright comes into existence automatically, but you need to be able to prove

artistic genius to 'The Man' has largely disappeared. Many established acts have turned down huge sums of money for the use of their songs in adverts, among them Tom Waits, who is quoted as saying: 'Apparently the highest compliment our culture grants artists nowadays is to be in an ad — ideally naked and purring on the hood of a new car. I have adamantly and repeatedly refused this dubious honour.' But what was once seen as selling out is now seen as just another means of promotion.

WHAT IS MUSIC COPYRIGHT?

As an unsigned artist, you shouldn't worry too much about protecting your copyright; in fact, you should release your copyrighted material into the public domain for little or no

> # What was once seen as selling out is now just a means of promotion

you own it. The easiest way to do this is to send yourself a copy of the recording by special delivery (which will be date stamped). When the package is delivered, keep the envelope sealed. You can also store a copy of the recording with a solicitor or bank manager. As owner of the copyright, you should use the copyright symbol – © – stating your name as the creator/owner of the work and the year of its creation. This states, beyond doubt, that you own the copyright on any material you have written. ★

Free Up Your Music

ROYALTIES WOULD BE NICE, BUT YOUR PRIORITY IS TO GET HEARD

E very time a copyrighted song is played in a public space, the songwriter earns a royalty payment. Anyone who wants to use copyrighted material – from public venues to companies who play music to phone-callers placed on hold – has to pay a licence fee to the MCPS (Mechanical Copyright Protection Society) PRS (Performing Rights Society) Alliance, which collects and distributes royalties.

The Alliance takes a small fee for its services and the rest of the money it collects is paid to the artist. But it will only collect and pay monies owed; it will not actively seek the accruement of royalties for an artist, so joining will not mean a sudden increase in your profile – and certainly doesn't imply instant wealth. You may also risk unbalancing any agreements you already have in place. For example, if you join the MCPS-PRS, it will normally ask your label for money that may be owed to you for the use of your copyrighted material. If you're signed to a small, independent label (which may own the copyright on the recordings, but not on the material that has been recorded), tight budgets will mean you have probably made a deal in which you only begin to earn once the label has recouped its costs.

It's always best to honour agreements you already have – or at least to make the other parties aware of your plans – before joining the MCPS-PRS. You don't want to risk ruining relationships. As an unsigned artist, or one signed to a small label, your priority should be to make your material freely available – not the pursuit of money. ★

Publish and Be Deemed a Good Bet

IMPRESS LABELS BY CASHING IN ON YOUR SONGS

A recording contract is usually one of the last components fitted into place by your team. The first priority of your lawyer or manager will be to find you a publishing contract. The reason for this is simple; you'll (hopefully) be making money well before you reach the recording-contract stage – from licensing, t-shirt sales and live appearances – and your team can use these earnings as leverage in their negotiations.

Larger publishing firms will offer you an advance on future earnings and, effectively, pay for ownership of your copyrighted material. They will also actively pursue accrued royalties on your behalf, unlike the MCPS-PRS (see page 157).

To protect and develop their asset, major publishers will pay you a living wage, offer you free studio time and pay for you to go on tours. They will also exploit your song material – via sales, performances and deals with TV producers, advertisers and movie producers – and try to secure a recording contract. Smaller publishing companies will still look after your copyright, but they will also try to sell on the publishing deal it has with you or sub-contract it to a larger company for a fee.

Most of the money in the music business is in publishing. Smaller companies may not be able to offer an advance on future earnings or have teams large enough to focus exclusively on your career development, but they will be more 'hands-on'. Larger companies may make you feel like a commodity, but they will have the funds to help you to pursue a recording contract while you develop artistically. ★

BOOKAZINES

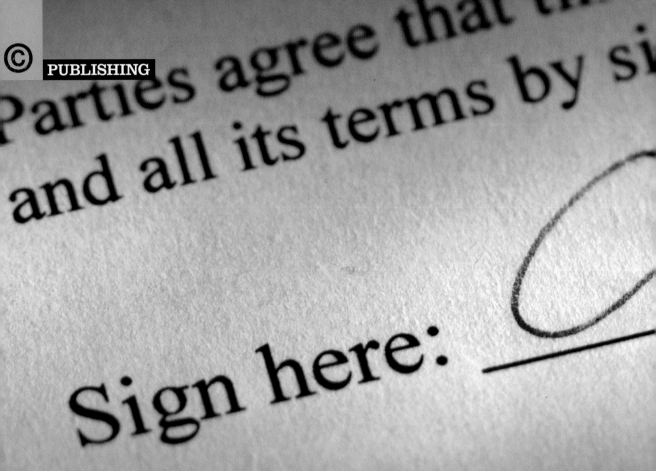

Contracts – Rights Here Rights Now

AVOID THE PITFALLS AND GET AHEAD IN PUBLISHING

Publishing companies actively seek out promising unsigned artists; they send scouts to gigs at venues across the country, follow up leads provided by trusted sources and scour MySpace for acts with marketable material. As a rule, expect them to contact you rather than you contact them. Publishing companies don't generally accept unsolicited material because they can rely on a stream of good-quality demos arriving from contacts in the business, including managers, lawyers and independent labels.

Any publisher willing to check out unsolicited material will make it very clear on their website; they'll explain that they are looking for new artists to work with and how best to contact them. Before you send out unsolicited demos, though, it's best to find out as much as you can about the companies you want to approach; make sure they specialise in your kind of music, look at their success rate, check how much attention individual acts appear to receive and take a peek at musicians' messageboards. This will save you writing a letter, burning off a disc, packing it up and sending it off, only to be ignored. A little research will increase your chances of the A&R department taking notice.

There is no guaranteed method of getting

a publishing contract and, to some extent, luck will always play a role. To improve your odds of winning big, you need to do your research, be professional, put everything you can into every gig and, most importantly, write at least one catchy song.

WHAT TO LOOK FOR IN A MUSIC PUBLISHING CONTRACT

Unlike record labels, who sign a band as a whole – with each member earning from recordings and live performances – the publisher concentrates on the songwriter. This can lead to tensions because the songwriter will always earn a larger

WHAT ABOUT...
The Kinks' album Lola vs Powerman, which satirises the music biz. The track Denmark Street brutally analyses publishing and the lengths to which artists must go for cash

PUBLISHING

About us : Contact us : Press : Jobs : Site map

LOGIN Email [_____]   Password [_____] ▶
sign up   forgotten password?

PLAYING, BROADCASTING AND ONLINE MUSIC | MUSIC FOR PRODUCTS | PRODUCTION MUSIC | MEMBERSHIP | M ONLINE

SEARCH [_____] ▶

Quicklinks [▾] ▶

MCPS-PRS

The MCPS-PRS Alliance is the home of the world's best songwriters, composers and music publishers.

We represent the world's music - that's 10 million pieces of music - and enable businesses and individuals to access all the music they need for use in their business, product or project in the most effective way.

THE IVORS

PRS chats to the nominees and winners at the songwriting awards for 2007

HAVE WE CONTACTED YOU?

Do you need a PRS Music Licence?

MAKE MUSIC?

MEMBERS
Being a member of MCPS-PRS means you are part of a 60,000 strong community earning royalties when your music is performed, broadcast or recorded.

See how MCPS-PRS membership can put a smile on your face...

[JOIN NOW] [LOG IN]

Getting to do what you love is amazing

Dan Le Sac Vs
Scroobius Pip

View more

WANT MUSIC?

CUSTOMERS
WHO ARE YOU? Select your business type here.

Select criteria [▾] ▶

CUSTOMERS
WHAT DO YOU WANT TO DO WITH MUSIC? Whatever you want to do, we've got the music for you.

Select criteria [▾] ▶

M ONLINE - THE LATEST NEWS AND EVENTS

What's this? | 🔊

24.07.2008 - Battle of the Rock Bands
2008 Classic Rock Roll of Honour nominations announced.

23.07.2008 - Black Kids play NY in-store show
Black Kids wow crowds at Virgin Megastore show in New York.

23.07.2008 - Mercury Nominations announced
Adele, Radiohead and Estelle amongst nominees for 2008 Mercury Prize.

22.07.2008 - Ting Tings to collaborate with Rascal
A collaboration between the recent chart-toppers is on the cards after Glastonbury encounter.

SEE/HEAR

What's this? | 🔊

Fringe Sunday 2008 Special - Part 2

Fringe Sunday 2008 Special - Part 1

MCPS-PRS New Member Podcast #15

HOT TOPICS

Why do you need to pay to use music?
MCPS-PRS Alliance explains why you need to pay to use music.

ProDub Licence
Licence for the professional use of music that has been copied onto an MP3 player or laptop.

---

percentage of the royalties than the other band members (equal shares of the songwriting credits may be the reason three of the world's largest bands – U2, R.E.M. and Radiohead – have survived so long). So, as well as being a fine test of intra-band loyalty, a good publishing contract will be your main source of income. You will share these four main income streams with the publisher.

1 MECHANICAL RIGHTS

These deal with the right to sell, download, license and reproduce music via mechanical means (for example, the production of CDs or vinyl records), with these products then being sold through retail outlets. Mechanical rights also control illegal copying of your music and forbid the distribution of copyrighted material without the express permission of the copyright holder.

USEFUL WEBSITES

WWW. ▶
mcps-prs-alliance. co.uk – MCPS/PRS
ipo.gov.uk – Copyright/Intellectual Property Office
mpaonline.org.uk – Music Publishers' Association; explains publishing law and has updates on the industry, event information and links to members' websites

2 SYNCHRONISATION RIGHTS (SYNCHING)

When copyrighted material is used for TV programmes, computer games, films and advertising, a production company will pay for the synchronisation rights by making 'synch deals'. Following the continued drop in CD and vinyl sales, synching is proving to be a steady means of income for publishers and a profit-generating method of promoting their artists. Synch deals can be very lucrative and they help established acts just as much as they could boost your career; Moby's 1999 album *Play* achieved sales in excess of 10 million, with every song on the album being synched to adverts and films. Synching also introduced The Dandy Warhols to mainstream success when their single *Bohemian Like You* was used on a mobile-phone advert.

ESSENTIAL DETAILS
KEY THINGS TO LOOK FOR IN A PUBLISHING CONTRACT

1 LENGTH OF THE INITIAL CONTRACT

This will usually be one year, with the publishing company having first option to renew or release you from the deal. Both parties must be able to work together, so if you are not being allowed to develop – or if you do not deliver a pre-agreed number of songs (normally no more than a standard-length album) – either one of you can walk away. After this initial period, the standard length of a publishing contract is 10-15 years; after this, you will regain the copyright of your published material and can then choose to renegotiate the deal, publish it yourself or go with another publisher.

2 TERRITORIES

Publishers may request worldwide exclusivity on your published output or they may allow you to reach agreements with other publishers depending on the territories your original contract covers. With a smaller publishing operation, you would be best advised to let them have the rights for Europe, then you can look for a separate deal to cover the rest of the world. If, however, a large-scale publisher, such as EMI, is interested in you, they will demand worldwide exclusivity – and it would be a wise thing to give it to them.

3 ROYALTY RATE

A standard rate is between 60% and 80% of gross income. When you first sign a publishing contract, you will be offered an advance to cover recording, touring and living costs. An advance is, basically, a loan and any royalties you receive will initially be used to repay it. If your material doesn't sell, you may be required to repay the advance at the termination of your contract.

4 PUBLISHER'S OBLIGATIONS

These specify the rest of the publisher's agreement with you. They will promise you as little as they can get away with, but expect this. Clauses to look out for include the freedom to sign to a record company of your choice; you might prefer a smaller company, whereas your publisher may want you to sign to a major. Also, as songwriter, you will want control over your copyrighted material in terms of changes to song structure or lyrical content.

Publishing is one of the most confusing aspects of the music business, but, with a basic knowledge of how it works, you should be able to structure a deal to meet your needs. And remember, always protect your copyright – in the music business, it's all you have.

3 PERFORMANCE RIGHTS

All public performances of copyrighted or published material are covered under the performance rights of an artist. Whenever recorded material is played – in retail stores, nightclubs, on the radio or live – the artist earns royalties for the use of their copyright. This includes songs covered by other artists. On large tours, artists have to submit their set list to the PRS after each live performance (but don't panic if you're in a covers band playing in a pub, the publishers won't be after you). For example, if Muse were to cover a David Bowie song at one of their gigs, they would have to pay royalties to Bowie's publisher. All outlets that play recorded music or put on live gigs, must have a music licence (renewable every year), from which published artists and members of the MCPS-PRS (see page 157) will receive a small percentage.

The songwriter will always earn more than the other band members

4 PRINT RIGHTS

The printing of contemporary sheet music – classical music will always sell large amounts of printed material – has grown as the number of people who play a musical instrument has risen. An artist with a publishing contract will have a printed portfolio and, depending on the success of their recorded output, this will be available to buy. This is now one of the smaller avenues of income for an artist, but it is where publishing began and companies still need to have their printed catalogue on sale. ★

INTERVIEW

The Magnificent Seven

THE PUBLISHER WHO LAUNCHED DIDO AND CARL COX WARNS OF THE PITFALLS OF PUBLISHING

Seven Webster has owned and run three music publishing companies, and managed and launched the careers of numerous UK artists and DJs, including Dido, Sasha, John Digweed, StoneBridge, Mason, McQueen and Carl Cox. He also books the Hard Rock Hell and Beachdown music festivals. Here, he gives an insight into the world of publishing, copyright and royalties.

Is it important that an artist retains the copyright on their written and recorded work?

If a writer assigns their songs to a good publisher, I don't think it makes a difference whether the publisher or songwriter owns the copyright, or how long they administer the rights for. The artist would still get the same money. As long as the publisher collects and accounts for all of the writer's royalties against their percentage, which is usually 20%, and the writer receives their 80%, everyone is happy.

If the writer retains the copyright, they will still need a good publisher to chase and track monies from collection societies around the world. They need to do a deal with a good administrative publisher otherwise they may find a lot of their income is never collected.

Ownership of recorded work is not a publishing issue; it is simply the reason an artist does or doesn't sign a record deal and, if they do, what assignment rights they have.

Would a new artist's career move forwards if they owned 100% of the copyright, but could not afford to put out a CD or fund a tour?

In short, no. The benefit of ownership of a recorded work is more complex. Record labels can provide everything from tour support to assistance in making a high-quality album. If, however, an artist is so proactive they

> **"Deal with a good publisher or you may find a lot of your income is never collected"**

manufacture their own CD, have the drive and funds to tour extensively, and can build their own business while maintaining and running an online store, they could definitely argue they are better off maintaining the ownership of recording rights. But it's a notoriously hard route and requires the artist to be talented in business or to have a good business partner.

If an artist owned their finished album, they could license it to a label to market and distribute, and have it revert back to them after a certain period. This is a good and favourable compromise.

An artist can join MCPS-PRS, so what is it a publisher does that they cannot do themselves?
The MCPS-PRS collects monies efficiently in the UK (see page 157) and registers your copyrights with parallel societies overseas. Some of these will pay your monies, but others won't and this is when having a publisher to track, chase and ensure your copyrights are registered properly is crucial, otherwise you could lose a good percentage of

your earnings. The MCPS-PRS also does not exploit your music – putting it into adverts or films, for example.

But it is important artists who have written songs that have been released commercially sign with the MCPS-PRS because, even if you are signed to a publisher, 50% of the performance royalties are directly paid to the writer (if you are unpublished, it is nearer 100%, less the society's token administrative percentage).

With the prevalence of synch deals and with the internet making music more freely available, has the publisher's role changed?
Not really. It's the same in as much as they exploit writers' copyrights, but the music industry now clamours for any sizeable revenue streams it can find and looks to break acts off the back of good placements on TV or in film. So good synchronisations are high on everyone's agendas.

The internet is generating more income through radio stations and retail outlets such as itunes and YouTube. It has also made it ●

easier for an artist to put up more of their copyrights for sale. These new revenues just mean publishers and societies have to track and chase smaller income streams, whereas they used to collect larger amounts of money on smaller numbers of copyrights exploited through physical sales. But monies from offline physical sales have plummeted because of file sharing, piracy and access to free music.

What is it publishers look for in an artist?

I look for great songs and songwriting ability. Being proactive as a writer and writing songs with different acts/writers will help you to create value. As these copyrights are released, publishers will look at you more seriously with regard to signing you.

What standard clauses would a publishing contract contain?

The key points are:

1 Term. This is the length of time you sign to the publisher for. It is usually for one year initially. If you do not earn any money, it is unlikely the term will run beyond one year. If, however, you have a hit, the term will most likely run for another year and, depending on your ongoing success, could run to three or five years.

2 Commitment. This refers to the number of songs you must write in a given period. Most commitment-based deals will require you to achieve a certain amount of released copyrights by a major or reputable label. Some deals do not have commitment and are based on a time period and what you earn in that period, with option triggers based on your success.

3 Retention Period. This is the length of time after the term that the publisher would continue to administer the copyrights written during that term.

4 Advances. This is the amount of money advanced by the publisher to a writer against future royalties earned.

5 Royalties. This would stipulate the percentage split with the publisher over rights. This tends to be about 80% in the artist's favour with breaks for

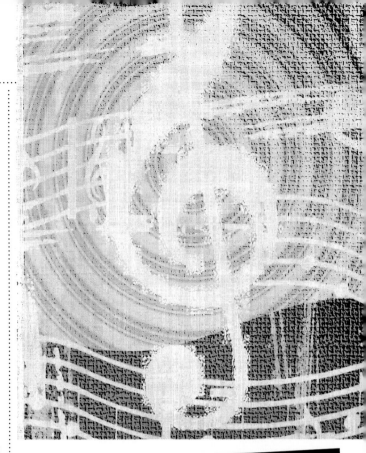

"Writers who assume they can do it all themselves would find things extremely difficult"

procurement of synchs and covers by the publisher.

As well as the above, you will usually find a contract contains details of warranties and definitions, as well as accounting periods and a schedule of songs written prior to the deal. Obviously, writers should seek good legal advice before signing any deal.

In what areas can an artist expect to generate publishing royalties and would they be able to exploit these without the use of a publishing company?

The main areas are:

- Performance income from radio-play
- Performance income from live performance
- Mechanical royalties from record sales (offline) and online sales

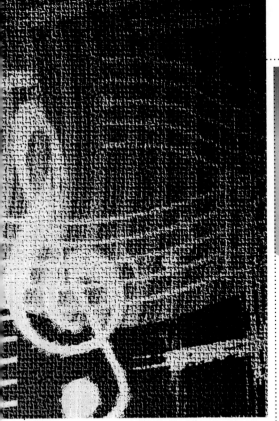

- Covers
- Synch fees
- Sheet-music sales

Writers who assume a publisher does nothing and that they could do it all themselves would find things extremely difficult. It would be like wiring the electrics of your house with no previous experience – not a good idea. It is worth paying someone experienced to do the job they know and understand, and that you do not. You could set up your own publishing company, but this would still have to be administered.

With regards to exploiting your music, you could go to independent synch agents, but they are few and far between and will most likely prefer to deal with people they know and who understand the cut and thrust of music publishing i.e. a publisher or an experienced management company.

Obviously, an artist could play lots of live shows without a publisher's help and achieve publishing income that way. A percentage of the door ticket receipts is paid to the PRS and, in turn, to the writer. However, if these

SEVEN WEBSTER

Seven Webster
seven@a7music.com
www.7pm
management.com
www.myspace.
com/7pmmanagement
www.suitsyou
music.com
www.a7music.com

shows were overseas, they would really need a publisher to chase and track these monies.

What is the future for publishing and has its importance increased or decreased over the past few years?

The music industry has changed radically in the past five years, so no one has a clearcut view about its future. All we can do is speculate and look for new ways to make money. The music publishing industry is probably going to continue to grow worldwide as more online revenue streams are recognised, but these will be based on the fact there are now millions more active copyrights. So it will be growth in terms of the quantity of active copyrights, but the amount of quality offline sales will most likely continue to decrease.

What traps should artists look out for in publishing?

I would suggest, to avoid traps, the artist gets good legal representation (see Lawyer Listings on page 112). That said, music publishing deals are relatively simple agreements. The main things to look at are:

1 Retention period (the period for which you are signing your rights to the publisher to administer). This is normally 10-12 years. If the publisher asks for longer, your lawyer will be best able to advise you on the circumstances of your deal. While publishing deals are simple, the relationship between a publisher and a writer is individual and should be treated as such.

2 The percentage split between writer and publisher. This should be about 80% in the writer/artist's favour with breaks of an extra 10-15% in the publisher's favour if they procure synchs and covers on the copyrights.

What advice do you have for artists who are struggling with the business?

Be proactive in all you do because this causes reactivity. Treat your artistry/songwriting as a business, apply basic common sense and grow it slowly. Launching any business is hard and the music industry is probably one of the toughest arenas in which to do it. Get good advice and good luck. ★

Music Maestros, Please

THESE GUYS WANT TO HEAR FROM YOU IF YOU HAVE A TALENT FOR SONGWRITING

4AD/BEGGARS BANQUET MUSIC LTD

Genres: Indie/pop
Address: 17-19 Alma Road, London, SW18 1AA
T: 0208 871 2121
F: 0208 871 2745
W: www.4ad.com
E: 4AD@4AD.com
Song submission: Check website for details
Artists: Blondie Redhead, Stereolab, Breeders

ASONGS

Genres: Dance/electronic/indie/R&B/rock/pop/urban
Address: ASongs Submissions, Fulham Palace, Bishops Avenue, London, SW6 6EA
T: 0207 384 7373
F: 0207 384 7375
W: www.asongs.co.uk
E: info@asongs.co.uk
Song submission: Via email or post
Artists: Fatboy Slim, Angie Brown

ALBERT MUSIC

Genres: Heavy rock/metal/rock
Address: The Basement, 57 Riding House Street, London, W1W 7EF
T: 0208 830 0330
F: 0208 830 0220
W: www.albertmusic.co.uk
E: info@alberts.co.uk
Song submission: Via form in the 'contact us' section of website.
Artists: 69 Eyes, Breed 77, The Answer

7HZ MUSIC

Genres: Indie/rock
Address: 4 Margaret Street, London, W1W 8RF
T: 0207 462 1269
F: 0207 436 5431
W: www.7hzmusic.co.uk
E: barry@7hz.co.uk
Song submission: Via email, with a link to your Myspace page/website and a list of live dates
Artists: The Films, Goldenhorse

A&G SONGS LTD

Genres: Indie/rock/folk
Address: 1st Floor, 5 Ching Court, 61-63 Monmouth Street, London, WC2H 9EY
T: 0207 845 9880
F: 0207 845 9884
W: www.agrecords.co.uk
E: roy@agrecords.co.uk (manager director)/sarah@agrecords.co.uk (A&R manager)
Song submission: Check website
Artists: Lou Rhodes, Bowling for Soup, The Cloud Room

A7 MUSIC

Genres: Indie/rock/pop
Address: A7 Music Ltd, PO Box 2272, Rottingdean, Brighton, BN2 8XD
T: 01273 304 681
F: 01273 308 120
W: www.a7music.com
E: info@atmusic.com
Song submission: Send demos, on CD or mini-disk, to the above address
Artists: McQueen, Sunset Strippers, Charlotte Church

ARLON MUSIC

Genres: Indie/Rock/Singer-songwriters
Address: 45-53 Sinclair Road, London, W14 0NS
T: N/A
F: N/A
W: www.arlonmusic.com
E: info@arlonmusic.com
Song Submission: Send any demos to the above address
Artists: Andy Fairweather Low, TY Songs, TD Lind

BDI MUSIC LTD

Genres: Indie/rock/pop
Address: Onward House, 11 Uxbridge Street, London, W8 7TQ
T: 0207 243 4101
F: 0207 243 4131
W: www.bdimusic.com
E: info@bdimusic.com
Song submission: Check website for details
Artists: Eskimo Disco, Beth Rowley

BOMBER MUSIC

Genres: Indie/Rock/Punk/Rockabilly
Address: N/A
T: N/A
F: N/A
W: www.myspace.com/bombermusic2
E: Via Myspace
Song Submission: Rather than sending a message Bomber prefer artists to friend them on Myspace, they will then have a listen to your tracks.
Artists: Lights Go Blue, Failsafe, Crazy Arm

BASEMENT MUSIC LTD

Genres: Indie/rock
Address: 20 Cyprus Gardens, London, N3 1SP
T: 0208 346 3969
F: n/a
W: www.basementmusic.co.uk
E: info@basementmusic.co.uk
Song submission: Check website for details
Artists: Willard Grant Conspiracy, Television

BELLA UNION
RECORD LABEL & PUBLISHERS

Genres: Indie/Alternative
Address: 63 The Arches, Cambridge Grove, Hammersmith, London, W6 0LD
T: N/A
F: N/A
W: www.bellaunion.com / www.myspace.com/bellaunion
E: info@bellaunion.com
Song Submission: Send a friend invite via Myspace.
Artists: Dirty Three, Laura Veirs, Explosions in the Sky, Midlake

BIG LIFE MUSIC

Genres: Indie/rock
Address: 67-69 Chalton St, London, NW1 1HY
T: 0207 554 2100
F: 0207 554 2154
W: www.biglifemanagement.com
E: reception@biglifemanagement.com/Jackie@biglifemanagement.com (publishing)
Song submission: Check website for details
Artists: Badly Drawn Boy, Snow Patrol

BUCKS MUSIC GROUP

Genres: Various
Address: Onward House, 11 Uxbridge Street, London, W8 7TQ
T: 0207 221 4275
F: 0207 229 6893
W: www.bucksmusicgroup.com
E: info@bucksmusicgroup.co.uk
Song submission: Post a 3-5 track CD to 'Demo Submission' at the above address. Further information on website
Artists: MC Hammer, Bert Jansch, Brian Eno

CHRYSALIS MUSIC

Genres: Indie/rock/dance

Address: The Chrysalis Building, 13 Bramley Road, London, W10 6SP

T: 0207 221 2213

F: 0207 465 6178

W: www.chrysalismusic.com.uk

E: info@chrysalismusic.co.uk

Song submission: Check website for details.

Artists: Aphex Twin, David Bowie, Black Keys, Blondie, The Cribs, Mogwai

COMPLETE MUSIC

Genres: Rock/indie

Address: 3rd Floor, Bishops Park House, 25-29 Fulham High Street, London, SW6 3JH

T: 0207 731 8595

F: 0207 371 5665

W: www.complete-music.co.uk

E: info@complete-music.co.uk

Song submission: Via email with online links to where your music can be heard

Artists: Go-Betweens, The Stranglers, Buzzcocks

D MUSIC

Genres: Various

Address: 35 Brompton Road, London, SW3 1DE

T: 0207 368 6311

F: 0207 823 9553

W: www.drecords.co.uk

E: n/a

Song submission: Send demos to the above address

Artists: Mercedes, Atar & the Funkadrome

EMI MUSIC PUBLISHING

Genres: Various

Address: 27 Wrights Lane, London, W8 5SW

T: n/a

F: n/a

W: www.emimusicpub.com

E: n/a

Song submission: EMI will only listen to songs submitted via a lawyer or manager, and/or at the recommendation of one of their existing artists.

Artists: The White Stripes, James Yuill, The Enemy, Depeche Mode

FAIRWOOD MUSIC

Genres: Dance/indie/rock

Address: 72 Marylebone Lane, London, W1U 2PL

T: 0207 487 5044

F: 0207 935 2270

W: www.fairwoodmusic.com

E: betul@fairwoodmusic.com

Song submission: Check website for details

Artists: Shapeshifters, JJ Cale

FAVORED NATIONS MUSIC

Genres: Pop/rock/dance

Address: PO Box 31, Bushey, Herts, WD23 2PT

T: 01923 244 673

F: 01923 244 693

W: www.favorednationsmusic.com

E: Jordan@favorednationsmusic.com

Song submission: Check website for details

Artists: Barry Blue, Viktoria Hansen

FRESHLY SQUEEZED MUSIC LTD

Genres: Various

Address: 116 Stanford Ave, Brighton, BN1 6FE

T: 01273 563 201

F: 01273 563 201

W: www.freshlysqueezedmusic.com

E: info@freshlysqueezedmusic.com

Song submission: Enquiries via email

Artists: Don Air, Lemon

GEORGE MARTIN

Genres: Indie/rock
Address: Lyndhurst Hall, Lyndhurst Road, London, NW3 5NG
T: 0207 384 9575
F: n/a
W: www.georgemartinmusic.com
E: info@georgemartinmusic.com
Song submission: Post demos to the above address or send links via email
Artists: Velvet Jones, Sandstone Veterans, Giles Martin, Tom Windriff

ISA MUSIC

Genres: Various
Address: 260 St Vincent Street, Glasgow, G2 5RL
T: 0141 248 2266
F: 0141 248 4333
W: www.isa-music.com
E: admin@isa-music.com
Song submission: Enquiries via email
Artists: Hot Love, Drop The Box, The Retrosexuals

KOBALT MUSIC

Genres: Rock/pop/indie/dance
Address: 4 Valentine Place, London, SE1 8QH
T: 0207 401 5500
F: 0207 401 5501
W: www.kobaltmusic.com
E: sales@kobaltmusic.com
Song submission: Kobalt does not accept unsolicited material. But if you have an existing catalogue or released songs for which you are seeking administration/collection services, email the above address
Artists: Gomez, Antony & the Johnsons, Interpol, LCD Soundsystems, NIN, The Hives

LEAP MUSIC

Genres: Various
Address: N/A
T: N/A
F: N/A
W: www.myspace.com/leapmusicltd / www.leapmusic.com
E: unsigned@leapmusic.com
Song Submission: Send website/Myspace links to the above e-mail
Artists: Owen Pallett

MCS MUSIC LTD

Genres: Pop/rock/jazz/reggae
Address: 10 Heathfield Terrace, London, W4 4JE
T: 0208 987 4150
F: 0208 987 4160
W: www.mcsmusic.com
E: info@mcsmusic.com
Song submission: Check website for details
Artists: Shaggy, The Pet Shop Boys, Metallica

MUTE SONG LTD

Genres: Rock/indie/dance/electro
Address: 1 Albion Place, London, W6 0QT
T: 0203 300 0000
F: n/a
W: www.mutesong.com
E: info@mutesong.com
Song submission: Check website for details
Artists: Nick Cave and the Bad Seeds, Brakes, Billy Childish

NU-SONG

Genres: Various
Address: 106 Canalot Production Studios, 222 Kensal Road, London, W10 5BN
T: 0207 209 9509
F: n/a
W: www.nu-song.com
E: info@nu-song.com
Song submission: Send demos to 'A&R@nu-song' at the above address
Artists: Neil Mclellan, Darren Moss

OUTCASTE MUSIC PUBLISHING

Genres: Acoustic/indie/rock/dance
Address: 43 Brook Green, London, W6 7EF
T: 0207 605 5808
F: 0207 605 5188
W: www.outcaste.com
E: Paul@mvillage.co.uk/mary-anne@mvillage.co.uk
Song submission: Send demos to Francisco Garcia at the above address.
Artists: Seth Lakeman. Cage the Elephant,

P&P SONGS LTD

Genres: Indie/pop/rock
Address: Hope House, 40 St Peter's Road, London, W6 9BD
T: 0208 237 8400
F: 0208 741 0825
W: www.pandpsongs.com
E: indo@pandpsongs.com
Song submission: Via online contact form or email. Check website for details
Artists: Ina, Jamie Scott, Sandi Thom

RAK PUBLISHING

Genres: Indie/rock/pop
Address: 42-48 Charlbert St, London, NW8 7BU
T: 0207 586 2012
F: 0207 722 5823
W: www.rakpublishing.com
E: info@rakpublishing.com
Song submission: Check website for details
Artists: David Saw, Ben Taylor, The Lovers

ANNIE REED

Genres: Various
Address: 'Little Shambles' 132 Top Lane, Whitley, Wiltshire, SN12 8QY
T: 01225 707847
F: N/A
W: www.anniereedmusic.com
E: annie@anniereedmusic.com
Song Submission: See website for details
Artists: Enzo Avitabile, Martyn Bennett,

P3 MUSIC

Genres: Rock/pop
Address: 4 St Andrews, Alyth, Perthshire PH11 8AT
T: 01828 633790
F: 01828 633798
W: www.p3music.com
E: n/a
Song submission: Via online contact form. Check website for details
Artists: Deacon Blue, Alison Burns

POLLINATION MUSIC

Genres: Dance/rock
Address: 30 Kilburn Lane, Kensal Green, London, W10 4AH
T: 0207 424 8665
F: n/a
W: www.pollinationmusic.co.uk
E: n/a
Song submission: Via on line contact form. Check website for details
Artists: Spiritualized, Warren Suicide

SEECA MUSIC PUBLISHING

Genres: Indie/rock/acoustic
Address: PO Box 885A, Kingston Upon Thames, Surrey, KT1 9JQ
T: 0208 398 2510
F: 0208 398 1970
W: www.seeca.co.uk
E: info@seeca.co.uk
Song submission: See website for details
Artists: The Most Terrifying Thing, Marc Ozall, The Toy Guns, The Lights

SONY/ATV

Genres: Indie/rock/pop
Address: 30 Golden Square, London, W1F 9LD
T: 0203 206 2501
F: n/a
W: www.songatv.com
E: Head of A&R Ian.Ramage@sonyatv.com/
A&R managers Flash.Taylor@songatv.com/
James.Dewar@sonyatv.com
Song submission: Send CD to any of the A&R
personnel above or email a link to web pages
Artists: Bob Dylan, Beck, Noel Gallagher

TASTE MUSIC LTD

Genres: Indie/rock
Address: Taste Music Ltd, PO Box 31797,
London, SW15 2XG
T: n/a
F: n/a
W: www.tastemusic.com
E: info@tastemusic.com
Song submission: Send a CD of no more than
three tracks to the above address and include
relevant photos, biographies and gig listings.
Alternatively, send your website/Myspace page
links via email
Artists: Muse, Shed Seven

WIPEOUT MUSIC

Genres: Punk/post-punk/indie/gothic
Address: PO Box 1NW,
Newcastle Upon-Tyne, NE99 1NW
T: 0191 266 3802
F: 01910266 6073
W: www.wipeoutmusic.com
Song submission: Via post or email
Artists: Devilish Presley, Embassy, Gold Blade

STAGE THREE MUSIC LTD

Genres: Indie/rock/acoustic
Address: 13a Hillgate Street, London, W8 7SP
T: 0207 792 6060
F: 0207 792 6067
W: www.stagethreemusic.com
E: info@stagethreemusic.com
Song submission: Check website for details
Artists: The Subways, CSS, Supatone,
The Boy Least Likely To

TOP CAT MUSIC

Genres: Indie/Rock
Address: Mill Side, Mill Lane, Box, Corsham,
Wiltshire, SN13 8PN
T: N/A
F: N/A
W: www.topcatmusic.co.uk
E: demo@topcatmusic.co.uk
Song Submission: Send demos to the above
address or Myspace link to the above e-mail.
Artists: Nicole Fermie, David Blazye

WARDLAW BANKS LTD

Genres: Various
Address: Park House, 111 Uxbridge Road,
London, W5 5LB
T: 0845 299 0150
F: 0207 117 3171
W: www.wardlawbanks.com
E: info@wardlawbanks.com
Song Submission: See website for details
Artists: Maxi Priest, Darryl Hunt

YELL MUSIC

Genres: Indie/Rock
Address: PO Box 46301, London, W5 3UX
T: 0208 579 8300
F: As above
W: www.yellmusic.com
E: jana.yell@yellmusic.com
Song Submission: See website for details
Artists: Alexis Blue, Midtown, Tenth Planet

RESISTING THE VINYL COUNTDOWN

BIG LABELS STICK IT OUT AS MUSIC-SCENE CHANGES POSE A NEW CHALLENGE

Announcements about the death of the record label are, maybe, a little premature. No matter what Radiohead did with *In Rainbows* (inviting fans to download the album for whatever price they wanted), it was the millions EMI put into recording and marketing the band's six previous releases (eight if you include the live EP and recent *Best Of*) that secured their success. As an unsigned artist, most of your material will also be available for free, but people aren't flocking to your website to download your music because you haven't had a multimillion pound, global corporation backing you for the past 15 years.

The funds and resources of record labels – including the back catalogues they hold – are keeping them afloat through the stormy seas the business is currently navigating. Labels have always had to ride incredible peaks and terrible troughs, dealing with periods of adaptation and then stability.

The difficulties of policing the internet and maintaining control of their copyrighted material are probably the biggest challenges labels have faced. But the industry has had to deal with piracy since music was first ●

printed; 19th-century publishers struggled to contain the reproduction of sheet music, while, in the 1980s, people recorded songs from the radio onto cassette. By using the New Model/360° marketing method (see page 192), labels – and unsigned artists – are finding other means of generating income.

HOW TO LURE A LABEL

Rather than approaching a record label, it's now more important for artists to build a team around them that will use their contacts and experience to secure a deal. This team should contain a lawyer, manager, publisher, booking agent and PR company, and their target should be to raise your band's profile while pursuing record-label A&R people.

Record labels will want guarantees of a return on their investment in you, so it's almost unheard of for them to sign an unknown artist on the strength of an unsolicited demo. A&R people rely upon

GETTING A RECORD CONTRACT

BOOKING AGENT
Books gigs/tours

MANAGER
Looks after the day-to-day running of an artist's career

PUBLISHER
Exploits an artist's copyrighted material

PR
Secures press coverage

THE ARTIST

LAWYER
Negotiates contracts

RECORD CONTRACT

contacts to feed them artists, to ensure demo recordings are of a high quality and contain at least one potential single, and to guarantee there's an audience for them to market to.

Unless you get very lucky and someone spots your potential at a gig, secure a team around you before thinking of a record contract because, the chances are, you won't make it on your own. As in any business, sometimes it's who you know not what you know – or how good you are. ★

Size Matters So Check The Labels

BIG OR SMALL, MAKE SURE THE FIT IS COMFORTABLE

Major labels can offer huge funding and total marketing exposure across every platform (TV, print media, internet), while giving bands the chance to work with experienced industry professionals; but it's easy to get lost among the huge lists of artists they have and heartbreaking to see your release swallowed up in the 15-25 albums they release each month. Subsidiary labels act independently, but are still answerable to corporate headquarters if their artists don't shift enough units, reviews are weak or tours are not selling out. ◗

SALES FIGURES

When an album makes a certain number of sales, the artist is presented with one of those familiar framed discs. The number of units that need to be sold to receive a disc are:

Silver: 60,000
Gold: 100,000
Platinum: 300,000

Alongside the four majors and their subsidiary labels, there is now a healthy crop of strong, independent labels. These tend to have smaller rosters of artists and, because they're not simply part of a massive corporate structure, they are able to give time and attention to every artist they work with, not just the bigger, marquee acts.

The independents don't have the funding or staff of a major label, but they are more able to focus attention on the artists they deal with – generally numbering no more than 30, whereas the majors each have hundreds of signed acts. Independents are more prepared

to allow a buzz to build around an artist before they release any recordings. Of course, an album still has to recoup its costs and bring in a profit, but the fact the artist is not part of a large, multinational company reliant on stock figures (when Coldplay delayed the release of their album *X&Y* in 2005, EMI's shares took a huge drop) means the pressure is not as great.

These are, though, generalisations; there are plenty of well-documented examples of independents not allowing artists time to develop a fanbase or grow musically, while, at the same time, expecting them to sell an

MAJOR RECORD LABELS AND THEIR SUBSIDIARIES

MAJOR LABELS		
Warners Music Group	Apple Records	Pinacle Records
Atlantic Records Group	Capitol Records	Silvertone Records
Roadrunner	Virgin Records	**Universal Music Group**
Elektra Records	Relentless Records	Def Jam UK
Atlantic Records	Hut Records	Island Records Group
Independent Label	Blue Note Label Group	Decca Records
Group	EMI Classics	Mercury Records
Asylum Records	Real World Records	Tamla/Motown
Triple Crown Records	Angel Records (US)	Universal Music Group
One Eleven Records	**Sony BMG**	Nashville
Warner Bros. Records	Columbia Records	MCA Nashville
Maverick	Aware Records	Verve Records
Nonesuch Records	Burgundy Records	Coral Records
Reprise Records	Epic Records	Blue Thumb Records
Sire Records	Caribou Records	
EMI	Ruthless Records	**LARGER**
Parlophone	GUN Records	**INDEPENDENT**
Angel Music Group	Ravenous Records	**LABELS**
Angel Records (UK)	RCA Music Group	Warp
Innocent Records	Arista Records	Domino
Hollywood Records	Zomba Music Group	XL
Capitol Music Group	Battery Records	Rough Trade
	Jive Records	

SHOW STOPPERS

KEEP THE CHECK-OUTS BUSY OR YOU'LL BE AN UNSIGNED ARTIST ONCE AGAIN

Even established musicians can find themselves out on their ear if they don't achieve sufficient sales.

The Eighties Matchbox B-line Disaster – Dropped by Universal/Island after two albums because of low sales figures and a lack of overseas success.

The Thrills –Their third album, *Teenagers*, was buried by Virgin and the band were dropped by the label soon afterwards.

Futureheads – Their second album 'only' sold 32,000, so the band and their label parted ways. The Futureheads formed their own label and retain a strong, loyal fanbase.

The Darkness – Unable to match the sales of their debut album, *Permission To Land*, with their second release, the band were dropped by Atlantic.

Annie Lennox – One of the biggest-selling female artists ever, Sony BMG decided not to renew her contract after it expired in December 2007.

The unwritten rule – you will be out the door if your album doesn't hit silver

unrealistic number of copies of their debut album (the unwritten rule is, you'll be out the door if your album doesn't hit silver).

No matter what type of label you sign for, the hard work begins once a deal has been penned, with the pressure and expectation suddenly far greater because you'll be in debt to a lot of people. ★

Good Things in Small Packages

ONE-OFF, GENRE-SPECIFIC RELEASES ARE NO BAD THING

Alongside the major and larger independent labels are several smaller companies that will release one-off albums, singles and EPs. The main form of distribution for these labels is via the internet, with releases sent out by post or made available as a download.

This is a great way to release your music to a wider audience, with each label helping to build awareness by listing your recordings for sale – or by making your songs available in a streamed music player – and by linking to your website from theirs. They should also include news of forthcoming gigs and releases in the newsletters they send out.

Unlike the majors, these smaller labels normally focus on one music style, building and retaining a fanbase for the artists they put out and for the label. In fact, for genres such as punk, rockabilly and folk, these labels have become many musicians' main source of income because most mainstream labels won't touch them.

You will get a few sales through the reputation of the label bringing traffic to your MySpace page or independent website, and this will give you the sense of satisfaction that comes from a little extra money being made from selling your material.

The details of any contract you sign with a label of this kind will depend on the type of deal you and the label are looking for. The company may choose to release existing recordings under a licensing agreement, whereby it buys the distribution rights, but not the copyright, of the recording and receives a small percentage on all sales.

The label may pay for the recording (with the artist earning money once the costs have been covered). It would own the copyright on the recording and you would retain the copyright on your songs. But, if you have the money to cover recording costs, ownership of everything could prove beneficial in the long term – if you're not happy with the way the label is handling your material, you would be free to take it elsewhere.

Some of these labels are so small that most people don't know they exist, but they provide another means of getting exposure, releasing your recordings and making them available to the public to buy. ★

WHAT TO LOOK OUT FOR IN A RECORDING CONTRACT
BE CAUTIOUS WHEN GIVING UP YOUR SIGNATURE

It's essential you read through your contract properly and employ a lawyer to do the same. Always try to retain your copyright and make sure you receive the majority share of any royalties. The contract will be worded in favour of the labels – standard practice in the business because it's their money you'll be spending. In addition, labels don't want artists suing them whenever they think a section of the contract has not been fulfilled. But, as long as you keep control of your interests, things shouldn't fall apart that easily.

Standard clauses

Length of contract: The number of albums expected rather than a time period. Most will be for 5-6 albums, with the label having the option to renew or drop an artist after the first (or second) album.

The number of recordings an artist has to deliver: The minimum is usually one album, which has to be delivered within a specified period of time (Term). A record company won't guarantee to release a recording – release is dependent on commercial acceptance after the label has listened to it.

Exclusivity: This ensures the label owns the rights to manufacture, distribute and sell any recordings within territories stated in the contract. The contract will also contain 're-recording restrictions', which will prevent the artist from re-recording previously released material. Guest appearances on another artist's recordings will also be at the label's discretion.

Artist royalty percentages: The amount an artist receives from every single/album sold will usually be 60-75% per unit. The royalty rate can be renegotiated when an artist's option is due for renewal and if they have shown sufficient return on material already released.

Advances: These are payments made against future royalties. Your manager will take 20% and the rest has to cover your living costs, recording, packaging, artwork, income tax etc. It can lead to artists being heavily in debt to labels if they do not make back costs, so generation of income from touring, publishing and merchandising is essential.

Other terms will include publishing, music-video rights, equipment, tour support, and creative and cost control.

Company Secrets

A&R EXPERT OLIVIER BEHZADI GIVES THE INSIDE TRACK ON ATTRACTING LABELS

aving been head of A&R for Sony International, Olivier Behzadi is now a consultant to record labels and to MTV, on which he co-presents *The A Cut* with Anastasia. He also oversees the A&R side of the business for new-media label Greengarden Records.

How should bands approach a record company?

Never over-package yourself or try to look more ready than you really are – good-looking packages are all too often let down by inferior music. Any photographs you submit should be neutral and not too stylised. The most important thing is that they capture the essence of your band. Try to grab the interest of A&R people by making your act as appealing as possible – it helps to be easy to deal with in the first place. Having an active MySpace page – showing press coverage, demonstrable gig experience and any DIY releases – is now expected before a band approaches a label. Creating the 'buzz' or the 'story' around you in advance has become very important.

How hard is it to sign to a major label?
Very. In 1996, Sony Columbia – just one label in the huge Sony stable – signed 26 bands. Sony is the smallest major, but, with its other imprints – such as Epic – this meant 250 bands were signed through the company in one year. That was costly back then and would be impossible now, when Sony Columbia signs perhaps 15 acts a year. These days, labels fight bidding wars over a very small number of exciting new bands. These wars are hotly contested and cut down on the time and money labels can devote to new acts. So signing to a major has become more competitive than ever.

Is a small label a good alternative?
Some things can't be done without the backing of a major company – the pop and soul sectors, for example. Both require big marketing spends and, sometimes, smaller

PLATFORMS FOR THE UNSIGNED

MTV's Get Seen, Get Heard (Oxjam)
XFM Unsigned
The A Cut (MTV International)
X Factor
Britain's Got Talent
O2 Undiscovered
O'Neils Undiscovered
City Showcase
ITC Manchester

outfits just do not have deep enough pockets. But rock and indie bands can use singles deals with small labels as a stepping stone to the majors. Fierce Panda is a good example; it is respected as an A&R source and its pedigree speaks for itself, having released successful singles by Coldplay, Air Traffic and others. It is a smart move for acts to do a small release through an independent label when starting out. Indies have experience and can be vital in providing advice and help. Starting small gives a band time to develop a 'story' for its target major label to hear. When signing to a major, elements of control are invariably lost; doing it this way allows a band to decide much for themselves.

What do A&R people actually do?
An A&R department relies on its contacts in the business to find, develop and build a buzz around new bands. A good A&R person will

CASH FLOW
FIND FINANCIAL BACKING

SLICE THE PIE
Harness your fans' money to finance an album. Bands with more than 5,000 fans can sometimes go straight to the finance stage; most start in the 'arena', where they enter a competition with 1,000 other bands to see who wins the deal. Innovative idea in its early days. *www.slicethepie.com*

SELL A BAND
Artists and their 'believers' raise cash for an album release. *www.sellaband.com*

CITY INVESTMENT
City firms now offer to invest in New Model companies, but funding is often dependent on being signed via companies linked to investment groups (such as Icebreaker, which needs to see £125,000 before they will look at stand-alone projects). In this respect, it can be similar to private investment schemes – some money may need to be raised first.

MEDIA COMPANIES
Media companies have invested in bands in recent years, using their various platforms as a launch-pad for new acts.

PRIVATE INVESTMENT
'Angels' invest in bands and their albums, providing them with enough money to record and release their music. Some schemes are self run, others are run via City investment firms (*see above*). Increasingly popular as part of the New Model and DIY approach, but at an early stage.

---

come up with novel promotional strategies and enhance your marketing online, on TV and on the radio. They can typically track down the right producer for you to work with and help to keep the quality of the project up to professional levels. A&R becomes more vital in the New Model. Bands can't achieve everything on their own and working through A&R people is less intimidating than dealing directly with multinational companies. A&R provides the connections, but no matter how well plugged-in you are – no matter how much your company spends – ultimately, the public decides.

The future?
I can see more 360° deals with a smaller number of major-label bands and, possibly, fewer big stars. But I don't expect bands to earn more money out of the revenue streams; it will still be between 20% and 24%. ★

TOP TIPS
TO LURE THE LABELS

1 Spend money on recording your music not on packaging it

2 Put energy into playing live and communicating with your audience

3 Establish a community and fanbase

4 Don't analyse the music business too much

5 Don't give money to compilations or to other get-famous-fast schemes – they don't work

Looking for the right labels

A SELECTION OF SOME OF THE BEST RECORD LABELS TO WORK WITH

1-2-3-4 RECORDS
Address: 27 Cowper St, London, EC2A 4AP
T: 0207 684 1126
F: 0207 613 5917
E: info@1234records.com
W: www.1234records.com
Accept unsolicited demos: n/a

ABSORB MUSIC
Address: PO Box 1089, Birmingham
T: n/a
F: 0121 247 6981
E: rod@fruitionmusic.co.uk
W: www.absorbmusic.com
Accept unsolicited demos: Send to the A&R at the above address.

1965 RECORDS
Address: PO Box 5060, London, W1A 0WN
T: 0207 734 2420
F: n/a
E: info@1965records.com
W: www.1965records.com
Accept unsolicited demos: Send to the above address.

AMAZON RECORDS LTD
Address: PO Box 5109, Hove, East Sussex, BN52 9EA
T: 01273 726 414
F: 01273 726 414
E: info@amazonrecords.co.uk
W: www.amazonrecords.co.uk
Accept unsolicited demos: Send to the above address.

AARDVARK RECORDS
Address: 65 The Terrace, Penryn, Cornwall, TR10 8EH
T: 01326 376 707
F: 01326 376 707
E: info@aardvarkrecords.co.uk
W: www.aardvarkrecords.co.uk
Accept unsolicited demos: Send to the above address, may take up to 1-2 months for a response due to volume received.

ATOMIC MUSIC
Address: Elme House, 133 Long Acre, Covent Garden, London, WC2E 9DT
T: 0207 379 3010
F: 0207 420 7979
E: info@atomic-london.com
W: www.atomic-london.com
Accept unsolicited demos: n/a

B-UNIQUE RECORDS

Address: 1A Cranbrook Rd, London, W4 2LH
T: 0208 987 0393
F: 0207 995 9917
E: info@b-uniquerecords.com
W: www.b-uniquerecords.com
Accept unsolicited demos: Send any demos to the above address.

BAD SNEAKERS RECORDS

Address: 1-5 Springfield Mount, Leeds, LS2 9NG
T: 0113 243 1481
F: n/a
E: info@badsneakers.co.uk
W: www.badsneakers.co.uk
Accept unsolicited demos: n/a

BELLA UNION

Address: 14 Church Street, Twickenham, Middx, TW1 3NJ
T: 0208 744 2777
F: 0208 891 1895
E: info@bellaunion.com
W: www.bellaunion.com / www.myspace.com/bellaunion
Accept unsolicited demos: No, but send a message via MySpace and they will try their best to have a listen.

BOY WONDER RECORDS

Address: 100 Hatfield Road, Hall Green, Birmingham, B28 0HP
T: 0121 370 0389
F: n/a
E: boywonder@botwonderrecords.com
W: www.boywonderrecords.com
Accept unsolicited demos: n/a

BRAINLOVE RECORDS

Address: 8b Cecilia Road, London, E8 2EP
T: vn/a
F: n/a
E: info@brainloverecords.com
W: www.brainloverecords.com
Accept unsolicited demos: Send an e-mail to the above address with links to where your music can be heard online.

COLUMBIA RECORDS

Address: Bedford House, 69-79 Fulham High Street, London, SW6 3JW
T: 0207 384 7500
F: 0207 371 9298
E: n/a
W: www.columbia.co.uk
Accept unsolicited demos: Visit www.columbiademos.co.uk for information on demo submission.

CONCRETE RECORDINGS

Address: 35 Beech Road, Chorlton, Manchester, M21 8BX
T: 0161 881 2332
F: 0161 860 7283
E: ms@concreterecordings.co.uk
W: www.concreterecordings.co.uk
Accept unsolicited demos: Send demos to the above address or email links where your music can be heard online.

COOKING VINYL

Address: PO Box 1845, London, W3 0ZA
T: 0208 600 9200
F: 0208 743 7448
E: info@cookingvinyl.com
W: www.cookingvinyl.com
Accept unsolicited demos: Visit www.cookingvinyl.com/contact for information on demo submission.

DANCE TO THE RADIO

Address: Floor 3, 36-38 The Calls, Leeds, West Yorks, LS2 7EW
T: 0113 246 1200
F: 0113243 4849
E: info@dancetotheradio.com
W: www.dancetotheradio.com
Accept unsolicited demos: Send demo and a blo to Ali Tant at the above address.

DELTASONIC RECORDS

Address: 102 Rose Lane, Mossley Hill, Liverpool, L18 8AG
T: 0151 724 4760
F: 0151 724 6286
E: demo@deltasonicrecords.co.uk
W: www.dealtasonic.co.uk
Accept unsolicited demos: Email links to where your music can be heard online to the above address.

DOMINO RECORDING COMPANY

Address: PO Box 47029, London, SW18 1WD
T: 0208 875 1390
F: 0208 875 1391
E: info@dominorecordco.com
W: www.dominorecordco.com
Accept unsolicited demos: Send demos to the above address or email links where your music can be heard online (check website for further information).

EARACHE RECORDINGS

Address: PO Box 144 Nottingham, NGE 4GE
T: 0115 950 6400
F: 0115 950 8585
E: mail@earache.com
W: www.earache.com
Accept unsolicited demos: Send demos to the above address or e-mail links where your music can be heard online. (Check website for further information)

FIERCE PANDA

Address: PO Box 43376, London, N5 2EA
T: 0207 704 6141
F: n/a
E: mrbongopanda@aol.com
W: www.fiercepanda.co.uk
Accept unsolicited demos: Send demos to the above address or email links where your music can be heard online.

FULL TIME HOBBY RECORDS

Address: 3rd Floor, 1A Adpar Street, London, W2 1DE

T: 0207 535 6740

F: 0207 563 7283

E: info@fulltimehobby.co.uk

W: www.fulltimehobby.co.uk

Accept unsolicited demos: Send demo and bio to A&R at the above address.

GUT RECORDS

Address: Byron House, 112A Shirland Road, London, W9 2EQ

T: 0207 266 0777

F: 0207 266 7734

E: general@gutrecords.com

W: www.gutrecords.com

Accept unsolicited demos: Go to the website and click the link 'Demos' for information on how to submit material.

INDEPENDIENTE

Address: The Drill Hall, 3 Heathfield Terrace, Chiswick, London, W4 4JE

T: 0208 747 8111

F: 0208 747 8113

E: ryan@independiente.co.uk / andy@independiente.co.uk

W: www.independiente.co.uk

Accept unsolicited demos: Email links to where your music can be heard online to the above addresses.

LOOSE RECORDS

Address: Pinery Building, Highmoor, Wigton, Cumbria, CA7 9LW

T: 016973 45422

F: 01673 45422

E: info@loosemusic.com

W: www.looserecords.com / www.myspace.com/ looserecords

Accept unsolicited demos: Email links to where your music can be heard online to the above MySpace.

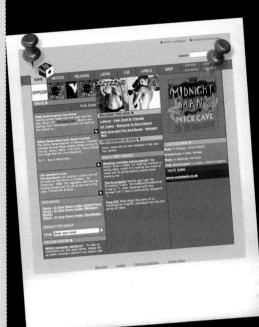

MUTE RECORDS

Address: 43 Brook Green, London, W6 7EF

T: 0208 964 2001

F: 0203 3008 6001

E: info@mutehq.co.uk

W: www.mute.com

Accept unsolicited demos: Send demo and bio to the A&R department at the above address.

MY DAD RECORDINGS

Address: 39 Barnfield Road, Hyde, Cheshire, SK14 4EL

T: n/a

F: n/a

E: info@mydadrecordings.com

W: www.mydadrecordings.com

Accept unsolicited demos: Send a demo to the above address.

REVOLVER MUSIC LTD

Address: 152 Goldthorn Hill, Penn, Wolverhampton, W.Midlands, WV2 3JA

T: 01902 345 345

F: 01902 345 155

E: Follow the link 'Contact us' on Revolver's website.

W: www.revolverrecords.com

Accept unsolicited demos: Click on 'submit your demo' which can be found on Revolver's website.

ROCK ACTION RECORDS

Address: PO Box 15107, Glasgow, G1 1US

T: n/a

F: n/a

E: info@rockactionsrcords.co.uk

W: www.rockactionrecords.co.uk

Accept unsolicited demos: Send demos to the above address or email links where your music can be heard online (check website for further information).

RED EYE MUSIC

Address: 24 Dinas Street, Cardiff, CF11 6QY

T: 02920 396 035

F: n/a

E: info@redeyemusic.co.uk

W: www.redeyemusic.co.uk

Accept unsolicited demos: Send MP3s or links to where your music can be heard online, with a short bio, to the above email address; post any demos to the above address.

ROUGH TRADE RECORDS

Address: 66 Golborne Road, London, W10 5PS

T: 0208 960 9888

F: 0208 968 6715

E: paul.jones@roughtraderecords.com

W: www.roughtraderecords.com

Accept unsolicited demos: Send any demos marked for the attention of Olly Parker to the above address, email any links where your music can be heard online to the above email.

REVEAL RECORDS

Address: 63 St Peters Street, Derbe. Derbyshire, DE1 2AB

T: n/a

F: 01332 556 374

E: tomreveal@mac.com

W: www.reveal-records.com

Accept unsolicited demos: Send a demo and brief bio to the above address.

SETANTA RECORDS

Address: 174 Camden Rd, London, NW1 9HJ

T: 0207 284 4877

F: 0207 284 4577

E: info@setantarecords.com

W: www.setantarecords.com / www.myspace.com/setantarecords

Accept unsolicited demos: n/a (check website for details)

SHIFT DISCO LTD

Address: Oxford Music Central, 1st Floor, 9 Park End Street, Oxford, OX1 1HH

T: 01865 798 791

F: n/a

E: Contact Shift via the 'Contact us' section of website.

W: www.shiftydisco.co.uk

Accept unsolicited demos: Go to the 'Contact us' section of the website and follow the link 'got something we should hear,' for further information on how to get your material heard.

SOUTHERN RECORDS

Address: PO Box 59, London, N22 1AR

T: 0208 348 4640

F: 0208 348 9156

E: n/a

W: www.southern.net

Accept unsolicited demos: Send demo and bio to the above address.

SPLIT RECORDS

Address: 13 Dagmar Terrace, London, N1 2BN

T: 0207 226 8706

F: n/a

E: emilykane@splitrecords.co.uk

W: www.splitrecords.co.uk

Accept unsolicited demos: Send a link to where your music can be heard online and a bio to the above email address.

SOUTHERN FRIED RECORDS

Address: Unit 3, Cranford Way, London, N8 9DG

T: 0207 384 7373

F: 0207 384 7392

E: n/a

W: www.southernfriedrecords.com

Accept unsolicited demos: Visit the website for further information on the label and where to send demos.

NEW MODEL

THE CHANGING FACE OF THE MUSIC INDUSTRY

These are interesting times for the rapidly evolving music industry, with new ways to hear tracks by fresh artists appearing almost every day. It's also an exciting period for musicians and huge opportunities exist for those who can successfully get their work 'out there'.

OLD MODEL

With the traditional model, artists were signed by record companies and negotiated separate deals covering publishing, live work and merchandise. As a rule, all important career decisions were made by the record company and the artist's management. Most artists presently signed to major labels would recognise this as their situation.

There aren't as many of this type of deal around these days; the first decade of the 21st century has seen the major labels, facing hard times, shed staff around the world and concentrate their investments on market-proven acts who are likely to return a profit.

Today's smaller, major-label rosters make this kind of deal an attractive choice for bands aiming to top the charts – and major labels may yet forge a niche marketing role within the new model because they have the expertise and reach that smaller companies can't match. Big labels certainly have the biggest budgets and any band competing for mainstream success will find the majors still dominate the stage.

INDEPENDENT LABELS

Before you sign anything, you must make sure you fully understand the kind of deal you're making. Independent labels usually allow bands more freedom than the majors and are not driven purely by the need to shift units. Most indies are members of AIM (the Association of Independent Music); they ●

Any band competing for mainstream success will find majors still dominate

BREAKING THE MOULD
RADIOHEAD'S GREAT MUSIC GIVEAWAY

When Radiohead's Jonny Greenwood wrote on their website 'the new album is finished and it's coming out in 10 days... we've called it *In Rainbows*', the music industry changed forever. The album was released as a digital download and fans could decide how much to pay for it. As one of the biggest bands on the planet, Radiohead could afford to have faith that their audience would want to pay for the music and, even though the band's management have refused to release sales figures (so it's unclear if the experiment was a success) this grand statement made the business take notice of the potential of the internet while embracing the new model of marketing.

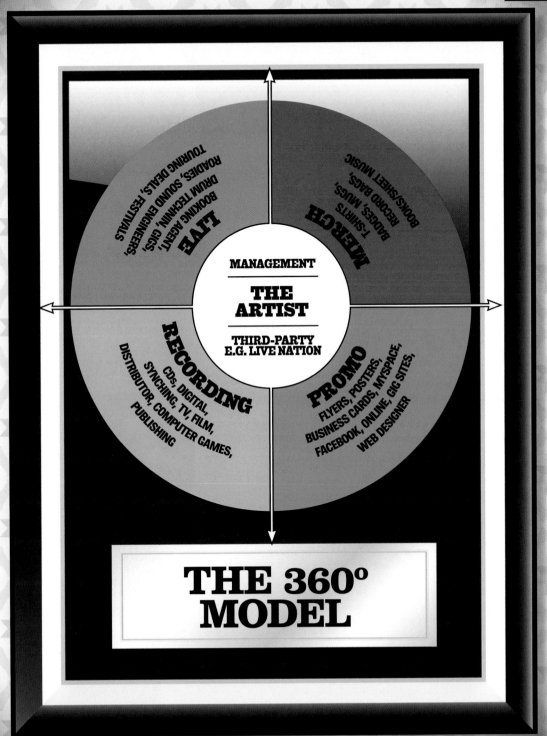

THE 360° MODEL

SAY WHAT?

"Rock 'n' roll was an outlet for some pure, natural expression of rebellion. It used to be one channel you could take without havin' to kiss arse." – Keith Richards

vary in size from small, development labels and community projects to far larger, chart-oriented companies. Some of the bigger outfits maintain respectably sized rosters and can even pay advances.

AIM promotes and celebrates the sector with an Independents' Day bash every July 4. Bands looking for a label that will let them grow while retaining their identity should check out likely candidates on AIM's website, *www.musicindie.org*. If you are already more involved with the DIY 360° model, you can track down licensing deals (which let you retain control of recording and content) with AIM-listed organisations – and, in theory, with the majors too.

NEW MODEL

The digital age has made it economically viable for bands to record and distribute their music themselves, and this has led to unprecedented upheaval in the industry. The

NINE INCH NAILS
TRENT REZNOR HAMMERS OUT A NEW DIRECTION

After Nine Inch Nails had completed their contractual number of albums for Interscope records – and lead singer/songwriter Trent Reznor had made his anti-label rant on the final date of their 2007 tour – the band focused on marketing and distributing new material via their website. *Ghost I-IV*, a 36-track instrumental album, was released in February this year for a minimum $5 fee to cover download costs. Then came the totally free release of NIN's seventh album, *The Slip*. Both albums are available in physical formats, but Reznor is focused on distributing his music via the internet and his embracing of digital technology is sowing the seeds for the rest of the industry.

enormous popularity of social-networking sites and of online sales systems, such as iTunes, has led to a global market for what would be 'unsigned acts' in the old model.

The growth of such sites has prompted the creation of so-called 'one-company' 360° deals, whereby artists pool all of their income streams in a deal with a single, multi-function company or they take control of those streams themselves – what's known as the DIY 360° Deal. This new model gives bands control of their destiny across all facets of their career, from selecting the studio to approving t-shirt designs.

CORE OF NEW MODEL – ONE-COMPANY VERSION

We are already seeing companies such as Live Nation offering artists complete package deals covering all areas of income. These are especially attractive to established major artists. The company will combine releases with tours and merchandise; this joined-up marketing should provide the artist with a big increase in their percentage of profits.

CORE OF NEW MODEL – DIY VERSION

The DIY model scales everything down, so even the smallest band can operate under it and take control of their career. Rather than

Artists are free to outsource specialist jobs, but they are always in control

signing several small record deals, bands can now license their music, set up their own label or publishing firm, and run their own concert diary. The internet also lets musicians distribute their product and sell it directly to shops.

From a band's point of view, the main advantage of this type of set-up is that they keep a higher percentage of any profits they make. Artists are free to outsource specialist jobs when necessary, but they are always in control. This model has now been successfully adopted across the entire music industry.

DOING IT FOR YOURSELVES
TOP TIPS FOR MAKING THE 360° MODEL WORK

1 GOOD MANAGEMENT
Get some

2 STAY ORGANISED
Organisation is vital. Jobs will need to be shared out among members of the band

3 BE REALISTIC
Without major investment, it's probably not going to be possible to grow too quickly

4 MAXIMISE
Make the most of all income streams within the New Model and always look for new ways to take your music to the public

5 KEEP YOUR FANS
Look after your loyal followers. They are your customers

6 KEEP ACCOUNTS
Make sure you follow all the legal requirements for running what is, essentially, a small business

7 USE EXPERTISE
Bring in people who really know what they are doing when you need it. Negotiate the percentages fairly, but remember to retain ownership of your work

8 MARKET WISELY
When distributing your music digitally, remember your track is only one of millions available in 'the shop'. Marketing is, therefore, essential to help your fans find your songs, so make the most of links and 'widgets' on your MySpace page and on other websites

DIGITAL DISTRIBUTION (DOWNLOADS)

Downloading now accounts for more singles sales than CDs, but the problem of illegal downloads remains very real, with innumerable file-sharing sites still operating and untold potential sales going astray.

The main player in the marketplace is iTunes, but there are many other companies, including 7 Digital, E Music and Ditto. Most tracks are individually priced, but some companies now offer unlimited downloads for a fixed, monthly payment. Developments have seen free downloads being offered by sites that use advertising streams to offset the cost of supplying tracks. Mobile-phone companies are also continually developing new ways of delivering music to their handsets; many offer downloads and most run SMS services.

Bands now have access to free distribution through aggregators such as The Orchard or stores such as Indie Store by 7 Digital. For a small fee, these companies also offer chart and ISRC registration for tracks. ★

Ned's Atomic Dustbin

THE 1990s CULT BAND COME FULL CIRCLE AFTER PIONEERING THE 360° MODEL OF DISTRIBUTION

N ed's Atomic Dustbin are a cult band from Stourbridge, in the West Midlands, who stormed the charts in the early 1990s with a barrage of hit singles and albums released on major label Sony in the UK and the US. Many bands in the punk/pop and skate genres cite the group as an influence. They split up in the mid-90s, but resurfaced in 2002 with three of the original band members. They had so much fun, they have continued to play occasional dates in the UK. Having reconvened for the 21st century, Ned's legend continues to grow.

THE PROJECT

Between 2004 and 2006, the band were filling venues around the UK. Fans were asking for new material and the group felt they should oblige. The groundbreaking strategy they came up with meant Ned's Atomic Dustbin were, possibly, the first 360° band to emerge in the UK.

Early in 2006, they assembled a group of experts from the new-media age to plan a different kind of campaign centred on marketing their first new release for a decade. With guidance from the band, the team's ideas were a big hit with Ned's fans, who helped to spread the word and distribute flyers, acting as a street team for the band. ★

NEW MODEL ARMY
THE PEOPLE AND PLAN BEHIND NED'S RETURN

Degrees of happiness

THE ORGANISATION

◼ THE BAND
www.nedsatomicdustbin.co.uk
Role: Creative input and project direction (the core)

◼ THE LABEL
www.7organic.com
Role: To release the single digitally and through mail order for chart purposes

◼ PR
Jon Penney (band) and Paul Harvey (Madison Management)
Role: To gain TV, press and radio coverage. Licensing

◼ MERCHANDISE
www.backstreetmerch.com

THE CAMPAIGN

◼ A three-track single: *Hibernation/Ambush/ Kill Your Television Remix*

◼ A two-day festival at Birmingham Barfly (filmed for DVD documentary release and directed by Carl Beebee)

◼ A launch event at the London Forum

◼ The single's vital first radio-play was on Steve Lamacq's

In any other week, the single would have been in the Top 40

T-shirts – the single included limited re-issues of the band's vintage designs

◼ LIVE EVENTS
www.myspace.com/rswconcerts
www.barflyclub.com
Role: To organise and promote the band's live events

◼ DVD DOCUMENTARY
www.twelve42.bigcartel.com
Role: To film, edit and release a full-length documentary about the band

◼ VIDEO FOR SINGLE
www.myspace.com/carlbeebee
A superb video was made by acclaimed filmmaker Carl Beebee

Radio 6 show and was followed up by interviews

◼ Various newspaper and magazine features in the run-up to and during the week of release

◼ Front-page advertising on 7 Digital, NME.com shop and NME

THE RESULT
◼ The t-shirts sold well and the band had two of the top five bestsellers in the NME and Back Street charts for three weeks, including a period at number one

◼ The Birmingham Barfly gigs were a huge success and, at the time of writing, Ned's Atomic Dustbin held the Barfly chain box-office record for the highest takings for tickets priced at £15 (£7-£8 is the normal Barfly price)

◼ The DVD *Don't Exist* has been selling successfully since its release in 2007

◼ The single sold large quantities for an indie release and, in any other week, would have been in the mainstream Top 40 and at number one in the indie charts. However, on the day of release, the link to the chart computer broke and 50% of that day's sales were not counted; the final chart positions (23 in the indie chart and 78 in the national top 100) were a disappointment and partly responsible for the band's decision not to record an album

◼ The process re-established the band as a major force, on stage and in record stores. Since the single release, Ned's have headlined one of the indie stages at Glastonbury and are planning an 'original line-up' reunion.

Going At It Hammer and Tongs

360° DEALS ARE THE FUTURE, BUT HARD WORK, SAYS CONSULTANT TIM ALDOUS

Y ou will have heard Bob Dylan's song about 'the times' and how 'they are a-changin'' and, unless you've spent the past few years exploring territory beyond the reach of a radio, you'll be aware its lyrics are particularly applicable to the music industry at the moment.

Once upon a time, you would have practised guitar licks till your fingers blistered, hammered keyboards till your fingernails fell off, sung till your throat was red raw or battered out paradiddles till your palms bled – dreaming and believing that, one day, a major record label would happen across your demo, or see you play live, and, in a haze of glitter and £50 notes, you'd be transported to a hedonistic life of platinum albums, sold-out stadia and champagne for breakfast, served by infatuated groupies.

Well, Cinderella, it was unlikely to happen then and it's even more improbable today, when labels are run by accountants. Conventional music sales are plummeting

and the days of record labels investing thousands of pounds in new signings in the hope of recouping their investment from CD sales and downloads are long gone. Today's majors have no interest in 'artist development' – the margins on the units they move don't allow for such a concept and they've sent it to the museum of rock 'n' roll history

WORK IT OUT FOR YOURSELF

Sending your music to major labels is a waste of your time and money. Between them, the majors receive about half a million demos per year. From those half a million hopefuls, maybe 200 will pick up a contract. Let's be generous and allow for 10% of these 200 achieving the kind of success you're looking for e.g. radio-play, features in the music press. Half of them will never make enough money to pay back the label's original investment, meaning, at the absolute maximum, only 10 will look back at the process and smile. Ten out of 500,000; you'd get a better return at

"Grasp your career by the knackers or you'll fall by the wayside"

the racetrack – and you wouldn't have to hump about speaker cabinets.

Big labels are now concentrating on artists who are likely to make them the most money as quickly as possible. Once the success of Amy Winehouse had identified a demand for big voices and drama, the industry quickly gave us the choice of Duffy, Adele and a whole sisterhood of bluesy white chicks. They found acts that matched Amy's in the demo bucket, polished them up and put them into stores and supermarkets to pick up a share of the spoils. Good returns and minimal risk.

Experts at identifying trends and pushing out product to match, the major record companies nevertheless missed the signs that consumers were changing their buying patterns. While they struggle to catch up and find ways to regain their role in supplying music to the fans, we're all losing out.

The indie labels were always a better proposition for newer acts, but they're thin ●

on the ground these days and competition from other artists is fierce. Even though the quality of UK music has never been better, the industry has let you down.

SO, WHAT SHOULD YOU DO NOW?

Today, the only worthwhile option for new bands is DIY. In fact, doing it yourself is a necessity because, if you don't do it, who will?

Major labels only want to sign artists who fit a proven profile. To pop up on their radar, you'll need to demonstrate you have a market by setting up your own label and signing yourself to it. This means you'll be ready when the big boys come sniffing around; instead of giving up the bulk of your rights, you'll be set up to license your music to them while retaining ownership of it.

Musicians and other artists have the right to make a living from their work, and they're increasingly able to negotiate – even compete – with larger companies. The disadvantages of being a small player in a field of major names are disappearing and, after a short period of adjustment and uncertainty, those with ideas and talent will shine.

Digital technology is on our side too: it's made recording and marketing inexpensive. We can all compete, provided we have talent,

> *"Those of us who didn't acknowledge the changes initially are beginning to catch up. Gone are the days of the 1960s and 70s, when artists had no clue about the business. Over the past two decades, there's been a movement of musicians being more aware of their careers from a business point of view."*
> **Jake Shillingford**

work hard and are continually innovative in our strategy. Clued-up artists are shunning the established industry routes to success and are doing it themselves, on their own terms. Owning their music helps them to steer clear of old-style deals and avoid joining music's endless list of ripped-off acts.

SO WHAT IS DIY?

To understand DIY is to understand that the music business is not necessarily the business of producing recorded music. As

Talking Heads' David Byrne puts it: 'Calling the physical product "music" is like having a shopping cart and calling it groceries.' A DIY artist is somebody who will recognise this and learn to maintain control of all facets of their output. By taking charge of your merchandise, your website, your live dates and, of course, your music, you are empowering yourself. As somebody who's in touch with their audience via social-networking sites, you can lay claim to knowing your fans better than anybody else. In that respect, the DIY philosophy is a noble one. You'll need to take a long, hard look at yourself, get a plot and stick to it. It's bewildering because there are so many options. It's all about cutting out the middleman and relating directly with your fans in every way.

Artists who choose DIY can make more money than your typical popstar. Though the sales are smaller by comparison, the actual profit per unit (sale) taken by the artist is larger. Also, you own the fruit of your labour and can develop at your own pace, and not be required to have a platinum album with your first release.

DIY takes staying power and it better suits certain types of act. With his extra-

> **HTML is as important a language as ABC. If you don't know how to do web design, recruit somebody who does – someone who doesn't necessarily play an instrument, but who is part of the team nonetheless."**
> *Jake Shillingford*

curricular activities eating into his time, Pete Doherty may be unable to apply himself in quite the same way that Trent Reznor, otherwise known as Nine Inch Nails, has done. The DIY ethic appears to suit a certain character and, while this may be unfair on the gentle flower who writes beautiful ballads, if you're too fragile and whimsical to grasp your career by the knackers, you'll fall by the wayside.

PUTTING DIY INTO PRACTICE

As boring as it may be, you need to realise you are involved in running a business. Yes,

you're a sensitive artist, but without a businesslike attitude – or someone on board to take care of the everyday stuff – you're doomed to failure and frustration.

If you've got the right attitude, though, the ways of making a living through developing the projects you believe in are limited only by your imagination. Obviously, social-networking sites are useful, but these should

> **"DIY is the only way you can go – a lot of high-profile A&R men only look at bands who have started a so-called DIY approach, who have put out download singles, done a bit of marketing and self-promotion, and shown their mettle."**
> *Jake Shillingford*

be considered as tools to aid your marketing rather than the centrepiece of your operation – picking up 1,000 followers on MySpace is no big deal; the skill lies in picking up genuine fans and convincing them to buy your next CD.

A major part of DIY is communicating with your fans and you have to take your website as seriously as you do the music you make with your band. If you have someone who is web-savvy on your team, you won't necessarily need an aggregator or middleman, which means more profit for you from t-shirt, CD and other sales. Your beautifully constructed website means you'll be able to sell directly to your fans and gain a bigger slice of the financial pie.

If this sounds daunting and there's nobody in your crowd to take it on, there are companies that offer support and guidance. The Independent Label Scheme (*www. independentlabelscheme.com*) helps DIY artists to set up their own businesses. 'If you are going to DIY, do it properly,' says company founder Dean Marsh. 'Get it right and you have the potential to sustain a career in music and to develop a valuable business.

'DIY is not easy. There are complex legal and commercial issues, and a lot of administrative stuff. It takes hard work, determination, resourcefulness and contacts.'

The punk ethic has returned. What are you waiting for? Let's have it! ★

Tim Aldous tim@indielabelscheme.com

Satisfy a Pressing Need

GET YOUR MUSIC ON TO CD AND THEN GET IT OUT TO A WIDER AUDIENCE

Record Pressing

BRANDED MEDIA

Address: Unit A, Lutyens Industrial Centre, Basingstoke, Hampshire, RG24 8LJ
T: 01256 355 533
F: 01256 812 668
E: sales@brandedmedia.net
W: www.brandedmedia.net
Rates: Phone, email or fill out online 'quick quotation' form

A1 DUPLICATION

Address: 2nd Floor, 2 Albion Place, Hammersmith, London, W6 0QT
T: 0208 748 0440
F: 0208 748 0412
E: sales@a1duplication.co.uk
W: www.a1duplication.co.uk
Rates: Phone/email to enquire

CD 2 CD

Address: 432 Perth Avenue, Slough Trading Estate, Slough, Berkshire, SL1 4TS
T: 01753 693 583
F: 01753 574 705
E: info@cd2cd.co.uk
W: www.cd2cd.co.uk
Rates: Phone or email to enquire

ALPHA DUPLICATION

Address: Unit 2, Halifax Road, Cressex Business Park, High Wycombe, Bucks, HP12 3SD
T: 01494 536 646
F: 01494 536 651
E: n/a
W: www.alpha-duplication.com
Rates: Fill out the online form in the 'contact us' section of website

CD COPY SHOP LTD

Address: Battle House, 1 East Barnet Road,
New Barnet Road, New Barnet,
Hertfordshire, EN4 8RR
T: 0208 440 5777
F: n/a
E: info@cdcopyshopltd.co.uk
W: www.cdcopyshopltd.co.uk
Rates: Phone or email to enquire

CD DUPLICATING

Address: Portsmouth
T: 02392 642 919
F: n/a
E: bob@soundcheckuk.com
W: www.cd-duplicating.co.uk
Rates: Phone or email to enquire

DISCUS GROUP

Address: n/a
T: 0871 220 199
F: n/a
E: n/a
W: www.discusgroup.co.uk
Rates: Phone or fill out the online form in the
'contact us' section of website

DVD QUOTE

Address: n/a
T: 01626 201 330
F: N/A
E: quote@dvdquote.co.uk
W: www.dvdquote.co.uk
Rates: Phone, email or fill in the 'contact us' form
on website

DISC WIZARDS

Address: Suite 11, Raymac House, 59A
Palmerston Road, Harrow, HA3 7RR
T: 0208 861 2349
F: 0845 045 4550
E: info@discwizards.com
W: www.discwizards.com
Rates: Phone, email or fill in the 'contact us' form
on website

HILTON GROVE

Address: 3 Greenwich Quay, Clarence Road,
London, SE8 3EY
T: 0208 521 2424
F: n/a
E: info@hiltongrove.com
W: www.hiltongrove.com
Rates: Phone, email or fill in the 'contact us' form
on website

ICC DUPLICATION

Address: Regency Mews, Eastbourne, East Sussex, BN20 7AB
T: 01323 647 880/0845 085 0055
F: 01323 643 095
E: Via online form
W: www.iccduplication.co.uk
Rates: Phone or fill out the 'contact us' form or quotation service on website

The Blood Brothers
"Young Machetes"

I DUPE

Address: Datacatch, Unit 4d, Follifoot Ridge, Pannal Road, Harrogate, HG 1DP
T: 01423 810 555
F: 01423 810 666
E: info@datacatch.co.uk
W: www.idupe.co.uk
Rates: Phone, email or fill in the 'contact us' form on website

MANIC FILMS

Address: 6 Lorna Doone, Moore Lane, Croyde, Devon, EX33 1NU
T: 01271 891 140
F: 01271 891 076
E: Via online form
W: www.manicfilms.com
Rates: Phone or fill out online contact form to enquire

MEDIA SOURCING

Address: n/a
T: 0845 686 0001
F: n/a
E: n/a
W: www.mediasourcing.com
Rates: Phone, register or fill out the instant quote form on website

S45

Address: 20 Oxford Road, Kidlington, Oxon, OX5 1AA
T: 01865 45 7000
F: n/a
E: info@studio45mediapromotions.com
W: www.studio45.org.uk
Rates: Phone or email to enquire

SHORT RUN

Address: Farfield Records, PO Box 152, Portishead, Bristol, BS20 7WD
T: 0800 011 2092/01275 460 261
F: n/a
E: info@short-run.co.uk
W: www.short-run.co.uk
Rates: Check website for details

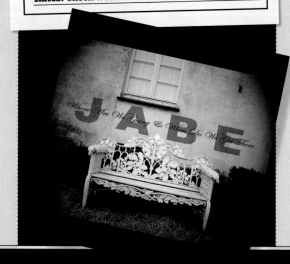

TECHNO VISUAL

Address: n/a
T: 0845 009 6147
F: n/a
E: contact@technovisual.co.uk
W: www.cdshortrun.co.uk
Rates: Phone or email to enquire

sam bigelow
the foundry

WE WOW

Address: The Digital Works, 1 Anne Gate,
Bradford, West Yorkshire, BD1 4ES
T: 0845 450 6262
F: 01274 301 415
E: sales@wewow.co.uk
W: www.wewow.co.uk
Rates: Phone, email, fill out online enquiry form
or complete the quick quotation form on website

ACTIVE MEDIA DISTRIBUTION

Address: Lower Farmhouse, Church Hill,
East Ilsley, Berkshire, RG20 7LP
T: 01635 281 359/377
F: 01635 281 607
E: Colin@amdist.com/Nigel@amdist.com
W: www.amdist.com
Info: See website for details

AVID GROUP

Address: 15 Metro Centre, Dwight Road,
Watford, WD18 9UL
T: 01923 281 281
F: 01923 281 200
E: info@avidgroup.co.uk or fill in the online
contact form
W: www.avidgroup.co.uk
Info: See website for details

Distribution

ABSOLUTE MARKETING AND DISTRIBUTION

Address: The Old Lamp Works, Rodney Place,
Wimbledon, London, SW19 2LQ
T: 0208 540 4242
F: 0208 540 6056
E: info@absolutemarketing.co.uk
W: www.absolutemarketing.co.uk
Info: See website for details

CARGO RECORDS

Address: Cargo Records, 17 Heathmans Road,
Parsons Green, London, SW6 4JJ
T: n/a
F: n/a
E: darrem@cargorecords.co.uk/john@
cargorecords.co.uk/craig@cargorecords.co.uk
W: www.cargorecords.co.uk
Info: Send finished samples (no demos) to the
relevant label manager, either by post or email.
Check website for further details

PURE REASON
REVOLUTION
THE DARK THIRD

EMPATHY RECORDS

Address: PO BOX 3439, Brighton, BN20 3439

T: n/a

F: n/a

E: info@empathyrecords.co.uk

W: www.empathyrecords.co.uk

Info: Send demos to the above address. See website for details

FORTE MUSIC DISTRIBUTION

Address: n/a

T: n/a

F: n/a

E: n/a

W: www.fortedistribution.co.uk

Info: See website for details

CD BABY

Address: n/a

T: n/a

F: n/a

E: Via online submission form

W: www.cdbaby.com

Info: One of the first and most popular online distribution companies. See website for details

KERASCENE

Address: 16 Russell Avenue, Dunchurch, Rugby, CV22 6PX

T: n/a

F: n/a

E: info@kerascene.com

W: www.kerascene.com

Info: Offers a wide range of services to help artists survive in the digital age

CODE 7 MUSIC DISTRIBUTION

Address: 23 London Road, Aston Clinton, Aylesbury, Bucks, HP22 5HG

T: n/a

F: n/a

E: Via online contact form in the 'contact us' section of website

W: www.code7music.com

Info: Independent, national music distributor. See website for details

KUDOS RECORDS

Address: 77 Fortress Road, Kentish Town, London, NW5 1AG

T: 0207 482 4555

F: 0207 482 4551

E: contact@kudos-records.co.uk

W: www.kudos-records.co.uk

Info: Digital music distributor. See website for details.

DITTO MUSIC

Address: n/a

T: 0121 551 6624

F: n/a

E: Via online contact form or through info@dittomusic.com

W: www.dittomusic.com

Info: Digital music distributor that specialises in independent and unsigned artists

PINNACLE ENTERTAINMENT

Address: Heather Court, 6 Maidstone Road, Sidcup, Kent, DA14 5HH

T: 0208 309 3600

F: n/a

E: n/a

W: www.pinnacle-entertainment.co.uk

Info: One of the UK's biggest independent distributors. See website for details

SHELL SHOCK

Address: 23a Collingwood Road, London, N15 4LD

T: 0208 800 8110

F: 0208 800 8140

E: info@shellshock.co.uk

W: www.shellshock.co.uk

Info: Mail a sample pack to the address above. Include artist biog – with phone number, address and email contact – background, press clippings and any additional information

RIGHT TRACK DISTRIBUTION

Address: n/a

T: 0203 3039 6661

F: n/a

E: info@righttrackdistribution.com

W: www.righttrackdistribution.com

Info: See website for details

SONG CAST

Address: n/a

T: n/a

F: n/a

E: info@songcastmusic.com

W: www.songcastmusic.com

Info: Sells your music on major download sites and provides customised codes to link your MySpace and other websites to stores. See website for details

THE ORCHARD

Address: n/a

T: n/a

F: n/a

E: Fill out online form in 'contact us' section of website

W: www.theorchard.com

Info: Controls and globally distributes more than one million songs through hundreds of digital stores

ROUTE NOTE

Address: 3 West End, Redruth, Cornwall, TR15 2RG

T: 01209 204 583

F: 01209 315 630

E: Fill out online form in the 'contact us' section of website

W: www.routenote.com

Info: Fill out online contact form in the 'contact us' section of website

TUNECORE

Address: n/a

T: n/a

F: n/a

E: n/a

W: www.tunecore.com

Info: Send your music to one or all of Tunecores partners, which include iTunes, Amazon, Lala, Napster, Rhapsody, Music.com, eMusic and GroupieTunes

CHAPTER 9

SAY
WHAT?
"Bands shouldn't compromise themselves for anything. Not for an audience, not for a record label. Because compromises mean fans won't believe in what you do." – Chris Cornell

CASTING
THE NET...

BROADCAST, PODCAST OR WEBCAST, BUT GET YOUR MUSIC TO THE PEOPLE

R adio-play remains the best means of exposure for an artist, but there are only a handful of nationally broadcast DJs who are willing to listen to every demo that arrives on their desk in their search for the next big thing. But there are numerous other ways to get your music heard. You can record a song in your bedroom and have it on your MySpace profile within hours; you can approach one of the hundreds of digital radio stations; or you can create your own podcast.

The internet, for better or for worse, is now flooded with music. This has created an open marketplace for unsigned artists to have their material played and has given audiences the opportunity to discover new music that may, otherwise, have passed them by.

The Digital Revolution

RADICAL CHANGES TO RADIO HAVE BROUGHT A NEW FREEDOM TO MUSIC

Until a few years ago, radio-play was almost exclusively for signed or established artists; unsigned acts, if they featured at all, inhabited the graveyard shifts. But the advent of digital radio has created hundreds of stations – covering all music genres – on which signed and unsigned artists can be heard.

Programmes can be accessed at any time through a website or as a downloadable podcast and, although the audience for each is unlikely to exceed a few thousand, it is still a great means of getting your music heard. Also, digital radio stations are broadcast throughout the world, so your music may reach Boston, Massachusetts as easily as it does Boston, Lincolnshire. Even if you never move beyond your local area, if you supply your contact details, you could push out a few extra sales or downloads.

Quite a few digital stations are open to playing unsigned artists, so check what genres they play and how best to contact them. Radio-play on one of these channels won't mean a big, fat record deal, but that your track was broadcast at all means you're heading in the right direction.

APPROACHING THE BIG BOYS

Listening figures for stations such as XFM, Capital, BBC Radio and Virgin tend to be at their highest for the morning shows, when you're likely to hear new releases from established artists or tracks from the current top 20.

It's crucial any demo you send to new-music shows (see below) is of the highest possible quality. Ideally, it should have been mastered (see p126). To gauge what is acceptable, listen to the tracks already being played or visit Steve Lamacq's MySpace page to hear a selection of unsigned artists he is favouring. But these shows receive thousands of demos and emails, so don't expect an immediate response. ★

ACCESS THE AIRWAYS
THE SHOWS THAT CHAMPION UNSIGNED ART

BBC
As an unsigned artist, there are two BBC 6Music shows (DAB, Freeview and online only) with which you ought to register: Steve Lamacq's *6Music Unsigned*, Monday-Friday, 4pm-7pm. www.myspace.com/lamacqunsigned and *Introducing: Fresh On The Net*, Saturday, midnight. www.bbc.co.uk/6musicintroducing

XFM
The station's *Mus...*
show selects track...
artists for radio-pl...
website www.xfm...
Artists create a pr...
include up to thre...
week, three artists...
and, from Monday...
a song by each is...
show. The public v...
favourite, which is...
Thursday. Listener...
of changes to prof...
access updated g...

SITES AND SOUNDS SOURCES

PODCAST HOSTING/ SOFTWARE

www.
podcastalley.com
dorada.co.uk
dopplerradio.net
podcastingworld.com
ipodderx.com
apple.com

EDITING PROGRAMS
Steinberg WaveLab
Essential 6
WavePad Sound Editor
Avanquest WebPod
Studio
Goldwave
Soundforge

EQUIPMENT
■ Alesis USB
Podcasting
Microphone Kit
■ Behringer
Podcastudio
■ Rode Podcaster
USB Microphone
■ Samson C010
Recorder Pack
■ Samson C030
Recorder Pack
■ SE Electronics
USB1000a
Microphone
■ ION UCAST
Podcasting
Microphone Kit

Like Peas in a Pod

REACH LIKEMINDED MUSIC FANS BY CREATING YOUR OWN RADIO SHOW

A podcast is a radio show that has been saved and distributed as an MP3 file. Once a listener has subscribed to their first podcast, their computer will automatically download a new one when it is broadcast.

You'll find loads of music podcasts on the internet – several promoting unsigned artists – so it may be difficult to decide which ones to send your music to. To get around this, why not create your own? It's relatively easy to do, offers you control of the production and gives you another way to promote your sound.

To draw in and retain an audience, the content of your podcast should not be limited to your own material: include other unsigned artists, information on your local scene and what gigs are worth checking out. In effect, you're creating a community in which your music, and that of other talented bands, is appreciated, so it shouldn't be all about you.

You could supplement your podcast with a blog and, maybe, spoken-word links, which are easier to create than you might think and are worth doing. To create content, you will need to install an RSS (Really Simple Syndication) feed, which will automatically send updates to your computer. An RSS feed is also a means of broadcasting and distributing created content, and allowing listeners to subscribe to your podcast and blog. You can download an RSS feed from several podcast websites, which will also host your podcast and give you the chance to advertise its content to potential listeners.

Content can be created on a computer with music-editing programs and voiceover links can be incorporated into the show – which can be a positive or negative thing depending on the quality of the microphone you use and the soundproofing of the room in which you record. Podcasts are not expected to be up to the standard of professional radio broadcasts; their appeal is in their 'mates talking in the pub about what's good and what's bad' feel. If you only have a basic knowledge of editing, your first few shows may be a bit rough around the edges, but as long as your topics and music choice are varied and entertaining, you can break material to a new audience. ★

**DO NOT
DISTURB**

**PODCAST
IN SESSION**

Become Socially Acceptable

NETWORKING WEBSITES ARE LAUNCHPADS INTO A WIDER MUSICAL SOCIETY

T he main place your music will be heard is on your MySpace page. Set up in 2002 as a social-networking site, MySpace has radically changed the relationship between an artist and their audience. It allows you to create, for free, your own, easily updated page and unique URL, so it's less crucial for you to have an expensive website (although you may still want to do this). MySpace has 250 million accounts (admittedly, many of these are fake or inactive), but that is still a massive potential audience.

It goes without saying the internet has revolutionised the music business, making songs freely and openly available to a much wider audience – and it's MySpace that has spearheaded this movement.

Three other major social-networking sites worth a look are Bebo, facebook and Last.FM. Artists can have their music played online with these sites and, again, reach out to a

USEFUL WEBSITES

www.
myspace.com
bebo.com
facebook.com
last.fm

mass audience. Signing up takes minutes and then it's down to you to keep your content (music, photos, gigs) updated. The superb Last.FM is billed as 'The Social Music Revolution' and is both a social-networking site and an internet radio station. Using an intelligent music recommendation system called Audio Scrobbler, Last.FM reads the music stored on your computer and creates a unique playlist from tracks that are part of the Last.FM music library. As an unsigned artist, you're able to incorporate your songs into this library and they will automatically be included on the playlist of listeners who have expressed an interest in artists of a similar genre. You'll collect royalties every time one of your songs is streamed or downloaded and you can promote any gigs you may have. Unlike on Bebo, facebook and MySpace – where people have to make the effort to find you – Last.FM takes your music directly to your target audience. ★

PLANT A PAGE

BOOST YOUR PROFILE WITH A BAND WEBSITE

CREATE A MYSPACE PAGE

Go to www. myspace.com and click on the link 'Sign In'. Once on the sign-up page, follow the link 'Musician or Band' (if you don't do this, you will end up with a standard MySpace page). Fill out all the necessary information, with music and pictures uploaded to the relevant sections.

Useful links:

www.pimp-my-profile.com – A profile-customising website
www.mybannermakers.com – Create personalised MySpace banners that link to websites from which your releases can be bought or downloaded
www.quackit.com – Hints and tips on HTML codes, which can be used to format text and create links to websites

CREATE A LAST.FM PAGE

Go to www.last.fm, click on 'Sign up' and fill in your information. Click on 'Download Software' to get Last.FM's Audio Scrobbler on to your machine. If your songs are on your computer, Scrobbler will create an artist page for you that you must claim before you upload music to the site. To do this, click on 'Are you this person?' underneath your artist name, fill in the information and then upload your songs.

INTERVIEW

Coming Up For Airtime

XFM'S JON HILLCOCK ON BREATHING NEW LIFE INTO RADIO'S STAID MUSIC AGENDA

aving worked his way from student radio in Loughborough to Virgin Megastores Radio, Jon Hillcock is now responsible for unearthing new music for Xfm. He provided the first UK radio exposure for bands such as Arcade Fire, Klaxons and CSS, and, in 2007, began a podcast, *New Noise*. This was then commissioned as a four-hour show on Xfm. *New Noise* aims to uncover and give exposure to some of the most exciting new music from across the globe.

What do you look for in a track before you'll play it on the radio and how important is recording quality?
I listen for a semblance of originality, but different things could catch my attention – from a simple, heavy riff or beat to a big pop hook or a genius lyric. The importance of quality of the recording depends on the style of music. Shiny pop music would sound rubbish recorded on a lo-fi tape deck, whereas crackly folk or electronica could sound better. But an intentionally lo-fi recording is completely different to a poor-quality MP3. Ultimately, though, a good song or idea can shine through a bad recording.

Is radio still the primary means of breaking artists, even though MySpace offers so much in terms of listening to new material/unsigned bands?
Radio is still a very valuable means of musical discovery, particularly for mainstream fans who don't look particularly hard or far to hear something new. The fact there is now so much opportunity to listen to,

read about and discover new music on the web means – more than ever – there is a need for a quality filter, which can be radio. If the listener can find a DJ or presenter with similar tastes, who can be trusted as a guide, there's no reason why that relationship cannot continue to thrive. Music radio should still offer the chance of not knowing what comes next. As wonderful as increased access to new and unsigned acts is, the amount of very mediocre music has grown accordingly – which is even more reason to tune in.

How should unsigned artists go about getting tracks played on the radio?
Email presenters and producers (but only those who are, realistically, likely to play your stuff) a simple message about who you

"There is so much new music on the web, there is a need for a quality filter"

are, where you're from and what you hope to achieve by getting in touch. A link to your MySpace page or website is essential and, maybe, a zShare/yousendit link to download material. Don't send large MP3 files because these quickly fill up an inbox, which is very annoying. If the DJ likes your sound, he or she will ask you to send more stuff. I often know if I'm going to like something before I've even put the CD in the player – a cheaply copied, scribbled-on CD-R sometimes has the most impact. Mystery is good!

Are there now greater opportunities for unsigned artists to break into the mainstream of music?

There are, undoubtedly, better opportunities to get their music heard, but, with that, comes a completely saturated marketplace, full of bands jostling for attention. A band can be recommended and dismissed in seconds, so do your best to make the few moments someone shows an interest in you a worthwhile experience. Sounding or looking like thousands of other bands won't help.

Are radio pluggers still dominant or do DJs have the freedom to pick and choose their own playlists?

Pluggers dominate to an extent, particularly on daytime radio, but specialist DJs – who are more likely to play new music first – receive a lot of stuff directly from the artists and from MySpace, shops and MP3 blogs.

LISTEN AND LEARN

Hear Jon's *New Noise* show on Xfm London (104.9FM) and Xfm Manchester (97.7FM), 9pm-1am Saturdays, and on Sky 0111, DAB digital radio and at www.xfm.co.uk

Should a debut single, especially from a new artist, be in the standard hook-verse-chorus-verse-chorus format or is there room to experiment?

This, surely, depends on what the band is trying to achieve and how much they are willing to compromise to achieve it. If their passion is verse-chorus-verse pop music, that's cool, but tailoring your style for a daytime playlist will just lead to an unfulfilling, superficial and, probably, short shelf-life. Make music you believe in. If you don't have 100% faith in it, no-one else will. If you want to make money, work in a bank.

Is it worth an artist's time and effort to get played on internet radio or should they focus on the national stations?

Any exposure is good exposure. What you need to know is, does the internet station have a track record for supporting bands who go on to be successful? Although the station may not have a particularly large listenership, these people matter when it comes to getting wider exposure for your songs – other presenters/producers/writers from bigger organisations could be listening. There doesn't have to be a great deal of effort put in to get your music to smaller internet stations, so what harm can it do? MP3 blog writers, especially those who regularly feature similar music to your own, are also well worth getting in touch with.

Have you seen a change in the music industry over the past few years and has this affected radio?
There have been hugely significant changes in the radio and unsigned music industries, although I'm not qualified to comment on how things compare to the 1980s and 90s. The very term 'unsigned' is becoming more and more irrelevant (and, probably, increasingly sullied by the relentless mobile-phone company campaigns trying to own the idea of 'discovering' new music) as bands and artists realise signing their lives away for very little return isn't the only option. Major

> "Artists realise signing their lives away for little return isn't the only option"

music labels have dealt with download culture in a wholly inadequate and ignorant way, and are now suffering as a consequence. If the creation of music is the sole aim of a band or artist, there are more opportunities to get it heard than ever before. If making money and forging a career is the objective, things become far more difficult. For a specialist radio DJ, there is now a brilliant opportunity to bypass labels, pluggers, managers and the rest of the industry, and go straight to the source of the music, thereby avoiding the hyperbole and extraneous guff that has, for so long, been an obstacle and a hindrance, rather than help.

How do you see the future of radio?
Radio has become increasingly homogenised,

HILLCOCK'S HANDY HINTS
SPIN WON'T WORK WITH THIS DJ, SO KEEP IT TRUE

☐ Believe 100% in the music you are making. If you don't, nobody else will

☐ Pursue a future in music for the right reasons. Money is not the right reason

☐ Don't pester or intrude upon people – if they like your music they will respond eventually

☐ Play as many gigs as you can, in as many places as you can

☐ Make sure people have a quick, accessible means of hearing your music

☐ Don't over-complicate the process of getting somebody to listen to you and your music

☐ Don't be too eager to sign up to any old label/deal

☐ Don't be too precious about people downloading your demos for free early on – the more people who own them, the more people who can listen to them

☐ Get an interesting name, especially if you are a solo artist (work under an enigmatic pseudonym that could just as easily be a band or a collective instead of 'John Smith')

☐ Don't have an expensive, black-and-white A4 band photo taken. It'll just be thrown away

with the same artists often appearing on playlists across several different formats and demographics (Gnarls Barkley, for example, could crop up simultaneously on daytime Radio 1, Radio 2, Magic, Heart, Xfm and local commercial and BBC stations nationwide). This lack of choice – coupled with a bland, generic 'hits' commercial-radio format, increasingly networked from London, and very repetitive, condescending small playlists across the industry – could drive music fans towards the internet and their MP3 players for good. The magic of music radio is not knowing what is going to come next and there are several healthily unpredictable specialist shows (albeit largely at night) that provide such a service at the moment. Ideally, this broader, more interesting and entertaining format should extend further into the daytime. But, for this to happen, the controllers, boards, bosses and shareholders of radio stations need to develop a greater level of trust and faith in their audiences' tastes and sensibilities, which is fairly unlikely. ★

Unsigned Radio Stations

THESE STATIONS PLAY MUSIC BY UNSIGNED ARTISTS – CONTACT THEM FOR MORE

ALL FM
w. ww.allfm.org

Description: Unsigned show for bands from Manchester and the surrounding areas.

EM TALENT
w. www.myspace.com/emtalentradio

Description: Free exposure for independent artists and unsigned bands.

BEACON RADIO
w. www.beaconradiowestmids.co.uk

Description: Weekly podcast for West Midlands based, unsigned artists.

HORIZON RADIO
w. www.horizonmk.co.uk

Description: Weekly unsigned show for artists based in the Milton Keynes area.

KERRANG! RADIO
w. www.kerrangradio.co.uk

Description: Every Sunday from 8pm, featuring both unsigned artists and those signed to small independents labels, send any demos to: UnsignedKerrang Radio, 20 Lionel St, Birmingham B3 1AQ.

KEY 103FM
w. www.key103.co.uk

Description: Radio Station based in the Manchester area.

LIVE AND UNSIGNED RADIO

w. www.myspace.com/liveunsignedukradio

Description: Live and Unsigned Radio is an exciting new Radio station dedicated to the promotion of unsigned artists.

MARS PLANETS MYSPACE RADIO

w. www.myspace.com/myspacemarsplanetsradio

Description: New, online radio station that's presented by XFM DJ Alex Zane. Follow the relevant links to submit your material.

MATT 'N' JACK'S UNSIGNED BANDS, 105.1FM

w. www.southendradio.com

w. www.myspace.com/mattandjackunsigned

Description: Unsigned radio show for artists in the Southend area.

NCCR UNSIGNED

w. www.myspace.com/nccrunsigned

Description: Unsigned radio show that's based in Gloucestershire

RADIO REVERB 97.2 FM

w. www.myspace.com/brightonreverb / www. radioreverb.com

Description: Brighton based radio station that focuses on local unsigned talent, see MySpace blog for contact details.

RADIO SAINT FM

w. www.saintfm.org.uk

Description: Radio Saint FM on 94.7 fm and online at www.saintfm.org.uk is a radio show that features songwriters, bands, musicians and artists that are local to the Maldon area.

TSM RADIO

w. www.tsmradio.net

Description: TSM Radio is dedicated to exposing unsigned acts and independent artists.

THE VOLT SHOW

w. www.thevoltsshow.com

Description: The Volts Show is about the promotion of new, unsigned talent via the means of Internet radio.

Record Label Hell!

the smiths

"WE WERE UNSTOPPABLE!"

THEIR RISE! THEIR FALL!

PLUS: THE **50** GREATEST

ALSO!
IKE TURNER
PAUL WELLER
KRIS KRISTOFFERSON
THE KILLS
DRIVE-BY TRUCKERS

ANNIVERSARY ISSUE

WU-TANG CLAN Inside A Hip Hop Dynasty At War

BY NUMAN

FLASH FORWARD
They were dropped be...
Now, says Sarah Boden,
can't move for fans cramm...

KEITH RICHARDS MEETS JOHNNY DEPP

BEATLES MAGICAL MYSTERY TOUR

BLUR REUNION OFF!

Print and the New Revolution

MUSIC MAGS WILL IGNORE YOU, SO MAKE USE OF THEIR DIGITAL FORUMS

A quick glance at the charts shows that transforming your band from unsigned unknowns into major-label, worldwide stars depends on something more than just talent. There's no guaranteed way onto the front pages of the press, but here's a sketch map of some routes that might work for you.

Newly formed rock acts chasing coverage in the major magazines that deal in their style of music – including Q, Mojo, NME, Kerrang, Metal Hammer, Classic Rock and Uncut – soon realise it's pointless. Unsigned artists in all other musical genres are also ignored by the press and find it just as painful to deal with the rejection.

Despite the widespread belief among musicians looking for a deal that there's a global conspiracy to keep new bands out of the public eye, the real explanation for this lack of attention is less exciting: unsolicited demos are rarely reviewed in print and most will never be listened to by anyone working at the magazine they're sent to. Your material will drown among the wealth of top-quality product that is hand-delivered to the right desk by thoroughly trusted sources.

Promo people are friendly and likeable for a living; they're experts in the music they push out and know their journalistic subjects. A writer facing a deadline in today's cut-throat publishing environment will almost always reach for the easy option. Competition like this – added to input from PR agencies, established contacts in the business and old-fashioned word of mouth – will reduce your lion's roar to an inaudible squeak. The major music titles can't cover the unsigned music scene; it's simply too vast.

No printed magazine can match the reach●

and potential readership offered by the internet, and the web is the best resource for unsigned artists looking to spread the word.

Your MySpace page is the natural home for reviews (not ones you've written yourself – that would be too sad) and the perfect place to advertise forthcoming gigs, instore appearances, t-shirt signings and so forth. But you need to look beyond the overcrowded social-networking sites for publicity and explore other methods to generate interest.

WHERE TO GO

As we go to press, MySpace is still the place most people will go to when looking for information about your band and a profile on there is essential for signed and unsigned artists alike. But MySpace is already overcrowded; its influence will eventually diminish, other sites will take over and you'll soon see it shouldn't be your sole means of promotion.

Only signed acts backed by major-league marketing budgets can afford to fully exploit MySpace – you haven't got the money for banner adverts and paid-for links from other pages that allow the big labels to inform the site's 150 million subscribers about new releases. A recent refinement to their technique is to create even more interest in performers by putting exclusive tracks, remixes and, sometimes, whole albums online to download for free through the artists' profile pages.

As an unsigned act, you will want to send people to your MySpace profile; it's the easiest way to keep in touch with fans, promoters and venues, and it's the best method of developing a network of like-minded artists. Canny management of your profile will plug you into a grid of acts and enthusiasts with similar music tastes to yours – just hit them with a Friend Request. Of course, you need to keep everything up to date, so stick up new recordings, write blogs and post flyers for gigs on your page. Don't forget to embed

All of the main titles have an online presence; some fund their own digital radio statio

flyers into the bulletins you send out and to post them into the 'comments' section on other users' profiles. Be polite though, and keep your flyers modest in size; most people don't mind you advertising gigs, but they do object if you take up half their page.

MySpace, then, is an essential part of your marketing, but it won't turn you into an overnight star; to pick up genuinely outstanding publicity, you'll need to take your material elsewhere.

All of the main music titles have an online presence that delivers more of an audience than their print version; some even fund their own digital radio stations. From a publisher's point of view, the advantages of a website are obvious; they can be updated instantly to carry the latest news, they can carry audio and video content, and they give readers the chance to interact with the magazine.

Despite their need for a constant stream of

PR AGENCIES
EMPLOY SOMEONE TO BLOW YOUR OWN TRUMPET

Music magazines receive most of their featured content from artists' PR agencies; and new artists don't normally bring a PR company on board until they have started to sign contracts.

Most independent labels will have a PR firm on their books and, at first, you'll want to use them as the best means of getting coverage. However as your career develops, recruit your own PR people onto your team.

It takes skill to develop your reputation and build an audience

for you, plus there will be about a year to fill between you signing a deal and releasing your first album. If the record company PR is going to fail you, it will happen during this recording gap.

In the 360° model of marketing, PR companies are important in whipping up interest from fans and labels. But remember, as an unsigned artist you're better off spending time with the underground magazines and online stations than waiting for the big names to notice you.

UNSIGNED MUSIC MAGAZINES

REVIEW YOUR STRATEGY FOR POSITIVE PUBLICITY

There is a growing community of online, underground magazines that regularly include content on unsigned artists. Even though it's not possible for them to run current news stories on every unsigned musician out there, picking up a positive review on any of these sites counts as a brilliant piece of promotion.

Check the 'contact us' sections of the following sites for information on where to send your demos and what the magazines' review policies are.

THE MAG
www.the-mag.me.uk

ROCK PULSE
www.rockpulse.co.uk

BEAT MOTEL
www.beatmotel.co.uk

GOD IS IN THE TV
www.godisinthetvzine.co.uk

MAXIMUM INK
www.maximumink.com

SANDMAN MAGAZINE
www.sandmanmagazine.co.uk

TOUR DATES
www.tourdates.co.uk

SHOCK
www.shockonline.net

STEREOHEAD
www.stereohead.co.uk

MUSIC NEWS
www.music-news.com

TIME OUT (LISTINGS)
www.timeout.com/london

news and features, the majority are still reluctant to carry stories about unsigned acts. Only Kerrang and NME run features about unsigned artists or hold Battle of the Bands competitions, and, even online, the coverage they devote to new artists is sparse and irregular. It's rarely more than a soundbite or a teaser article to entice you to buy the print version.

Like the rest of the music industry, then, the specialist press is embracing digital technology. It's a comparatively low-cost, low-risk investment for the big names, an effective way of expanding their brand. Still, you're more likely to win a small byline crediting your input on nme.com than you are to scoop the front cover of the weekly NME on the newsstands – and that byline, linked to your MySpace page or band website, will help you to pick up coverage and generating a 'buzz'. ★

Computer Connections

THE INTERNET PROVIDES A FORUM TO GET KNOWN AND GET KNOWLEDGE

WWW.LEMONROCK.COM

Listings website containing gig guides, venues, reviews, forums, recording studios, rehearsal spaces and other useful bits and pieces. Membership is £14.99 per month.

WWW.OVERPLAY.CO.UK

Music site dedicated to the development and exposure of unsigned artists.

WWW.TOURDATES.CO.UK

Website of the free music magazine *London Tourdates*. Artists can log in and create their own profile page containing MP3s, pictures and upcoming gigs.

WWW.UNSIGNED REVOLUTION.COM

News and reviews of signed and unsigned artists.

WWW.LEEDSMUSICSCENE.NET

News, reviews, interviews, MP3s and gig guides for signed and unsigned artists based in the Midlands area.

WWW.SOUNDONSOUND.COM

Website of the monthly magazine *Sound on Sound*. Contains news and articles that cover just about every aspect of the music business, from recording demos to signing contracts.

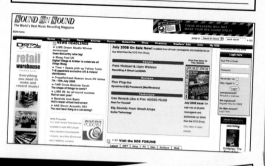

WWW.VIRTUALFESTIVALS.COM

Contains news, photos, videos and useful information/line-ups for festivals in the UK and Europe.

WWW.MUSICPROMOTION MEDIA.CO.UK

Based in the UK, Music Promotion Media is an established unsigned-band promoter that deals with many of the well-known record labels, covering all genres.

WWW.MUSICTECHMAG.CO.UK

The magazine/website for producers, engineers and recording musicians.

WWW.BBC.CO.UK/RADIO1/ ONEMUSIC

Contains several detailed articles covering every aspect of the music industry.

WWW.MUZIKVOICE.COM

Online promotion for unsigned bands.

WWW.THEMIXBUS.COM

The purpose of The Mix Bus is to inspire and help audio engineers in the dog-eat-dog world of the music industry.

WWW.ENTSWEB.CO.UK

The directory of entertainment, music and leisure.

WWW.MUSICMANAGERS FORUM.CO.UK

The MMF gives music managers an opportunity to share and learn, and also provides a much-needed voice within the industry. Also contains useful information for artists.

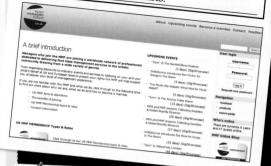

WWW.GIGWISE.COM

News, reviews, features and lots more, and unsigned artists are able to create and update their own profile pages.

WWW.TELIVO.COM

Domain names, web hosting and more.

WWW.JIGSAWDESIGN STUDIO.CO.UK

Websites from £39 per month.

WWW.RCRDLBL.COM

RCRD LBL is an online record label releasing exclusive and free music from emerging and established artists.

WWW.BMR.ORG

Website for the British Music Rights organisation, which was established in 1996 to speak on behalf of the UK's songwriting, composing and music publishing community.

WWW.NME.COM

News, reviews, features and lots more, with unsigned artists able to create and update their own NME 'breaking bands' profile page.

WWW.KEYNOTE UNSIGNED.CO.UK

Keynote provides an online stage from which unsigned musicians can share, promote and sell their music and merchandise.

WWW.AMPLIFEYE.COM

An online resource for unsigned artists, DJs and the music industry to promote themselves using the web.

WWW.TOTALLY UNSIGNED.CO.UK

Unsigned artists' website that contains videos, interviews, reviews, events, a forum and a radio station. Acts are also able to create their own profile page, through which they can sell their material online.

WWW.CDUNSIGNED.COM

Provides links to a number of useful websites for unsigned artists.

WWW.123PHOTOGRAPHY.CO.UK

Music and band photographers based in the Leeds area.

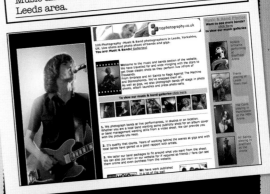

WWW.GUARDIAN.CO.UK/ TECHNOLOGY/DIGITALMUSIC

Up-to-date, detailed articles about the current state of the music business.

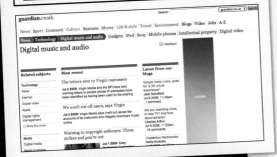

WWW.MYSPACE.COM/ ROBERTMCHALE

London-based photographer.

WWW.MUSICWEEK.COM

One-stop resource for up-to-date information on every aspect of the music business.

WWW.ALISONPETTY.COM

Band photographer based in London and Brighton.

WWW.UKMUSICSEARCH.COM

Online music directory.

WWW.MYSPACE.COM/ LIBRASNAKE

Live music photography.

"Break windows, smoke
cigars and stay up late. Tell
'em to do that, they'll find a
little pot of gold."
– Tom Waits

CHAPTER #10

ACTIONS SPEAK LOUDER

WORDS ARE ALL WELL AND GOOD, BUT YOU GOTTA MAKE IT HAPPEN

So you've read every page and you know it all now, yeah? Well, think again. Every chapter offers a wealth of information from experienced musicians and industry experts, but, the truth is, even if your act has got what it takes to make it in music, you'll still have to work extraordinarily hard to prove it.

As a gigging musician, you're out there playing because you love to do it and – like every other artist who has ever stepped into the glare of a spotlight – your goal is to turn your passion into a career. But that's not going to happen just because you love gigging, no matter how well received you are. As we have illustrated with the New Model, it's crucial you understand the business side of things, too. Contracts, liabilities and rights will come back to haunt you if they're not ▶

properly addressed in the first place.

The music industry is undergoing possibly the most significant shake up in its history and even people with years of experience struggle to keep up with the constant changes. However, with the DIY/360° model being embraced by signed and unsigned artists, the playing field is wide open. In fact, it could be argued there are more opportunities than ever before to be successful because you have access to more tools. You can build a respectable profile in a relatively short time by adding new media and social networks, such as MySpace, to your regular promotional duties of gigging,

Hi Mum, we've made it to the big time!!

There are more opportunities to be successful because you have access to more tools

pressing flyers into the hands of an audience, handing out free copies of your CD and taking part in talent competitions.

There's fun to be had in helping to create must-have merchandising that compensates for the comparative drudgery of collecting names for your mailing lists. Seeing your music appear on digital download sites is always satisfying and you might even discover a motivational talent by asking your friends to form your first street crew.

The internet plays a central role in all of this; artists can release new music and listeners can make their own discoveries before the conventional filters (radio-playlist selectors and their ilk) get in the way. It's resulted in unbelievable opportunities for unsigned, talented musicians to get the recognition they deserve without needing an expensive advertising campaign.

Music always has been – and probably always will be – a strange business, but never has the time been more favourable for unsigned artists. You'll play good, bad and ugly gigs, but, if you put in the hard work, act like professionals, believe in what you play and don't let your head drop, who knows what may happen? It's in your hands. Now, one more time from the top – a-one, a-two, a-one-two-three-four! ★

INTERVIEW

High Voltage

THE VOLT WERE WINNERS OF MTV'S *GET SEEN, GET HEARD* CONTEST. WE ASK THEM ABOUT THEIR ROUTE TO THE BIG TIME AND STAYING GROUNDED

T alented four-piece The Volt have had a crazy 12 months. The band from Bath won MTV's unsigned talent search, *Get Seen, Get Heard*, before storming Koko and rocking Glastonbury. They are involved in promoting their own shows and their onstage energy fuelling wild reactions from their audiences.

Where did you meet and how long have you been playing together?
Phoebe and I have been playing guitars together since we were tiny, and we decided to start a band. We asked Sam, our singer, to join, and, a year later, we auditioned Dom to be our drummer. So it's been just over a year.

How long did you spend rehearsing and writing before playing your first gigs?
After we auditioned Dom, we only had two weeks to get the material up to standard, but, fortunately, we managed it.

Was coming to London always a priority or was it more important to build a name for yourself on the local scene?
It was always very exciting coming to London to do gigs and we always had a good time. We also had a few friends in London who would

come to watch us, but we've only recently started to notice a large fanbase back in Bath.

Is the songwriting shared among the band or does one person come in with an idea that is then worked on?
One of us normally has a chord progression or a melody and then we all put our parts in and see what we get out of it.

How important is the internet to you in terms of promotion?
It has helped us tremendously. We can let people know when our gigs are and it was the only way for people to know about the MTV competition we were in.

How did you come to enter MTV's Get Seen, Get Heard. Where did you first hear about the competition?
Sam told us about it. We had to upload a video of us playing at an Oxjam gig to the MTV website. We then got everyone we knew to vote for us and ended up being shortlisted, along with 23 other bands. MTV came to film us around Bath and interview us for a two-minute profile. Five industry judges then put us into the semi-finals with four other bands and we went to the MTV Studios in Camden, and played a gig at The Fly in Soho. Ross

SAY **WHAT?**

"People ask me, what was the best year for music? I always say, this year is the best year for music. Prior to that, it was the previous year."
– John Peel

from The Futureheads was one of the judges and our allocated mentor, so he came to watch the gig and give us advice. MTV then told us we were through to the final, which was exciting, but very scary. We played our two tracks and won, which was amazing.

Did it take a while for everything to sink in?

It did, but we weren't allowed to tell anyone for about a month, until the final programme was aired, but then we went mad and told everyone we could.

How did it feel to play a venue the size of Koko after being used to playing much smaller venues on the circuit?

It was the high point of our career so far. It was one of the most amazing feelings and we all played our hearts out.

Things are moving so fast for you at the moment, is it difficult to keep grounded

"Whenever we do gigs, we always have a good time, no matter what or where it is"

and also to keep up with it all?

It's not hard to come back down to earth. After each gig, we go back to Bradford on Avon and carry on doing the things we have to do, such as work and college. But it's good our lives have stayed like this because it means, when we do play live, we always have a good time – no matter what it is or where.

So what next for The Volt?

We all want to keep the momentum going and to make a living out of this. Whether it's touring the country doing club gigs or headlining the Pyramid Stage at Glastonbury, it doesn't matter – as long as we are having fun. ★

For more on The Volt visit www.myspace.com/thevolt

You don't get me I'M PART OF THE UNION

LIFE AS A JOBBING MUSICIAN CAN BE HARD AND LONELY, BUT THERE IS HELP AT HAND

The music industry can be a challenging environment in which to work and professional musicians, regardless of their experience or the genre of music they play, can come across any number of problems during their career. The Musicians' Union (MU), which was established in 1893, aims to protect the rights of musicians while providing any resources they may need to fight their corner. The MU employs several specialist, full-time officials to deal with issues arising from performing on stage, working in the studio or from a musician's written material.

WHY JOIN?

Developments in the music industry – from use of samples to online distribution – have meant the MU has had to evolve to retain and protect its members' rights. If your ambition is to make all or part of your living from music, you'll need the services and assistance of the MU.
To join, visit the website at www.musiciansunion.org.uk and follow the link 'Join The MU'. The annual fees are based on your previous year's gross earnings from music and are payable in advance. The cost structure is as follows:

MORE THAN £15,000 IN PREVIOUS 12 MONTHS
£22 per month, £66 per quarter, £264 per year (direct debit); £269 per year (cheque/CC).

LESS THAN £15,000 IN THE PREVIOUS 12 MONTHS
£12 per month, £36 per quarter, £144 per year (direct debit); £149 per year (cheque/CC).

STUDENT/IN FULL-TIME EDUCATION
£5 per month, £15 per quarter (direct debt); £60 per year (cheque/CC/direct debit).

Membership provides you with free access to the services provided by the MU, the members' handbook, updates on industry developments and a monthly magazine.

BENEFITS AND SERVICES

The MU offers a range of services and assistance to its members, while also encouraging their development as an artist.

CAREERS AND BUSINESS ADVICE

Help with developing your music career and increasing your job opportunities.

LEGAL ASSISTANCE/ CONTRACT ADVISORY SERVICE

Recovery of fees for live and recorded engagements and help with contracts, intellectual property and personal injury.

RIGHTS PROTECTION

Because of the development of online distribution, the protection of artists' copyrighted

Online distribution means protection of copyright is more important than ever

material is more important than ever. The MU offers advice on this.

MEDIA AND SESSION SPECIALISTS

The MU negotiates agreements with broadcasters, film producers and record companies to collect and send musicians' fees.

INSURANCE SCHEMES/ INSTRUMENT PROTECTION

Exclusive insurance schemes that cover musical equipment, including home studios.

TAX-SAVINGS GUIDE

As a self-employed, professional musician, get advice on tax, national insurance and VAT.

CAMPAIGNS AND LOBBYING

The MU campaigns on behalf of their members at a local and national level.

LIFE-LONG LEARNING

Training and guidance is on offer to members so they can develop their skills.

SALARY AND RATE NEGOTIATION

The MU negotiates salaries and working conditions on behalf of its employed members.

PERSONAL INJURY

The union offers insurance packages that cover loss of earnings if a member is injured, whether at work or during their own time.

DISCOUNT SCHEMES

Members can access discount schemes for instruments, music shops and magazines.

FEE COLLECTION AND DISTRIBUTION

The union's media rights department collects and distributes fees and royalties.

FEE RECOVERY AND DISPUTE RESOLUTION

The MU can assist members with small-claims litigation to recover unpaid gig and cancellation fees.

CONTRACTS AND SPECIMEN AGREEMENTS

The union offers a variety of standard contracts for live, teaching and media work.

The music world can feel like a very lonely place to a jobbing musician. The Musicians' Union can make it seem a little less daunting by looking after your rights and addressing any issues you may have. ★

www.musiciansunion.org.uk

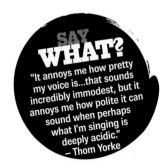

INTERVIEW

Yuill's Tide Turns

SINGER-SONGWRITER IS HAVING TO ADJUST TO SUCCESS AFTER MANY DARK DAYS ON THE ROAD

J ames Yuill has a passion for the emotional atmospherics of artists such as Nick Drake, Radiohead and Sufjan Stevens, as well as the visceral dynamic beats of Justice, Chemical Brothers and Aphex Twin, and has fused these disparate influences into a magical sound of his own. With two self-released albums and years of gigging experience, Yuill's craft is well honed. His second single, *No Pins Allowed*, is now available through Mushi Mushi records. ●

How long have you been playing live?

I've been on the singer/songwriter scene since 2005. I started with some very small acoustic nights, about once a month, and I now play, on average, 10 shows a month.

What drove you to get up on stage in the first place and how did you carry on playing through the dark days?

I don't really know what made me decide to start gigging. The idea of getting up on stage in front of people fills me with dread and I always get insanely nervous before I go on, so it must be that I am addicted to the feeling of euphoria I have after I come off stage! By dark days, I assume you mean bad gigs and

"It was exciting. At last, someone other than your mother thinks you're good"

empty gigs. Yes, it's hard, but, to some extent, that's what it's all about – it makes the good gigs seem even better.

Has a laptop, containing pre-recorded backing tracks, always been a part of your performance? Do you find the backing tracks constrain your performances by cutting out the ability to improvise?

The laptop started to make an appearance in 2006, just after I'd finished my first album. I was looking for a way to recreate soundscapes from the album in the live performance environment. It has gradually evolved into just another instrument and, although it does just provide a backing track, there is a certain amount of freedom to manipulate it. The software I use means everything can be controlled via a midi input; the only problem is not having enough hands.

Have you had any nightmare situations with your laptop, when everything has crashed or it wouldn't switch on – and what have you found to be the best solution to these problems?

For a while, I had a habit of holding the mouse over the 'jump to next track' marker. During one of my more energetic songs, I accidentally hit the mouse button with my palm and it suddenly jumped to the next track. Not only did this sound pretty bad, it also meant I had to go back and start the track again. In the end, I had the skip button programmed into my midi controller. I'm now in the process of incorporating a midi foot pedal into the line up and this should, hopefully, rule out any kind of accidental clicking in the wrong place.

Would you say your music is dance, folk or a mix of the two; and have you found it easy to appeal to both audiences?

I'd say my music is, at the moment, folk, but I'm trying to improve my dance-production skills so they both have an equal presence. I was recently asked whether I want my audiences to dance or to stand and listen. I think my answer was dance – mainly for the reason that people tend not to stare and examine what you're are doing on stage if they're dancing.

How big a risk was it for you to quit your day job and do music full time, and are there moments when you panic about your decision?

Well, it was a risk – I had to give three months' notice at my job and had no idea what I would do once I'd left.

I had saved up for a while; enough to last me a few months, so, when I left, I set about getting a manager and contacting music lawyers. My new journey was made easier by the fact I already had two finished albums for people to listen to. I only panic when I think of the number of nice people who have put so much time and effort into my career so far. I don't want to let anybody down.

How did it feel when your career took off and contracts were thrust under your nose; was it a sense of relief that things were happening or were you nervous that you had to live up to expectations?
At first, it was very exciting. Here's something you've dreamed about for years finally happening. At last, someone other than your mother thinks you're good. Now it's just daunting as more people start working to help me – I feel a massive debt is building up.

ADVICE TO ARTISTS

Record your music and make sure you're happy with it

Play lots of gigs to get known and improve your performance

Don't contact labels or publishers until you're really ready – and, then, contact a music lawyer first

www.myspace.com/jamesyuill

Has it been strange seeing your face in the papers and hearing your songs on the radio – do you feel you've 'made it'?
It was strange at first, but – and this is going to sound bad – you kind of get blasé about it. I've unconsciously detached myself from the realisation that the picture or the name in the magazine is me – and, when I listen to the odd bit of radio-play I get, all I hear are the mistakes and errors in the mix. I'd like to think that's pretty normal. I certainly don't have the sense that I've made it. My manager asked me recently what would be the point at which I'd think that and I guessed it would be when I'm walking along the street and hear my tune on the radio in someone's passing car. It would be even better if they were singing along.

What does the future hold for you?
The album comes out, more singles, gigs and remixes, Hopefully more albums, too. ★

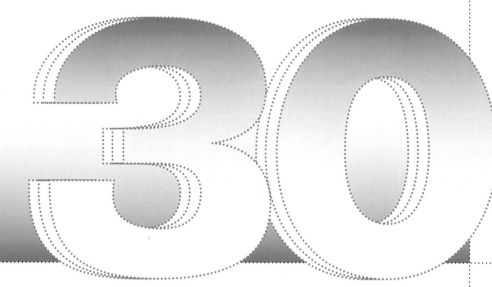

30
RECORDINGS YOU MUST LISTEN TO

A SELECTION OF ALBUMS THAT CHANGED MUSIC FOREVER

ROBERT JOHNSON
KING OF THE DELTA BLUES SINGERS

(various recordings, 1936-1937): The story of Johnson selling his soul to the devil at the crossroads to become the greatest blues guitarist is ingrained in musical folklore and the few recordings he made during his life – he died at 27 – have influenced every blues/rock guitarist.

THE KINGS OF RHYTHM
ROCKET 88

(Single, 1951): Written and produced by Ike Turner, this standard 12-bar blues song was given a raw sound and pounding backbeat to drive on Turner's piano, while distorted lead guitars (the first time this effect had been used on a record) pull the song forward to create the first rock 'n' roll song.

KARLHEINZ STOCKHAUSEN
GESANG DER JÜNGLINGE

(1955-1956) An early masterpiece of electronic music, it splices together three tape loops – a boy soprano singing, sine tones and repeating pulses – to create one piece of music. A huge influence on The Beatles, the German's music was years ahead of its time.

ELVIS PRESLEY
ELVIS PRESLEY

(1956) There may have been better singers, there were better guitarists and he rarely wrote his own songs, but there will never be a better interpreter and performer of rock 'n' roll music. His debut album shivers with the energy of youth and passion, and helped to define a generation.

MILES DAVIS
KIND OF BLUE

(1959) There is a saying, 'if music is a journey, jazz is where you get lost'. Now sadly more associated with identikit coffee shops than with dark and smoky bars, Davis's *Kind of Blue* still stands up as a masterpiece of the genre and as a brilliant example of song construction and improvisation.

VARIOUS
MOTOWN GOLD

(1959-1972): Every track Motown released is an example of great, sometimes genius, songwriting. This compilation doesn't contain everything, but all the classics are present along with several lesser-known gems. If you're a songwriter – or you just want to hear perfection – you owe yourself this album.

BEACH BOYS
PET SOUNDS

(1966): This album is full of examples of incredible harmonies, perfect structure and annoyingly catchy songs. Not only is it Brian Wilson's masterpiece, it is one of the finest albums ever released. *Pet Sounds* saw the Beach Boys move away from the lightweight pop of their early career and become masters of their craft.

THE BEATLES
REVOLVER

(1966): Probably their greatest record, it has more classic songs than any other album they released. From George Martin's brilliantly written and recorded strings on *Eleanor Rigby* and George Harrison's tambura-led *Love To You*, to Lennon and McCartney's tape-loop masterpiece *Tomorrow Never Knows*, *Revolver* still influences artists.

BOB DYLAN
BLONDE ON BLONDE

(1969): The final part of Dylan's mid-60s trilogy of albums that marked his change from acoustic to electric guitar (the others being *Bringing It All Back Home* and *Highway 61 Revisited*) this album is one of the finest examples of songwriting and musical arrangement you will find. The perfect introduction to Dylan's work.

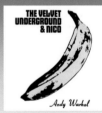

THE VELVET UNDERGROUND
THE VELVET UNDERGROUND AND NICO

(1967): The album flits between moments of darkness (*The Black Angels Death Song*) and sweetness (*Sunday Morning*) and, at first, didn't sell well. But it was once said that 'everyone who bought a copy started a band' and its influence can still be felt today. ●

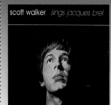

SCOTT WALKER
SCOTT WALKER SINGS JACQUES BREL

(recordings 1967-69): This collection of Brel songs, recorded for Walker's first three solo albums and then compiled onto this disc, are beautiful, epic and funny. His voice floats on lush orchestration and the songs are wonderful observations of the human condition.

THE KINKS
THE KINKS ARE THE VILLAGE GREEN PRESERVATION SOCIETY

(1968): If you want to know what England sounds like, listen to this album. Ray Davies' homage to village life contains some beautifully constructed songs, perfect examples for anyone who wants to study the craft of one of the greats.

MC5
KICK OUT THE JAMS

(1969): This debut album by Detroit's MC5 is as blistering and powerful as any punk record that followed it. The howl by lead singer Rob Tyner at the start of *Kick Out The Jams* is rock 'n' roll at its most primal. A raw and unpredictable album, the musicianship may not be amazing, but the attitude is.

THE STOOGES
FUNHOUSE

(1969): All that can be said about *Funhouse* is it's, without doubt, the greatest rock 'n' roll album that has ever been recorded.

JONI MITCHELL
BLUE

(1971): Perfect, beautiful songwriting, amazing lyrical construction and singing that reaches beyond the natural human range. Any singer-songwriter should invest money, time and energy into this work, which transcends specific genres to create something unique.

DE LA SOUL
3 FEET HIGH AND RISING

(1989): Released amid the first wave of gangster rap, *3 Feet High and Rising*, at least musically, is an incredibly positive and upbeat album that just happens to contain songs about failed sexual experiences. De La Soul, along with Public Enemy, prove hip-hop isn't always what you expect.

DAVID BOWIE
THE RISE AND FALL OF ZIGGY STARDUST AND THE SPIDERS FROM MARS

(1972): The album that broke Bowie into the mainstream in the UK and the US. From opening track *Five Years*' piano-led story of the end of the world to the pure rock of *Suffragette City*, Bowie and guitarist Mick Ronson spearheaded the glam scene and, in Ziggy, created an icon.

ROLLING STONES
EXILE ON MAIN STREET

(1972): Influenced by gospel, blues, country and rock 'n' roll, this album has lead guitarist Mick Taylor beautifully playing off Keith Richards' great riffs, Mick Jagger's lyrics and vocals at their sleazy best, and drummer Charile Watts cementing his reputation as one of rock's greatest.

NICK DRAKE
PINK MOON

(1972): Only 30 minutes long, *Pink Moon* is a starkly produced album, with Drake's voice backed only by an acoustic guitar – the piano on the title track is the one overdub on the album. The honesty on display is occasionally painful, but the universal nature of melancholy can be sensed throughout this album.

RAMONES
RAMONES

(1976): An album that can be summed up thus: 1,2,3,4 shouted really quickly, riff, verse, chorus, verse, chorus, riff, two minutes later the end. If you want to know where English punks got their ideas, listen to this album, then copy everything the band are wearing, learn three chords, add a load of attitude and you'll be there.

KRAFTWERK
THE MAN-MACHINE

(1978): Containing the one Kraftwerk song everyone knows, *The Model*, this album's impact on electronic music can not be underestimated. Pioneers of a genre and masters of the instruments it is played upon, *The Man-Machine* is the easiest point at which to start your journey into the world of Kraftwerk.

FLEETWOOD MAC
TUSK

(1979): A work of insane brilliance and an act of career suicide that followed the massive-selling *Rumours*. The band's songwriters were barely talking to each other, so each of the 20 tracks is a piece of an artist's personal crisis. There are flaws, but the Mac can't be faulted for ambition.

THE CLASH
LONDON CALLING

(1979): An album that respects everything that has gone before while very definitely being an era-defining work. Maybe one of the least punk albums released by a band who rose to fame during the punk movement, *London Calling* throws in dub, rockabilly, soul and classic rock to create a work of brilliance.

MICHAEL JACKSON
THRILLER

(1982): The roll call of artists that have been influenced by this album sounds like a run down of every hit pop star from the past 26 years. Quincy Jones' slick production makes every track leap with energy. Thriller will continually be discovered by hungry for pop perfection.

PUBLIC ENEMY
IT TAKES A NATION OF MILLIONS TO HOLD US BACK

(1988): Dense and sample heavy, with Chuck D's energised raps, this is one of the best and most influential hip-hop albums. Buying and exploring this record will open your eyes to how powerful and aggressive music can be while still retaining accessibility.

LED ZEPPELIN
PHYSICAL GRAFFITI

(1975): If you're looking for an example of a four-piece rock band playing just about every genre of music there is, this album is the best place to start. With blues, heavy rock, folk, rockabilly, rock 'n' roll and everything inbetween, this is the album every rock band should buy, study and then try to reproduce.

JEFF BUCKLEY
GRACE

(1994): The only album released in Buckley's lifetime, *Grace* is a work of timeless beauty. His epic vocal range sweeps through every song and the musicianship, in terms of songwriting and arrangement, contains echos of his influences while also being truly unique. An album that is destined to be discovered by generations to come.

NINE INCH NAILS
THE DOWNWARD SPIRAL

(1994): An album that perfects a unique style. Incredibly dense and aggressive – with vocals that go from primal screams to faint whispers and song structures that pitch from heavily layered beats to single guitar lines – the studio technique on display is both singular and brilliant.

RYAN ADAMS
HEARTBREAKER

(2000): A massive influence upon the singer-songwriter scene, Ryan Adams' debut solo album documents the break-up of a relationship. His voice cracks with raw emotion and, as a songwriter, Adams hasn't again reached the peaks of this album – but the ability he displays on *Heartbreaker* is simply breathtaking.

RADIOHEAD
KID A:

(2000): *Kid A* is the Radiohead album no-one expected. Following up two successful, guitar-led albums (*The Bends* and *OK Computer*) with one influenced by Brian Eno's ambient works and Aphex Twin's crazed dance music is insanely brave, but Radiohead created a complex, wonderful and unique piece of work. ★

MOTLEY CRUE –
THE DIRT

BY NEIL STRAUSS AND MOTLEY CRUE

ISBN: 978-0060989156 (£12.99)
Not so much a guide in how to
make it, rather what not to do if
you do make it. Incredibly funny,
slightly horrific and amazingly
debauched this is a must read for
anyone with a passing interest in
the hedonistic lifestyle of the
touring Rock'n'Roll band.

RIP IT UP AND
START AGAIN – POST
PUNK 1978-1984

BY SIMON REYNOLDS

ISBN: 978-0571215706 (£10.99)
The seven years after punk's
explosion in 1977 was one of the
most vibrant periods in music.
Simon Reynolds' exploration of
this period perfectly sums up the
buzz that was then running
through the industry.

A ROCKING
GOOD READ

BEHIND-THE-SCENES INSIGHTS
FROM THOSE WHO WERE THERE

A quick browse of the shelves of any
good-sized music retailer – not to
mention your online bookstore of
choice – will offer you dozens of
'How To...' titles, mainly written by
people you've never heard of. Most of these
books are so specific, so out of date or so
badly researched that it's a waste to spend
time or money on them.

In general, you should avoid anything with
a big star's name on the front – any self-
respecting rock 'n' roll millionaire is going to
have far better things to do than write a
book. Instead, follow the sound, if less
exciting or debauched, guidance of people
who've manufactured success from behind
the scenes. ★

PLEASE KILL ME:
UNCENSORED ORAL
HISTORY OF PUNK

BY LEGS MCNEIL AND GILLIAN MCCAIN

ISBN: 978-0349108803 (£10.99)
Put together by two key figures
within the scene and told through
interviews, this is the full,
decadent story of the New York
punk movement. It beautifully
captures the period's thrilling
highs as well as the painful lows.

PSYCHOTIC
REACTIONS AND
CARBURETOR DUNG

BY LESTER BANGS

ISBN: 978-1852427481 (£8.99)
This collected works of rock
journalist Lester Bangs' reviews,
articles and general thoughts
presents a twisted insight into the
rock scene of the 70s and early
80s. You'll never look at this
period of time, and those artists
who defined it, in the same way.

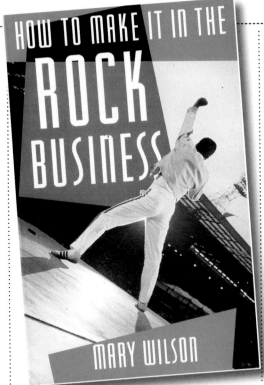

HOW TO MAKE IT IN THE ROCK BUSINESS

BY MARY WILSON

ISBN: 0-86287-316-9 (currently out of print)

Mary Wilson was a mainstream journalist who worked on most of the national newspaper titles in the late 1970s and 80s. Her other career, on the periphery of the music business, came about because of her partner's failed attempts to make it in the industry as record company executive and rock manager. The book is a treasury of stories from grizzled managers, roadies, publishers, musicians and the many other people involved in the wonderful world of pop, and is based on interviews with those who, unlike her partner, made a living from music.

After a brief, scene-setting introduction, Wilson's chapters unfold in a no-nonsense manner, from 'Getting Started' to 'Lawyers and Accountants', and cover all of the basics in detail, while being light and readable.

She even covers some of our territory; her 'Doing It All Yourself' section is based on the experiences of The Icicle Works, a band that enjoyed reasonable sales and a degree of credibility in the mid-80s. Although the prices quoted and the primitive technology referred to put this firmly in the 'vintage reference' sector, Wilson's advice on dealing with the people that inhabit the music world is unbeatable.

THE MANUAL [HOW TO HAVE A NUMBER ONE THE EASY WAY]

BY JIMMY CAUTY & BILL DRUMMOND

ISBN: 1-899858-65-2 (currently out of print)

Only sporadically available in the shops, with second-hand copies offered online for about £100, this rare tome by the KLF is now available to read on the web – a copyright-busting irony that must have the old zenarchist pranksters crying with laughter.

Its treatment of home technology is a little dated, but most of the wisdom it contains remains relevant. Jimmy Cauty and Bill Drummond show how talent is unnecessary, musicianship a mere distraction and even having a decent song isn't much help when you begin the process. Their ultimate advice is leave absolutely everything to those who know what they're doing. Blag what you need – from studio time to CD pressing – on credit until your suppliers can't afford to cut off their support and they're obliged to keep helping you.

The Manual is deliciously Macchiavelian and a fine back-pocket read for all wannabe rock stars. It only guarantees to give you a number one in the pop charts; it says nothing about a career in music, respect from your peers or even a crowd at your gigs. If you buy it, do exactly what it says and don't get a chart-topping hit, they'll refund your money. What more could you ask? ★

THE MANUAL
(HOW TO HAVE A NUMBER ONE THE EASY WAY)

JIMMY CAUTY   BILL DRUMMOND

Bands worth listening to

A VARIETY OF BANDS FROM ALL GENRES

This is a section of bands currently playing on the scene. Some are signed to small independents, a couple have been picked up by the mainstream music press, but all are on the scene, living gig by gig and picking up fans as they go.

ANDREW BALKWILL
Genre: Piano Rock
Description: A mixture of Stevie Wonder and Ben Folds wrapped up in a unique, piano rock, pop style.
MySpace: www.myspace.com/andrewbalkwill

BREAKFAST IN BED
Genre: Pop/Rock
Description: Endearing, English roustabouts equally influenced by Ian Dury, London buses and cafeterias which smell like the inside of ancient handbags. These guys write catchy, hooky, nicely nicely indie music.
MySpace: www.myspace.com/letshavebreakfastinbed

BOURGEOIS AND MAURICE
Genre: Pop/Punk
Description: 21st Century cabaret stars like no other.
MySpace: www.myspace.com/bourgeoisandmaurice

COCOS LOVERS
Genre: Roots music
Description: Roots collective that play traditional Americana mixed with English, folk sensibilities.
MySpace: www.myspace.com/cocoslover

FOX CUBS
Genre: Rock
Description: The very definition of polished modern indie, Fox Cubs display a sharpened sense of sounds, epic hooks and subtle lyrical twists that escapes their chart based contemporaries.
MySpace: www.myspace.com/foxcubs

GOLDHEART ASSEMBLY
Genre: Country/Rock
Description: Brilliant harmonies and wonderfully constructive songs.
MySpace: www.myspace.com/goldheartassembly

GOOD TIME GOOD TIMES
Genre: Blues/Folk/Country
Description: Good times Good times throw these blues on the carnival bandstand and dance around them with a smile from ear to ear. A beautiful defiance of and lust for life.
MySpace: www.myspace.com/thisisgoodtimesgoodtimes

HENRY AND THE BLEEDERS
Genre: Rockabilly/Punk/Country
Description: An up-to-date version of the Sun Records sound circa 1956, played by drunken drop-outs for punk rockers, greasers, psychos, skins, teds and anyone who'll listen.
MySpace: www.myspace.com/henryandthebleeders

IMELDA MAY
Genre: Rock/Blues/Rockabilly
Description: Dublin-born Imelda May is fast becoming regarded by fans and critics alike as one of the finest vocalists currently emerging out of the UK roots music scene. She's a rockin' little minx; tough, sassy, sexy, classy. A big voice on a fine tiny frame.
MySpace: www.myspace.com/imeldamay1

IMPERIAL LEISURE
Genre: Rap/Ska/Punk
Description: One of the best live bands currently playing on both the signed and unsigned scene, a brilliant, unique mixture of Ska and Punk.
MySpace: www.msyapce.com/imperialleisure

JONNYGONEHOME
Genre: Acoustic/Rock
Description: Formed on the banks of Clapton Pond, jonnygonehome sing songs about frustration and plaster. Danny Elfman meets country rock, mixing the lime, shouting at youth, and a great day with Ant.
MySpace: www.myspace.com/jonnygonehome

JUKEBOX VANDALS
Genre: Indie/Pop/Rock
Description: Infectious indie pop with jagged, uneven guitars and unexpected chord changes, plus there's a late 60s garage pop thing going thru early Who righteousness.
MySpace: www.myspace.com/jukeboxvandals

LAST DAYS OF LORCA
Genre: Indie
Description: Floods of jagged guitars set off like an emergency alarm while a sense of urgency persists throughout their records.
MySpace: www.myspace.com/lastdaysoflorca

LOS JAILBREAKERS
Genre: Rockabilly
Description: A Spanish frontman for this North London stompin rockabilly trio with a punk attitude, floor shakers and high voltage rock and roll
MySpace: www.myspace.com/howiethe5050s

LOUISE CAIRNS
Genre: Blues/Jazz
Description: Well felt songs with feelings and meanings to the words. You don't get much of that in today's music in the UK.
MySpace: www.myspace.com/loucairns

MATT KEBBELL
Genre: Acoustic/Blues
Description: An avalanche of a voice, brooding, widescreen songs and scything lyricism – the brutal simplicity of Kurt Cobain, with the dark humour of Leonard Cohen and the grit of Johnny Cash.
MySpace: www.myspace.com/mattkebbell

MONSTERS IN THE ATTIC

Genre: Rock

Description: Pure, heavy punk rock with a live show that's full of destructive passion, an English version of US cult rockers Rocket from the Crypt.

MySpace: www.myspace.com/monstersintheattic

MR B THE GENTLEMAN RHYMER

Genre: Hip-Hop/Comedy

Description: On a one-man mission to introduce Hip-Hop to the Queen's English, Mr B is delighted to present Chap-Hop.

MySpace: www.myspace.com/mrbthegentlemanrhymer

MY ELEMENT

Genre: Indie/Pop/Rock

Description: Their broad range of influences and backgrounds mean that the songs vary in style from one to another - one minute calming you with their melodic four part harmonies, the next making you want to dance around the room like a loon.

MySpace: www.myspace.com/myelementmusic

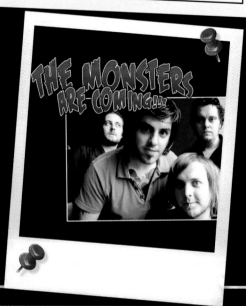

NATE PILGRIM & THE MAGNIFICATZ

Genre: Rockabilly/rock'n'roll/countrypunk

Description: Fast, slow, old new covers, originals and hot... keep it rockin

MySpace: www.myspace.com/magnificatz

NATELY

Genre: Indie/Rock/Acoustic

Description: Nately are a two-piece from London. They are currently 'in between' drummers and are thus honing their acoustic craft at venues like the 12 Bar Club and the Betsey Trotwood in London although they've also been known to stray as far as the Night & Day Cafe in Manchester and Bestival on the Isle of Wight.

MySpace: www.myspace.com/natelydotnet

NIGEL BURCH AND THE FLEA-PIT ORCHESTRA

Genre: Folk/Punk

Description: A cross between the music of Ian Dury, Brecht and Weill, an Irish pub band and a 1950's skiffle group. Songs of urban-alienation with plenty of fierce spontaneous playing.

MySpace: www.myspace.com/nigelburch

NOTE TO SELF

Genre: Folk/Acoustic/Indie

Description: Solo, acoustic blissful-ness.

MySpace: www.myspace.com/notetoselfsongs

OLI WENNINK

Genre: Blues/Jazz

Description: A collision of Nina Simone's piano playing attached to the voice of Jeff Buckley.

MySpace: www.myspace.com/oliwennink

ONE EYE BLUE

Genre: Rockabilly/Pop

Description: With a little bit of Rock and a little bit of Roll, a little bit of Blues and a little bit of Soul One Eyes Blue's unique blend of popular music has bought them to the fore-front of the Midlands music scene.

MySpace: www.myspace.com/oneeyeblue

QUICKBROWNFOX

Genre: punk/rock n'roll

Description: Unstoppable girl/boy punk rock n roll two piece. Stripped down to the bare essentials, this duo create a dynamic noise of thunderous proportions.

MySpace: www.myspace.com/ quickbrownfoxmusic

RYAN O'REILLY

Genre: Folk/Country/Blues

Description: Evocatively sublime and perfectly paced, an unhurried and effortlessly bewitching take on Americana.

MySpace: www.myspace.com/ryanoreilly

SATURDAYS AND SUNDAYS

Genre: Rock/Pop/Indie

Description: Three piece, indie pop, rock that are making noise a lot of noise on the live scene.

MySpace: www.myspace.com/saslive

SINNERSTAR

Genre: Rock/Punk/Acoustic

Description: Heartfelt Rock'n'Roll, played straight from the soul, with rock from the heart and guitar slung low.

MySpace: www.myspace.com/sinnerstaruk

SMOKE FAIRIES

Genre: Country/Blues

Description: Slide, blues duo that own the stage wherever they play, unique, beautifully constructed melodies tied around wonderfully, playful lyrics.

MySpace: www.myspace.com/smokefairies

SMOKE FEATHERS

Genre: Alternative/Lyrical/Soul

Description: Groove-heavy roots-rock, reggae, alt-soul and sunshine pop from the brilliant Smoke Feathers.

MySpace: www.myspace.com/smokefeathers

STANTON DELAPLANE
Genre: Folk/Acoustic
Description: Brilliant and unique mixture of live vocal loops and picked acoustic guitar.
MySpace: www.myspace.com/stantondelaplane

SUPER NASHWAN
Genre: Gospel/Rockabilly
Description: Underground anthems and supercharged love songs from an unhinged anti-hero. Super Nashwan are a rebellion tearing into this digital world with razor lyrics, euphoric gospel melody and songs just bursting with tender soulful cool.
MySpace: www.myspace.com/supernashwan

TEN CITY NATION
Genre: Rock
Description: Tight rock n roll circa 'Bleach' Nirvana, the spirit and passion shines through.
MySpace: www.myspace.com/tencitynation

THE BIRTH OF BONOYSTER
Genre: SKINK (Ska/indy/Punk)
Description: The Birth of BonOyster play SKINK, a finely blended mix of epic rock, beaty pop-ska and gritty punk.
MySpace: www.myspace.com/thebirthofbonoyster

THE GRAVEROBBERS
Genre: Garage rock
Description: The Graverobbers handle their songs like prime cuts of rotten flesh, grind them to a pulp and stamp on the remains with utter irreverence until it squeaks, squeals and begs for mercy.
MySpace: www.myspace.com/theegraverobbers

THE HIGH SOCIETY
Genre: Rock/Glam/Punk
Description: With a classic album's worth of tracks that just screams to be played on vinyl this Birmingham band are ones to look out for.
MySpace: www.myspace.com/highsociety

THE JACKS
Genre: Pop
Description: Songs full of catchy hooks and unashamed pop medleys.
MySpace: www.myspace.com/thejackstunes

THE LAMY BROTHERS
Genres: Alternative/Blues/Country
Description: Melodramatic and melancholy, a virile and brittle bitterness pervades their landscape; a landscape that can only be appreciated by those who are not yet accustomed to the injustices of life. More importantly, the Lamy Brothers are sometimes as clever as they think they are.
MySpace: www.myspace.com/lamybrothers

THE PENNY BLACK REMEDY

Genre: Country/Rock

Description: The Penny Black Remedy don't really play venues, it's more like they storm them. Winners of best alternative act 2008 at the Indy music awards.

MySpace: www.myspace.com/pennyblackremedy

THE SCOURGE OF RIVER CITY

Genre: Punk rock

Description: A rip-roaring nitro-fuelled thrash through blues, punk, rockabilly and melodic hardcore that hits all the right buttons.

MySpace: www.myspace.com/thescourgeofrivercity

THE SLOW BLADE

Genre: Alternative/Rock/Electronica

Description: Electro/Gothic rock that are making waves on the London scene, a band to look out for in the future.

MySpace: www.myspace.com/slowblademusic

THE WHYBIRDS

Genre: Rock

Description: All four members of the band are singer/songwriters – with influences including Bruce Springsteen, Steve Earle, The Band, Pearl Jam and Whiskeytown – giving the group a diverse range of songs and vocal styles, but without straying from The Whybirds' sanguine brand of rock 'n' roll.

MySpace: www.myspace.com/thewhybirds

THEE SINGLE SPY

Genres: Gothic/Rock/Country

Description: Arthouse gothic-folk and clarinet-fuelled rioting. Songs about drowning towns, lyrical Christian campfire traditions and the smoking of herbal anxiety medications prevail, drawing comparisons with Tom Waits, Smog, Bright Eyes and Beirut. Thee Single Spy is the spirit of older, cracklier times and rhymes throughout.

MySpace: www.myspace.com/theesinglespy

THINGUMABOB & THE THINGUMAJIGS

Genre: Vaudeville cabaret showtunes

Description: "With their amazing facial hair and singalong ukulele music they put a great big smile on the otherwise moody face of the Manchester music scene." Stuart Avery, SA Promotions (one of Manchester's longest running independent music promoters).

MySpace: www.myspace.com/thingumajigs

VESUVIAN

Genre: Psychedelic rock

Description: Loud, heavy thunderous rock. One of the best bands currently playing both their native Scotland and the rest of the UK.

MySpace: www.myspace.com/vesuvian

WIN

A NINTENDO Wii FEATURING GUITAR HERO III

Enter our competition today and you could win not one, but three fantastic prizes. First up we are giving away a Nintendo Wii with Guitar Hero III: Legends of Rock. Crank up the volume and get ready to rock like never before. We're also giving away an iPod Touch 8GB and Sony's PCM-D50 portable audio recorder, which is perfect for making and recording live music.

To enter this fantastic competition, answer the question at *www.howtomakeitinmusic.com*

Question: What band is featured in How To Make it in Music?

A Ned's Atomic Dustbin

B Ultravox

C Showadawaddy

Closing date: 14 August 2009
For full terms and conditions go to:
www.dennis.co.uk/comp/terms

PRIZES WORTH £850